UNCERTAIN CORRIDORS

Gideon Haigh has been a journalist for nearly thirty years, contributed to more than a hundred newspapers and magazines, and written twenty-eight books and edited seven others.

Also by Gideon Haigh:

Sphere of Influence

On Warne

GIDEON HAIGH

UNCERTAIN CORRIDORS
Writings on modern cricket

**SIMON &
SCHUSTER**

London · New York · Sydney · Toronto · New Delhi

A CBS COMPANY

First published in Great Britain by Simon & Schuster UK Ltd, 2014
A CBS COMPANY

Copyright © 2013 by Gideon Haigh

1 3 5 7 9 10 8 6 4 2

Simon & Schuster UK Ltd
1st Floor
222 Gray's Inn Road
London WC1X 8HB

www.simonandschuster.co.uk

Simon & Schuster Australia, Sydney
Simon & Schuster India, New Delhi

A CIP catalogue record for this book is available from the British Library

Cover and text design by John Canty © Penguin Group (Australia)
Front cover image: Michael Dodge/Stringer/Getty Images
Cricket ball image: C Squared Studios/Getty Images

ISBN: 978-1-47113-280-3

CONTENTS

A WORLD GAME?

END PIECES

INTRODUCTION

In 2007, I published a collection of journalism called *The (Green &) Golden Age*, encompassing a decade of work about the long period of Australian cricket ascendancy. Why? I had a strange sense of living in end times. Strange because at the time the teams led by Ricky Ponting appeared unassailable, with the Ashes, the Frank Worrell Trophy and the World Cup all in safe and undisputed keeping, and new caps such as Mike Hussey, Stuart Clark and Andrew Symonds already nicely bedded down. All the same, Shane Warne, Glenn McGrath and Justin Langer were gone, and Adam Gilchrist and Matthew Hayden would not be long behind them. It seemed like an opportune moment to capture the past, and to pay tribute to this team of the talents before it receded entirely from view. And though I could hardly have forseen the magnitude of the forthcoming revolution, I also intuited that in T20 the game had a vibrant, lucrative and potentially discombobulating variant. The last few pages of *The (Green &) Golden Age* were devoted to a preview of the first World T20 in South Africa, with the prophecy that 'the face of the game is about to change', albeit that success might prove a 'mixed blessing', and for Australia a particular challenge.

Don't worry if you didn't read this; not many did. But here, despite popular demand, is a sort-of sequel: *Uncertain Corridors*, the title pertaining both to those of technique outside the off stump and those of power in which administrators make decisions concerning cricket's future. It offers a sample of what might be loosely described as 'stuff' I have written about the twilight of Australia's great era, and this cricket country's attempt to find its way in a T20-centric world. For, as we now know, that inaugural instalment of the World T20 was won by India, which promptly embraced a format it had previously scorned, and parlayed it into the money machine of the Indian Premier League, thereby consolidating the economic thrall in which it keeps the rest of the cricket world. Australia has struggled to keep up in every respect, on the field and off, commencing a painful rebuilding of its talent stocks even as it has undertaken a top-to-bottom refit of its cricket system in emulation of the IPL, each rather complicating and compromising the other.

For much of the time, Australia's team was marshalled by captain Michael Clarke, coach Mickey Arthur, and the still striving Ponting and Hussey, all to specifications laid down in an August 2011 report by a panel of eminences, the so-called Argus Review. At one point, Australia threatened to outdo Arthur's former side, South Africa, going within an ace of victory during an unforgettable Test at Adelaide Oval. But when Ponting then Hussey went, Clarke struggled with the additional burden, and Arthur paid with his job – the first Tests of his successor Darren Lehmann I will report in a forthcoming chronicle of the back-to-back Ashes of 2013–14. So *Uncertain Corridors* amounts to another time capsule, of middling success, with both highs and lows attained against

India, and muddling strategy, at times just too clever by half.

To be fair, we are all of us groping our ways forward. A French *philosophe* once quipped that the English invented cricket because of their non-religiosity, to give them a sense of the eternal. But there has been nothing eternal about the six years since Sreesanth caught Misbah ul-Haq to afford India victory over Pakistan at Wanderers, and some falls have been especially precipitous: in May 2013, Sreesanth was one of three regulars of the Rajasthan Royals arrested on charges of spot-fixing in the IPL, midst allegations of fathomless corruption. A fan out of touch with cricket since Australia's last World Cup win would quickly lose their bearings in the modern landscape. Who are these players, these teams? What are these events? Where did these schedules come from?

Because you can regard all this as the outworkings of animal spirits liberated by Kerry Packer thirty-six years ago, I include a speech delivered last year on that great time tunnel, *Howzat*; my most recent subject, Shane Warne, also looms large. And because it's also a big wide cricket world these days, *Uncertain Corridors* includes glimpses of some esteemed Australian opponents, plus despatches from cricket's high councils (the International Cricket Council, the Board of Control for Cricket in India) and far-flung satellites (Afghanistan and Papua New Guinea). These suggest some foundation for the truism about money being like muck: best when spread. For cricket has found its new riches acutely problematic, in their tendency to prop up dysfunctional autocracies and bureaucracies whose chief interest is their own perpetuation, to offer instant riches to unfinished players and subtly marginalise those with traditional ambitions, to puzzle and alienate cricket's core supporters in quest of fabled 'new markets'. We might even wonder whether cricket would not be a happier game were it less wealthy, or at least more equal, as heretical a notion as this may sound to votaries of the remorseless logic of late capitalism. In search of a more positive conclusion, the book ends with some reflections on two cricket forms: the club game and the Test match, opposites where I feel most at home. Perhaps you do too.

Uncertain Corridors is offered with thanks to my most excellent colleagues at *The Australian, The Nightwatchman, Wisden Cricketers' Almanack, The Cricketer* and *The Global Mail,* where these pieces were previously published, and to my wife Charlotte and daughter Cecilia, who waited very patiently for me to finish them.

GIDEON HAIGH

Melbourne, July 2013

A LONG TIME
RETIRED

1977 AND ALL THAT

In 2005, Matthew Hayden mentioned to the broadcaster Alan Jones that he had long nursed a desire to meet Kerry Packer, then in poor health, and destined not to last the year. It turned into a dinner chez Packer attended also by Justin Langer, Steve Waugh, Shane Watson and Brett Lee. It was around the time that the doughty Langer had developed an unfortunate propensity for ducking into bouncers; Packer admonished him that he could not be watching the ball. Later in the evening, Packer began to dilate on a favourite subject: luck. Packer family lore is that Kerry's grandfather derived his first capital from spotting a ten-bob note on the ground and placing a successful bet at a Tasmanian racetrack. Warming to his theme, he turned to Langer again: 'And son,' he said, 'you'd know all about luck. If Tony Greig hadn't developed helmets, you'd be fuckin' dead.'

Everyone laughed, and everyone implicitly acknowledged the subtext. For, as any fule kno, Tony Greig developed those helmets while in Kerry Packer's employ, as captain of the World XI, one of the three teams that composed his World Series Cricket. Packer might have gone further in a list of the things his cricketers were lucky to enjoy as a result of WSC: the chance to play cricket as a full-time professional, the opportunity to participate in day/night cricket in coloured clothing with white balls and field restriction circles, the whole lavish corporatised television spectacular that modern cricket had become. Aye, it was Kerry Packer's world: Langer and his teammates just lived in it. But nobody *really* needed to mention this, because it was somehow understood, something the cricketers acknowledged by their act of homage to this maker of the modern game.

Seven years on and the nation has now paid collective homage, by watching in the millions the two-part *Howzat: Kerry Packer's War*, on his former network, Channel Nine. Many who watched would not have been born at the time the events dramatised took place, being introduced to the facts by the legend, as it were. If you were watching very closely as the credits rolled, you'll have seen my name with the fancy title 'script supervisor'. This is a bit of a misnomer. I didn't supervise anything, let alone the script, which I did not read; nor did I see the series in advance, otherwise I might have persuaded Rick McCosker to shave off his moustache and Clive Lloyd to bat the right way round. Instead, the producers, Southern Star, paid me a modest emolument so that the scriptwriter Chris Lee could consult my book *The Cricket War* and my memory as he wrote his screenplay – which he did, in quite granular detail, both for what went to air, and also for a book-length exposition with the same title as the series.

Howzat was not, I might say, an adaptation of *The Cricket War*. Perhaps the crispest distinction is that the subject of my book is cricket, while the subject of Chris's screenplay is Kerry Packer. Naturally I dealt with Packer and Chris with cricket, but *The Cricket War* sees events from a cricketers' perspective, while *Howzat* aims to bring a rumbustious Australian character to life – and thanks to Lachy Hume's scenery chewing portrayal, I think it succeeds, and memorably so. Both our narratives were seasoned by subsequent events, mine by the fact that Packer became the most powerful figure in Australian cricket, Chris's by the fact that Packer subsequently became Australia's wealthiest man. But the process has made me more than usually aware of the trade-offs involved in the accretion of historical information, the process of historical analysis and the dissemination of historical narratives. Kerry Packer's World Series Cricket has become a perdurable mythology served by both its participants *and* its interpreters, each informing the other, each adding complementary, competing, overlapping ideas. It's not a stationary object at which we're taking ever more accurate aim; it's a firing range of moving sharpshooters aiming at constantly shape-shifting targets. I want to talk tonight about the origins of that mythology, and what *Howzat* might tell us of its evolution.

Anyway, it's getting blurry round the edges of the screen. Yes, we're slipping back in time. Can you hear the strains of *Countdown?* 1977: Elvis Presley either dies or embarks on a career in hospitality; many people hate Malcolm Fraser who'll later like him, and vice versa. Mankind is so primitive, to invoke Douglas Adams, that it still thinks digital watches are a good idea. So how did the cricket world look, apart from the fact that the players wore safari suits and the groupies looked like Delvene Delaney?

Test cricket, 100 years old, was stable, secure, comfortably but not hugely profitable. It had originated in Australia in 1877, under a colonial governance structure that was highly decentralised: a swirl of clubs, associations, ground authorities and, above all, commercially minded players, who formed themselves into the original teams that toured England with legend-building success.

Federation of Australia in 1901 had then had a correspondingly centralising influence, causing the state associations to band together in the foundation of the Australian Cricket Board, which gradually wrested administrative and financial power from the players, assumed responsibility for the organising of Test matches, and distributed the profits amongst the membership, where they were directed to the upkeep of the game.

Two things are worth noting about the Australian Cricket Board in 1977, and they are in tension. It remained a federation, a non-profit entity distributing all the revenues it earned. It had neither reserves, nor premises, nor employees. Australia's only paid full-time cricket administrators were the secretaries at each association, one of whom, Alan Barnes of New South Wales, acted additionally in the role for the board, based in an office in Sydney where he kept the files on the floor and his scotch and cigarettes in the filing cabinets. To be fair, Barnes was formidably organised. He was known as 'Justa', for the fact that in response to every enquiry he would scuttle round the floor of his office saying: 'Just a minute. Just a minute.' It was *never* more than that because he knew where everything was. But the board itself was strictly part-time and unpaid, composed of honorary appointees elected by the associations from among their first-grade club delegates.

The board was *also* a monopolist. All cricket in Australia took place under its auspices. It set the market rates for all cricketers. When a player was picked to wear the green and gold, he was not offered a contract; he received what was called an invitation to play, basically for a week. He was offered a modest fee, but it was up to him to organise time off work, to guarantee his availability and fitness. He had no agent to assist him, no collective body to represent him: he accepted the invitation, or he did not play. In an infamous effusion, Barnes told *Cricketer* magazine: 'The players are not professional. They are all invited to play and if they don't like the conditions there are 500 000 other cricketers in Australia who would love to take their place.'

Your view of Australian cricket in 1977 probably depended on which of these two qualities of the Australian Cricket Board you emphasised: the board as high-minded custodian of a game beyond price, or the board as feudal overlord oblivious to the value of its players, or the board as a fusion of the two, a kind of benevolent dictatorship. There's some detail worth adding, though, because it goes to one of the biggest single fallacies about World Series Cricket, which is that Kerry Packer took a moribund, hidebound game and *made it popular.* On the contrary, cricket was *massively popular already*, and hadn't been so popular since the era of Bradman. It was precisely *for this reason* that Packer coveted the rights to broadcast it.

There was a variety of reasons for cricket's lustre. Foremost among them, of course, was the Australian team – a once-in-a-generation combination of aggressive, charismatic, larger-than-life, hairier-than-a-hearthrug cricketers, generalled by the Chappells, bristling with the mercurial talent of Lillee, Thomson, Walters and Marsh, but invested also with the more homely presences of Max Walker, Ian Redpath, Ross Edwards and Rick McCosker – a rare combination of stars and characters, stars who were characters, and characters who were stars.

There were also some other reasons, which we should not overlook. One was the robust pyramidal structures of junior, club and interstate cricket which conduced to the preparation of such great players, maintained by numberless thousands of devoted amateur administrators. Another was Australian cricket's historic endowments, most especially the national pride and goodwill inhering in 100 years of Test cricket, celebrated in 1977 by the Centenary Test at the MCG. Still another was Australian cricket's accessibility, reflected in the fact that since the advent of radio the game had enjoyed an honoured and unquestioned place in the schedules of the ABC. The football codes were still obstinately, ostentatiously parochial; not even Olympic gold rivalled the atavistic pleasure of beating the Poms.

So it was a combination of contemporary vibrancy and traditional prestige that had made Australian cricket such an attractive commercial proposition in the decade before Kerry Packer's arrival. And while it's commonly argued that the board did nothing but sit on its pinstriped posterior in this period, that's not *really* true. In 1968, the board commenced a domestic one-day knockout competition, and arranged a sponsor for it, V&G Insurance, later succeeded by Coca-Cola, then Gillette. In 1971, when the Melbourne Test was washed out, the board initiated the inaugural one-day international against England, sponsored by Rothmans. Later that year, when the South African tour was cancelled for political reasons, it arranged a tour by a Rest of the World team, sponsored by the Herald and Weekly Times. Most importantly, in January 1974, the board signed a long-term sponsorship deal for the whole of Australian cricket with British American Tobacco, anxious to find avenues to promote its Benson & Hedges cigarettes as the company's advertising options were closed off.

At the same meeting that confirmed that sponsorship, furthermore, Victorian board member Len Maddocks successfully moved the following motion: 'That the Board officially adopt the policy of paying players, in one form or another, the maximum amounts possible from time to time, consistent with the Board's responsibility of assisting the states to promote and develop cricket in Australian [sic] in the long-term.' You might ask why this needed enunciating. The reason is one I mentioned before: that the board was a federation whose first duty was to its member associations, whose dividends were virtually their sole source of income. You understand just how significant this was when you read on a few pages to *this* note: 'That in considering the above the board should assess the associated advantages to be gained from establishment of separate finances controlled directly by the board, and approve the fundamental change in financial policies which would arise there-from.' In other words, the board would need to do something never done before, which was keep some money back rather than disgorge it to the states.

These are carefully worded and non-binding resolutions, but if you read them in the context of board minutes, which can go for pages talking about the specifications of a blazer pocket, they stand out like copperplate. I was unaware of them in 1992 when I researched *The Cricket War*, because the Board declined to give me access to their records; I read these minutes only five or so years ago when I was asked to write the Board's official history, and inter-viewed Len Maddocks, who mooted the idea. Sir Donald Bradman aside, Len was the only former Test cricketer on that board. He had been blessed with an indulgent employer, APM, who paid him half salary when he was absent on cricket tours. But he knew of the pri-vations his teammates faced, and was also a good friend of Ian Chappell's – in fact, it was at Maddocks' urging that Ian, recently retired, played the season of 1976–77 at North Melbourne. An actor playing him makes an unnamed appearance in *Howzat* too, chatting to Ian Chappell at a North Melbourne grade match. But there's no more detail, and *Howzat* certainly does not mention that when win-ning bonuses are factored in, fees per Test for Australian players grew sharply between 1974 and 1977; the players on the 1977 Ashes tour received four times as much as on the Ashes tour just two years earlier. The base was low but the rises were steep.

So why did relations between the board and the players break down? The more I've reflected on this, the more I've concluded that

World Series Cricket was a social as well as an economic upheaval. In the 1970s, it was common to talk about 'the generation gap'. A yawning one had opened up in Australian cricket. In 1976, Len Maddocks was the youngest member of the board: he was fifty. The majority were over sixty. Sir Donald Bradman was approaching seventy. They had experienced a Great Depression, they had experienced the Second World War, they were husbanders rather than builders of resources, they hastened slowly, they did not really grasp the ruinous effects of inflation on real incomes in the first half of the 1970s, they were out of touch with the quotidian reality of the lives of young male athletes and their families. Clem Jones, the Labor Lord Mayor of Brisbane, who grew up in a family that sang 'The Internationale' around the piano, once told me a flavoursome story of the Pax Menziana that prevailed round the board table. The day he joined, Bradman came over at morning tea and said: 'I just want to tell you that while you are a member of this board, you will receive all the respect due to you. But we can *never* be friends, because I abhor your politics.'

Ian Chappell, by contrast, was thirty-two when he retired from Test cricket in 1976, and in Australian cricket terms he was old. Rewards were too little, touring requirements too onerous and tenures too insecure for players to linger longer. The player who felt this most keenly was Dennis Lillee, who a year after becoming the world's best fast bowler had suffered a devastating back injury that kept him out of cricket for eighteen months. He rebuilt his back and his career by sheer willpower, but earning a subsistence income from working in a bank, then with a travel agent, then in a contract cleaning business, was an ignominious fate for a man at the top of his cricketing craft. Players were conscious that individuals in other sports were considerably better off: Rod Marsh had a brother Graham, a good golfer but not a great one, who earned more than the Australian team put together. But anger was fomented by the sense of impotence that official cricket was *the only cricket*, that there was no rival employer to use as leverage. When Dennis Lillee appointed the former Subiaco footballer Austin Robertson as his manager, it was not to go to the board to demand a better pay deal from the board, but to help him earn money from non-board sources. One thing, as we know, led to another. Austin Robertson had this mate, John Cornell. John Cornell worked with Paul Hogan. And Paul Hogan had this new boss, Kerry Packer . . .

In *Howzat*, there's a scene with two English journalists in a newsroom preparing to write a profile of Kerry Packer, and finding a fat file – but it's about his father Sir Frank, one of Australia's mightiest media moguls, proprietor of the *Daily Telegraph*, Australia's most powerful tabloid newspaper until he sold it towards the end of his life in May 1974. We make a mistake, I think, if we evaluate Kerry Packer in terms of the man he became. The figure we see in *Howzat* was in his late thirties, married with two small children, still overshadowed by his father's legacy, still something of an unknown quantity, at least to the outside world.

Packer had distinguished himself at this stage in one small corner of the Consolidated Press group, founding *Cleo* and reviving *Women's Weekly*. He had moved from there to Cons Press's broadcasting arm, Publishing and Broadcasting Ltd, and launched them into primetime drama with *The Sullivans* and *The Young Doctors*. But he was still making his mark. Even within the organisation, many looked for counsel to his deputy Harry Chester, a long-serving lieutenant of Sir Frank's. Interestingly, not one of the cricketers who later signed to play with his enterprise recognised Packer's name when first they heard it.

Why did Packer aspire to broadcast cricket? Some of you will remember the scene in *Howzat* where Packer is strolling round

Lord's, and avers with great conviction that his father loved cricket. In fact, and I've since discussed this with his biographer, while Sir Frank was a tremendous enthusiast for racing, for yachting and for polo, he was no more than averagely fond of cricket. In his autobiography, the English cricket writer E W Swanton describes a dinner with Sir Frank in 1966 in which the Australian bet that cricket here was doomed, and would in the next decade be overtaken in popularity by baseball. So I don't think the proposition that World Series Cricket was an act of filial piety has much to recommend it. The reasons were more prosaically commercial. Television and sport had been long-term acquaintances; they were starting to pay one another more attention. In 1975, for example, TEN-10 in Sydney, then owned by a consortium of AWA, Email, CSR and Bank of New South Wales, agreed with the Australian Rugby League to a mid-week made-for-television tournament, the Amco Cup. Cricket was actually an even more attractive television prospect – longer, larger, genuinely national and sewn with naturally occurring ad breaks. It's TCN-9's Bruce Gyngell who probably deserves credit for setting Packer's cogs ticking, when he pointed out that the ABC obtained a 21 rating at midnight for the 1975 World Cup final, live from Lord's. Whatever the case, cricket's potential for a commercial broadcaster was enormous – providing, and it was quite a proviso, that the rights to it could be held exclusively.

In the very first scene in *Howzat*, even before the credits, Kerry Packer strides down a hallway and bursts through ornate doors of oak and frosted glass at the Victorian Cricket Association to make two officials an offer they can't refuse: $2.5 million over five years for exclusive rights to broadcast top-class cricket in Australia. Bob Parish and Ray Steele, respectively the chairman and treasurer of the Australian Cricket Board, inform him that they have shaken hands on a deal with the ABC for the next three seasons, but that he is welcome to offer for the non-exclusive commercial rights. Packer fumes: there is no point in broadcasting in parallel with the ABC, as the natural preference of every viewer would be a commercial free feed. They're sorry, the administrators say. You will be, mutters Packer under his breath.

Now, a lot about this is correctly depicted. A meeting took place on 22 June 1976 at VCA House in Jolimont Street. It was attended by Packer, Parish and Steele. Packer was also accompanied by a loyal retainer, Alec Baz; Parish and Steele by Len Maddocks. When the administrators professed to being committed to the ABC, Packer did *indeed* assert: 'Come on, gentlemen, we're all whores. What's your price?' And the board members did *indeed* decline a fee many times what was on offer from the national broadcaster.

Nonetheless, some additional context is useful. First, since the inception of television in Australia, the Australian Cricket Board had sold rights to *both* the ABC *and* commercial broadcasters. The ABC was always there. It covered everything including the Sheffield Shield, and took great pains to provide interstate relays of its broadcasts, using circling aircraft where it could not rely on cable transmission. Commercial broadcasters . . . well, they liked the Ashes, and they liked the West Indies. Such was the public enthusiasm for the 1960–61 series against the West Indies, for example, that GTV-9 broadcast the final Test; HSV-7 covered the 1975–76 Worrell Trophy Series, and would also broadcast the Centenary Test.

But, and it was a big but, these channels came and went; they were excited some years, indifferent others. This being so, the traditional arrangement for television rights was that the ABC was dealt with first; then, and only then, were expressions of interest heard from commercial broadcasters. So when Packer made his offer those many years ago, it was unprecedented not just in quantum but in nature. No commercial broadcaster had *ever* expressed dissatisfaction with a non-exclusive deal; no commercial broad-caster had *ever* presented itself as an alternative to the ABC; and while we're inclined to use the expression 'Nine Network' as a generic, it does not mean what it does now. Thanks to an antique statute called the 'two-station rule', PBL only owned two television stations: TCN-9 in Sydney, GTV-9 in Melbourne. It networked through other independently owned Channel Nines, but a good deal of regional Australia was beyond its reach. Packer was offering a lot. He was also asking a lot. This was a meeting of oil and water, never likely to mix.

Secondly, remember what I said earlier about the Australian Cricket Board having no premises, no reserves and no employees. That's why the meeting was at VCA House, because the board sub-committee that dealt with television was the three Victorian board members. VCA House? It's shown as rather splendid. Long corri-dors. Marble floors. Ornate doors. In fact, it was an old carpet showroom. The VCA had just sold an old city office block it had owned since the 1930s, and moved into these newer but smaller premises in order to bolster its liquid assets. It suits dramatic pur-poses to present Parish and Steele as living in wood-panelled splendour, but it's far from the truth. Parish ran a family timber importer; Steele was the son of a blacksmith and railway worker who studied law on a scholarship while playing on a halfback flank for Richmond. They were the club delegates of the Prahran and Hawthorn–East Melbourne cricket clubs respectively: Parish con-tinued to run the scoreboard and serve the drinks at Toorak Park even after he became board chairman. Between them, they'd give a century of unpaid labour to cricket administration in Australia. So if not vestal virgins, these were not men likely to answer cheerfully to the description 'whores'. Not so long ago, David Richards, then VCA secretary, told me a sequel to Packer's visit. Richards was in the

US, on a trip to study American sports marketing techniques, with an eye to how they might be used in relation to the Centenary Test – another interesting fact that belies the assumption that the board was commercially dormant in the mid-1970s.

On making a routine call to the VCA, he was forced to listen for an hour as Parish poured out his indignation at Packer's boorishness and bullying. When he checked his hotel bill, Richards was embarrassed to find that the conversation had cost $110, and wondered how on earth he would explain it. The story seems to me highly symbolic. A volunteer body that counted every penny was about to run smack bang into a business tycoon for whom money was no object.

Howzat does an excellent job thereafter, I think, of explaining the confluence of events and characters that helped Packer nurture his own cricket attraction. The role of John Cornell, Paul Hogan's partner in comedy, as impresario. The participation of Austin Robertson, Dennis Lillee's manager, as intermediary. The recruitment of Ian Chappell, whose involvement gave the enterprise a decisive endorsement, such was his stature among the players of his generation. The enticement into the fold of Tony Greig, who, although *Howzat* leaves it out, was Packer's other vital recruiting sergeant: it was Greig who visited the Caribbean on his new bosses' behalf in April 1977 and wooed the West Indian and Pakistan teams, then flew on to London to sign the South Africans. *Howzat* does well, too, in conveying the simmering discontent among the players integral to their signing with such alacrity.

It's worth making a couple of observations about that alacrity, in fact. The sums of money Packer offered were no better than full – roughly what a top professional in law or medicine might receive. Rod Marsh's fee in 1977–78 was $35 000, an eighth of what his brother won on the professional golf tour. Yet I know of no player saying to an agent of Packer's that an offer was insufficient, or too onerous, or too comprehensive. A sizeable majority signed without so much as reading their contracts, something which seems astonishing in an age when footballers' contract negotiations run into multi millions of dollars, involve multiple parties, and can drag for whole seasons.

Nor does there seem to have been any particular curiosity among players about what they were signing up to. There'd be some games. They'd be on TV. No dates, no venues, no team names; it wasn't even clear whether they would clash with the Test and first-class seasons. The players kept their contracts secret because they were advised to, not because they thought there was that much wrong with them. Jeff Thomson, the only Australian player at the time apart from Lillee with a manager, did not even tell him: 'I was with a few blokes at the time and it seemed OK,' he explained.

Nor was that mystery dispelled when the story of Packer's initiative broke prematurely in England on 9 May 1977. Contra *Howzat*, the revelation did not make front pages round the world. It did not even make the back page lead of *The Age*, whose Peter McFarline shared the scoop. Thundered the mighty broadsheet on the day in question: 'Once again Collingwood is a great side, and coach Tom Hafey has told his players there are bigger and better things to come.' It was another week before Packer had very much to say at all, when the cover of his magazine, *The Bulletin*, was given over to: 'The Great Cricket Story: The Inside Facts.' This revealed a good deal about the recruiting process, and hardened many attitudes in administrative circles by revealing that many players had signed up in the shadow of the Centenary Test. But it gave away precious little about how Packer intended to deploy his all-star troupe, whether it would be directly in opposition to or alongside establishment cricket. At that stage, I'm not sure Packer knew, or even whether he was entirely committed to the venture.

That wasn't until 23 June 1977, a year and day since his abortive encounter with Parish and Steele, when Packer met them again, this time as members of what was then the International Cricket Conference at Lord's. Packer actually seems to have been decidedly conciliatory at that meeting. The minutes include Packer's comment that he had 'no desire to run international cricket' and 'what he really wanted was to become involved in the television rights of cricket' – specifically to be guaranteed 'exclusive television contracts to cricket in Australia at the conclusion of the Australian Board's contract with the ABC in 1978–79'. His only remark that could be construed as remotely menacing was a warning that 'the moment that any one of his players was barred from international cricket was the moment that the governing bodies would see him as an enemy'. Half an hour was all it took for the ICC to make up their mind; Packer was told that while the Australian Cricket Board would 'consider the principle of exclusive television rights', it could only afford him 'the opportunity to bid for these rights on an equal basis with others'. At the subsequent ICC annual meeting, members voted to deem Packer's signatories 'disapproved persons' for the purposes of selection. In effect, it was not Kerry Packer who declared war on cricket, but cricket that declared war on Kerry Packer. As he famously said afterwards: 'It's every man for himself and the devil take the hindmost.'

This, and not the meeting a year earlier, was the authorities' disastrous miscalculation. It was an escalation, I think, borne of rage and betrayal, at how eagerly it seemed that the players had turned their back on traditional cricket, and how ungratefully they appeared to regard those efforts that *had* gone into improving their financial lot. Packer was as good as his word, taking two steps in retaliation. He decided that each of what he was calling Supertests would be staged on exactly the same dates as the Test matches of the ensuing Australian summer. He also took the ICC to the court, and thence to the cleaners, because Justice Slade sided with him. In perhaps the single most important legal judgement in cricket history, Slade concluded that while administrators might have believed that they acted in 'the best interests of cricket', their retaliation had 'strained the bounds of loyalty': 'The very size of profits made from cricket matches involving star players must for some years have carried the risk that a private promoter would appear on the scene and seek to make money by promoting cricket matches involving world-class cricketers.'

The former expedient did not pay off. Despite the galacticos in action, the Supertests of that first summer were sparsely attended. But the latter tactic of going to court, which Packer was not obliged to do, and which he undertook I think mainly as an act of good faith with his players, ramified for the next two years. The costs of that case, borne equally by the member nations of the ICC, drove a huge wedge into their ranks. Countries outside Australia and England felt, not unfairly, that they had been dragged into the middle of a domestic television dispute down under. There was never again quite the same solid front in the establishment and, as the good book tells us, a house divided itself cannot stand.

The effort of putting what became World Series Cricket together was, of course, stupendous and unprecedented, anticipating the whole grammar of modern cricket. Barred access to Australia's cricket grounds, Packer settled instead for the Sydney Showground, for Aussie rules football grounds in Melbourne and Adelaide, and for a trotting track in Perth. Each required pitches to be laid – at Waverley's VFL Park, they were grown in hothouses, then dropped into the middle of the ground, a precursor to the modern drop-in pitch.

Travelling light, without any of the cultural or institutional baggage of the traditional game, Packer was also free to innovate. So many cricketers had he been able to sign, he could field not the standard single opponents for Australia but two: the World and the West Indies. Packer's programme relied heavily on one-day cricket: an underexploited variant of the game. Australia and England had played the first one-day international, as I noted before, in 1971, but in the ensuing six years Australian audiences had been treated to a further two only, despite the success in 1975 of the inaugural World Cup in England. And blessed at VFL Park with lights, just erected for night football, Packer immediately conceived of staging one of these limited-overs games in the evening using a white ball.

Packer, in other words, could do what he liked. He did not need to consult – indeed, he was not by nature a consulter. He didn't really have to worry about public relations – he could fashion his own, in television and magazines. Approaching the game as a visual spectacle, he was particularly eager to experiment with its coverage: multiple cameras, constant replays, explanatory graphics, pitch microphones, field restriction circles to encourage big hitting, more accessible commentary to reach wider, non-expert audiences. The most profound and revolutionary aspect of Packer's presentation of the game was, however, perhaps the simplest: the decision to place cameras at each end, so that action could always be watched from behind the bowler's arm. Think about that a moment. Until that stage, television coverage of sports events had been about replicating as close as possible the experience of being at the ground, which, of course, involved sitting in one seat. All of a sudden, thanks to Kerry Packer, the home viewer enjoyed *for free* a luxury unavailable to the most privileged live spectator.

Unconstrained by any politesse about the game being beyond value and the players being flannelled gods, he was also content to see them commercial entangled, whether it was Tony Greig advertising Waltons or Nutri Grain, or Len Pascoe and Wayne Daniel flogging McDonalds. Above all, he did not have to worry about money. The scenes in *Howzat* where wise old Harry Chester says to Kerry that he's betting the whole of Cons Press on WSC are, politely, an exaggeration. Chester had reservations about WSC's management, which was chaotic, precisely because it was basically unilateral. But the costs of WSC were straightforwardly amortised across the huge Consolidated Press and PBL group. In a very good 1978 interview by Terry Lane, now available as a podcast on the *Inside Story* website, Packer says: 'My father was a gambler. Every man who ever created anything was a gambler. I am, also, but there's a difference. What I risk on World Series Cricket is not going to put this company into jeopardy. It's not going to send it broke. I could close it down and the place would not even hiccup.' He wasn't bluffing. And in showing off the market power of an integrated media conglomerate, WSC also began revealing the weaknesses of the board's old monopoly. The traditional game was profitable, but only thinly so. International cricket made good money, but its revenue base was narrow: cash came in mainly from the turnstile, a growing amount from sponsorship, relatively little from television. There were, moreover, a lot of mouths to feed. There was a Sheffield Shield to sustain. There were six state associations dependent on their dividends, two of them, in South and Western Australia, paying for the upkeep of expensive, underutilised grounds. What *just* worked as a monopoly market began to unravel as a duopoly.

Packer then did something that showed real cojones. In the first season of WSC, he had been content to emphasise the quality of the star names in his stable. It had not really resonated with a public accustomed to the idea that players were driven by more exalted motives than money, like honour and glory. For the second season, he sought to enlist the public in a patriotic vision. 'C'mon Aussie C'mon', the advertising theme devised by Allan Morris and Allan Johnston, is the original and perhaps still the best marketing campaign for cricket ever devised. It was bold as brass. In 1978–79, the Australian Cricket Board was hosting England, the old enemy, for the mother of all international cricket rivalries. But somehow, Packer would convince fans that his was the real Australian team. That sales pitch was made more convincing by access to the Sydney Cricket Ground. After the SCG Trust had gone to law to keep Packer off the great ground, Packer's friend, NSW premier Neville Wran, sacked them, going to the further trouble of having light towers installed that enabled night cricket. *Howzat* rightly identifies the night of that first WSC international at the SCG as the tipping point in the campaign, Packer, his retinue and 50 000 fans storming the establishment's sanctum sanctorum.

That season of 1978–79, the Australian Cricket Board staged the biggest international summer in history: eight Tests and four one-day internationals – the first in Australia for three years. It was also our least successful: six of those Tests ended in defeat, before progressively poorer crowds. That's also because there was an even bigger summer taking place simultaneously: WSC played five Supertests and twenty-seven games in its one-day International Cup – from 17 January 1979, he even introduced deliriously coloured uniforms. Free to play where he pleased, Packer also confined WSC almost entirely to the eastern seaboard, serving its bigger publics and bigger television audiences. As he cut *his* losses, those of the board and its members grew.

What's often underestimated about Packer was that by the middle of that second season, he was in a position to effectively run world cricket. Having carried on his recruiting, he had the sixty best players from Australia, West Indies, South Africa, Pakistan. New

Zealand's Richard Hadlee had played; India's Bishan Bedi and Sunil Gavaskar were in his sights. He had a Caribbean tour in the works with the consent of the West Indies Cricket Board; there was a World Cup round the corner which depended on the presence of the top stars, all of whom were on his books. It was in Packer's reach to become to cricket what Mark McCormack had become to tennis and golf – a truly global mogul.

Packer said that he had never admired his father more than in the sale of the *Daily Telegraph*, the thing in the world he most loved, but for which Rupert Murdoch had offered a knockout price. While Packer enjoyed World Series Cricket, he never lost sight of his original purpose, which was not after all to build a cricket attraction, but to obtain exclusive broadcast rights for cricket in Australia; he had always been prepared to sell the players back to the game as part of a quid pro quo. Now that his quid was flourishing, he could demand a mighty quo. It was called the 'peace agreement', but it wasn't so much an armistice as an unconditional surrender. PBL was to receive what were called 'marketing rights' to Australian cricket for ten years; the responsibility for the televising, promotion, merchandising and sponsorship of international cricket, leaving the board to basically pick the teams and man the turnstiles.

The legal reason for doing it this way was that the *Trade Practices Act* made it 'an offence to have any agreement, understanding or arrangement which has the effect of lessening competition', reserving particular asperity for long-term deals. But the commercial reason from Packer's point of view was that he gained a much greater degree of control over what he was putting to air. The fees payable, inclusive of sponsorships from Benson & Hedges and new domestic one-day sponsor McDonald's, excluding relatively minor monies from merchandising, would rise from $1.3 million in 1979–80 to $1.86 million in 1988–89. It was more than the Board was used to, of course, but their obligations were onerous. In return, they had to procure a minimum of two touring teams a summer, to compete with Australia in Tests and in a tri-cornered one-day competition with a minimum number of twenty matches – the World Series Cup.

In a June 1977 interview with the ABC, Packer can be heard talking about the parsimony of the Australian Cricket Board towards its players. 'So,' asks the ABC reporter, 'does that mean that your venture is half-philanthropic?' 'Half-philanthropic?' replies Packer. 'That makes me sound more generous than I am.' Quite so. Packer did the business deal of a lifetime in his rapprochement with the board. At a time when broadcast rights and sponsorship monies were just beginning the upward trajectory that continues to this day, Packer capped his outgoings for a decade.

Packer sensed, rightly, that the board were desperate men, who just wanted their precious game back, who could see the endowments of generations being laid waste, who did not understand how all their good intentions had come to nought. As they wised up, resentments began to fester. Those who defected to WSC were forgiven but not forgotten. The defectors themselves could not overlook who had been on which side of the barricades. Vestigial traces of the animosities between WSC and the board were lived out in the travails of Kim Hughes, felt by the returned servicemen of WSC to have sided with the board a little too ardently, and also in the thwarted ambitions of Rod Marsh, thought by the board to have been just a little too passionate in speaking Packer's part.

The players – well, Packer used them too, in a way. The brief upward financial influence on player payments of WSC became, when monopoly was restored, the downward commercial pressure of PBL. For all that he had broken open cricket's monopoly, Packer restored it rapidly afterwards, with his the most powerful voice, insisting that selected star cricketers be contracted through 'Key Player Agreements', under which, in return for a guaranteed minimum income, they assigned their general marketing rights to PBL for promotional use. No-one was going to do to him what he had done to the board. Ian Chappell's dream of a players' trade union remained unfulfilled until the mid-1990s, and not until the first Memorandum of Understanding between the board and the Australian Cricketers Association did first-class cricketers in this country earn better than subsistence wages.

The game? I don't think there can be any dispute it benefited. WSC precipitated more innovation and experimentation in two years than establishment cricket had in probably the entire three decades since the Second World War. It was an education in the priorities and potentialities of broadcasting and mass marketing. Cricket had given star players and their hold on public imagination relatively little thought; Packer, because television lived and died by providing bigger stars and more excitement than network rivals, provided a salutary reminder that neither big names nor big crowds were to be taken for granted. The day/night limited-overs match in coloured clothing with field restriction circles became the killer app of modern cricket – so successful it almost ate the game alive. Post-WSC, in fact, the game rather lost impetus in Australia, as though it needed time to digest the stupendous change of the preceding two years. With one key sponsor, Benson & Hedges, cosily ensconced, and an external promoter, PBL, focused primarily on its bottom line, cricket fell into the habit of repeating the same effects with diminishing returns. Between 1980 and 1996, West Indies teams visited ten times for Tests and/or one-day internationals; India came thrice. When cricket authorities took back control for the marketing of the game in Australia, they did so in a rather half-hearted way. Competition between them made the football codes ambitious, expansionist, responsive to the public; thanks perhaps to a perceived lock on summer, coupled with on-field success, cricket rather marked time. Next month, cricket will finally leave behind a governance structure that has remained essentially unaltered since before female suffrage. It has proven as resilient as lantana.

A J P Taylor once explained that much of the talk of the decline of civilisation among his colleagues at Oxford in 1950s meant only that 'university professors used to have domestic servants and now did their own washing up'. My perspectives on Kerry Packer's enterprise are likewise personally seasoned, because it has intersected with my life at three discrete intervals. When I went to Kardinia Park to watch one of the first WSC games, I was an eleven-year-old at Geelong's Manifold Height Primary School; when I started *The Cricket War* in 1992, I was a 26-year-old journalist attempting my first cricket book; in this era of *Howzat* two decades later, I'm about to publish my eighteenth cricket book, one of which was the history of what is now Cricket Australia.

In 1977, I might say, I was repelled and fascinated by WSC. I did not go so far as my old friend Mark Ray, who wore a T-shirt that read 'Death to the Circus', but I was appalled that players could have been so disloyal as to turn their backs on the glory of the game. No-one is so primly shockable as a youthful prude. By the same token, who couldn't be excited by cricket on two channels? Yee hah. It wasn't channel surfing because remote controls did not yet exist; more like channel trundling. But it was new and different.

During the 1980s, I grew increasingly interested in WSC's unacknowledged legacy. So much of the game I was watching was a fruit of the WSC years – one-day games at night, mass marketing, supercharged television presentation, supersaturation advertising. Yet nobody, it seemed, wanted to talk about that. In fact, as I found when I started researching the subject, there remained deep wounds in the game, even fifteen years on. Players remembered being 'disapproved persons'. Administrators hung onto senses of betrayal. Kerry Packer had by this stage suffered the public odium of the 'Goanna' affair and, I heard later, sent down the line that I was not to receive any cooperation. I'm not sure he had terribly much to fear. At the time, I might say, I was simply a low-level hack being paid a pittance by an obscure monthly magazine and living on breakfast cereal. I would take my office's Mac Classic home at weekend to my one-bedroom flat, keyboard under one arm, monitor under the other, mouse between my teeth; I would be rejected by eleven publishers before *The Cricket War* became a reality.

That I got anywhere at all was due primarily to Ian Chappell. Chappelli's attitude was that WSC had been the hardest cricket he had played. Relentless fast bowling, untrammelled aggression, unparalleled concentration of talent. Yet, he complained, none of it counted – not in Test records, not even in first-class records, and it had been virtually ignored by the mainstream media. Talk to me? Of course, he'd talk to me, and he did, for hours, candidly and vividly, for his memory is the most compendious of any cricketer I have ever met. But even Ian could not persuade, for instance, Rod Marsh to talk. Another cricketer of my acquaintance told me of a dinner where he overheard Ian counselling Marsh: 'You should talk to this guy, Bacchus. He's OK.' Marsh continued demurring: 'Naaah, he'll be just like the rest.'

The board, meanwhile, was little less hostile to the idea of the book, and also discountenanced having anything to do with it – one board officer told me I was 'a disgrace to cricket'. Funnily enough, Bob Parish and Ray Steele, by then some time retired, were not themselves prickly. They still bore some scars of the events, and they were frank about them, but in person they were two decent, honest, kindly men of cricket. Some of you will have noted the characterisation in *Howzat* of Bradman, who never actually appears, but is represented by a disembodied voice at the end of a phone. It springs more or less directly from a remark of Ray Steele's. He mentioned *inter alia* that there had been some talk of Bradman going to London in August 1977 to testify in the High Court case brought by Packer against the authorities to overturn the ban on his players. This, said Steele, had been quickly nipped in the bud. 'The Don'd load the bullets,' Steele chuckled, 'but he'd leave us to fire them.' The line is paraphrased in *Howzat* and, from memory, put in the mouth of Bob Parish. It's a thought-provoking sentiment. Though not the chairman of the ACB in 1977, the Don remained Australia's most substantial cricket personality. Fascinatingly, he never made a single public comment about WSC, preferring to wield his influence more subtly. One wonders how events might have been different had Bradman not been wearied by a lifetime of scrutiny, had he elected to make a public stand against Packer's irruption. It's possible it would have made little difference, but it might have made some, both at the time, and to our sense of him now. As it was he remained above the fray.

The Cricket War celebrates WSC. Why? Partly because, at the time, it was *not* celebrated, and because if anything I tend to lean a little against prevailing points of view, to try to move the terms of public debate along a bit. That puts me in an interesting position now that WSC *is* celebrated, indeed has been adopted as part of the official story, not surprisingly considering that its dramatis personae occupy so many enduringly powerful positions in the administration, presentation and interpretation of the game. Kerry Packer is a synonym for cricket innovation – he is invoked as freely in India, now the bastion of made-for-TV cricket, as in Australia. He's a hero even in establishment cricket. On news of his death in 2005, the players in a Boxing Day Test formed two solemn lines during a minute's silence, and the chairman of the board that had resisted his encroachments every step of the way now seated him in the pantheon alongside the Don: 'That cricket is today taken for granted as a natural part of the Australian way of life is in no small measure due to his influence. The so-called "Packer Revolution" in the 1970s has left a lasting legacy in the way the game is played, administered and presented to the public via the influential Channel Nine telecast.' He stopped short at least of claiming that Oceania had always been at war with Eurasia.

I'm sure that nobody would be more surprised than Packer at his sentimentalised posthumous reputation as entrepreneurial derring-doer. He deplored the Australian attitude to wealth, and much preferred the American. He said that when an American saw a flash car, his attitude was to approve of the owner, who had obviously worked hard to deserve such a car; Australians, he complained, were inclined to grumble about such ostentation. Have we come around, then, to his way of thinking? I wouldn't be so presumptuous. But it may be time to move the terms of the debate along again. Kerry Packer's insurgency in 1977 did indeed revolutionise cricket, but that was not his intention. His objective was to wrest a commercial property, broadcast rights, on terms advantageous to his interests, for the least expenditure with the greatest flexibility. Mission accomplished, he moved on: the last scene of *Howzat* evokes this rather well, Packer being seen on the phone already in the throes of his next deal, like the proverbial capitalist shark, remaining in motion in order to survive, surviving in order to remain in motion. In the rush to agree that cricket did well from Packer, we're at risk of overlooking how well Packer did from cricket. Half-philanthropic? Not even Packer thought so.

Address to History Council of Victoria, September 2012

Shane Warne

THE SHOW MUST GO ON

'Fair set of cheeks on it,' said Jason Warne. It was a bright summer day just before Christmas, and we were looking up at the statue of his brother Shane that had just been unveiled near Gate 2 of the Melbourne Cricket Ground. Fair indeed – one and a half times life size, and rather a contrast to the self-sculpting of the features of Australia's greatest living cricketer by assiduous dieting and well-chosen unctions.

Warne himself was busy being photographed *en famille*, arm draped round the waist of his fiancée Elizabeth Hurley, whose smile flickered as if in harmony with the flashbulbs. He looked good, too. Snug Dunhill suit, conservative tie, fashionably mussed hair. He even made a self-deprecating joke about the sculpture's obviously more generous figure: 'That's 300 kilograms, so it's pretty lifelike from when I played.'

There was actually a bit of a back-story to this. A couple of weeks earlier, I had visited sculptor Louis Laumen in his studio, a Footscray warehouse, in which the wax husk of the bronze cast still towered, and the original model from which the final image had been worked up via a giant pantograph remained on display. Laumen recounted meeting Warne at the end of May in an office at the Melbourne Cricket Club to take measurements for his vast idol of the idol, the first in a new series of casts destined to line the walk to the MCG across Jolimont Park. Laumen pored over his subject, meticulously documenting each proportion, photographing his head from sixteen different perspectives. Some subjects, he finds, writhe in discomfiture as they are boiled down to their dimensions and captured in all their imperfections. Warne did not; he was enthusiastic and engaged throughout, tweeting excitedly on his smartphone: 'Feel very privileged and honoured to join so many amazing and wonderful sportsman in the way of a statue at the mcg – thankyou – humbled !'

'He was really likeable, really pleasant, really approachable,' said Laumen. 'Just one of those guys you know it would be impossible to stay mad with. Five minutes with him and it feels like you're old buddies; he seems to like everybody, so it's just impossible not to like him. I think if I'd asked him to strip he'd have done it.' Only once, Laumen recalled, did Warne look slightly perturbed. 'You're not going to do me fat, are you?' he asked, a little anxiously. Laumen placated him: 'What I want to do is show you at your best as a player.' They discussed how his playing weight had tended to fluctuate, and the periods when he had been happiest with his physique. Looking over the images later and comparing them to images from Warne's career, Laumen was actually impressed: 'One thing about Warnie was that whenever he was carrying any weight at all, it went to the throat and neck. So in order to lose it, he's had to work really hard, and become quite gaunt.'

It was the representatives of the Melbourne Cricket Club who demurred. They looked askance at Laumen's slimline model of

Warne in action, insisting on further layers of upholstery, particularly round the face. Laumen strove to keep faith with subject and client: 'I've put weight on, without going too far. There's a hint of paunch without it being overly developed. He's just a bit comfortable. The curve of the belly is there, the pants are down low.' He honoured, too, Warne's immemorial habit at the point of maximum exertion of letting his tongue protrude: 'The MCC people didn't like it, but I still had to give a hint of it, just behind the teeth; it's part of the cheek of the man.' And now, of the cheeks.

On perhaps no Australian do so many people hold views as Shane Warne; as the foregoing implies, sometimes they cannot even agree what he looks like. Twenty years of fame will do that to you. Most athletes dwindle in their profile and recognisability when their playing days expire. At what he called 'a young forty-two', Warne has perhaps never been neither more successful nor more sellable. He leads a jet-set existence flitting between hemispheres; he is engaged to be married to one of the world's most beautiful women; yet Old Warnie maintains a residual hold on imaginations even as New Warnie stretches them.

This summer, NW has filled the breach left by OW. Five years after his Test farewell, Warne returned to big cricket by stepping out with the Melbourne Stars, one of the eight teams involved in Cricket Australia's new city-based T20 competition, the KFC Big Bash League. He became, again, headline news, whether jousting with cyclists, jesting with commentators or nesting with Elizabeth Hurley, dragging along more than 650 000 people in his Twitter slipstream, @Warne888; he felt good enough at one stage to contemplate a return to the green and gold; he rested content in the end with producing perhaps summer's most telegenic moment. Above all, by resuming as a cricketer, Warne showed by just how far he had left that simple designation behind: we watch him now just being himself. 'Shane is best at doing those things he enjoys,' says his manager James Erskine. 'And the thing he is best at is being Shane Warne.'

Whenever someone has a brainstorm about Warne – whether they'd like him to drive an $850 000 yellow Lamborghini Murcielago, which he agreed to, or to promote a herbal remedy for erectile dysfunction, which he didn't – it's with Erskine they make an appointment. Likewise if they have an idea for Harry Kewell, Matt Giteau, Mark Nicholas or Michael Clarke, whom Erskine's Sport & Entertainment Ltd also manages. But it's Warne whose signature is most sought after: without needing to hurry or hustle or pursue every opportunity, he rakes $5 million in a year easily.

When I meet Erskine at SEL's East Sydney offices, he is enjoying his boss's prerogative by wearing shorts and a polo shirt while a young, fresh-faced and crisply laundered staff toil at their workstations. We adjourn to 'The Library', a comfortable, partitioned anteroom with armchairs, couches and bookshelves heavily stocked with the works of Michael Parkinson. Rightly so: it was selling Parky to Channel 10 in Australia just over thirty years ago that put Erskine, sent out from London in September 1979 to run the Sydney office of Mark McCormack's International Management Group, on the map Down Under.

Warne entered Erskine's orbit at a similarly seminal stage, shortly after Erskine had struck out on his own at SEL with former IMG colleague Basil Scaffidi and the ubiquitous Allco financier David Coe. Warne's erstwhile spin bowling partner Tim May had just founded a cricketers' trade union, the Australian Cricketers' Association, to negotiate a collective bargaining agreement with a disapproving Cricket Australia. May asked SEL to advise them. The ensuing argy-bargy brought Australia's cricketers to the brink of a strike, with Warne perhaps as militant as anyone.

At the time, Warne was managed by Austin Robertson, previously agent to Dennis Lillee and Allan Border. It was not until the 2005 Oval Test that Warne and Erskine chummed up. Warne was at a personal nadir that English summer: his wife Simone had taken their children back to Australia after wearying of his compulsive infidelity; even his great patron Kerry Packer had lost faith, tearing up a commentary contract worth about $300 000 a year. Yet as was often the case with Warne, his cricket burned all the brighter and his popularity in England was probably at its zenith. In the 150 metres it took Erskine and Coe to walk with him to an Italian restaurant, Warne was stopped five times. The Italian waiters there all recognised him and his phone rang incessantly – to the point that Erskine had to ask him to turn it off. Harness that irrepressible personality and natural popularity, thought Erskine, and here was a remarkable client in the making. 'I'll represent you on one condition,' he told the cricketer. 'That you will listen.'

Which Warne has, says Erskine, even if he does not always hear. Erskine, for instance, would much prefer that Warne did not tweet, something he only began in order to promote his involvement with the British online gaming company 888 Holdings plc, which began four years ago, but which he now does compulsively. 'Shane thinks it's wonderful,' says Erskine. 'I think it's asinine.' In general, though, it's been a happy and lucrative partnership. With the end of Warne's international career, he segued seamlessly into the new world of supranational T20, becoming the captain-coach of the Rajasthan Royals at an official figure of $450 000 a year but enhanced by other arrangements including a 3.5 per cent stake. He mended fences with Nine; he walked into commentary with Sky and writing columns with London's *Daily Telegraph*. And things kept coming along that simply do not befall the average sporting great. It was Erskine, for example, who persuaded Warne to see the fun in Eddie Perfect's *Shane Warne: The Musical* three years ago. Sensitive to 'unauthorised' portrayals, Warne was reflexively hostile to the project and even fantasised of stopping it legally. On reading the script, Erskine counselled him: 'They can do it, Shane. You can't do anything. And my advice would be to embrace it. After all, how many cricketers have had a musical done about them? And by the way, it's bloody funny.' Warne agreed to attend a preview at which he was spotted at the interval by two septuagenarian theatregoers. 'You must be very proud,' they told him, in all seriousness. 'Do you think so?' Warne wondered aloud. On opening night, he joined Perfect on stage, and as the theatre rocked with cheers looked bashfully chuffed.

Not everything has succeeded. Perhaps the worst misadventure was *Warnie*, the stale, formulaic talk show which topped a viewer poll last January as Australia's worst Australian television programme. 'We made a huge mistake, for which I blame myself,' agrees Erskine. 'My idea when I went to Nine was to do a kind of *Larry King Live*, based on cricket, but also including other people and things. It could basically be at the ground. But we were all too busy and I got talked by Gary Burns and his offsider at the time into a big production with a studio audience . . . They tried to do a *Footy Show* and it didn't work.'

Warnie was a strangely telling experiment, nonetheless. Warne, who seems born to television, who has likened his life to a soap opera and refers to its superintending 'scriptwriter', who has more screens on his walls at home than he does paintings, was buried beneath his show's layers of production, contrivance and corniness: the exercise probably told you more about television than about Warne. Erskine's strictures notwithstanding, *@warne888* seems somehow truer to Warne's nature – his spontaneity, his sentimentality, his ingenuousness, his impetuosity, his utter everydayness, whether he is soliciting views about budgie smugglers, mentioning his dreams featuring Scooby-Doo, exchanging lovestruck notes with Hurley, or simply chewing the virtual breeze ('UNSTACKING DISHWASHER !!!!!!!!!!!!!!', 'How much does it hurt when you cut your finger nails to short !!!!'). Sachin Tendulkar's tweets soon petered out thanks to the unappeasable cravings of his two million followers. Warne, with the aid of his personal assistant Helen Nolan, keeps the faith with a rapt audience who cheerfully retweet everything from his philosophies of life to pictures of his son's Lego creations: packing his three children off on their new school years took four continuous tweets that would have struck a chord with any parent. Twitter helps Warne corral and control his fame, while radiating an air of accessibility.

Warne's breezy comfort with mainstream and social media also draws commercial opportunities. To use an idiom of public relations, Warne has 'cut-through'. When the Australian arm of Mattel went looking for an Australian personality for the Hot Wheels 'Designed By' series last year, for instance, it faced an immediate problem. In other markets, Mattel had used a motor sport hero to promote the series: MotoGP champion Jorge Lorenzo in Spain, F1 driver Felipe Massa in Italy, NASCAR's Danika Sue Patrick and Dale Earnhardt Junior in the US have all worked with Mattel designers to produce personalised toy cars. The possibilities in Australia, says Pulse Communications account manager Steve Munachen, were altogether thinner: 'There was Mark Webber, who spends ninety per cent of his time overseas and lives in Switzerland. There was [V8 Supercars'] Jamie Whincup, who doesn't really have a big profile. Not all that much else.'

Then Munachen thought of Warne, with whom he had worked on a promotion, the Pop-Up Pub, for VB in 2009: 'He was really good, a nice guy, easy to deal with – I never had a bad experience with him. Very personable, chatted to everyone.' Like his Porsche-driving father Keith, Warne has an abiding fetish for cars: he used to own a Brock Commodore which his wife Simone called the 'Bogan-mobile'. Mucking round with his children, too, has become a recurring theme of *@warne888* ('Played laser force with kids So much fun. Now 10 pin bowling I just bowled a gutter & yep the rails are up – kids laughing at me – classic !!'). What could be more ideal? 'Not only is Shane probably our most high-profile domestic sports-man,' says Munachen, 'but this was a car that was going to be available in all markets, including England and India, as well as Australia. Shane worked well almost everywhere.' A toy car is a toy car. A toy car associated with Shane Warne is paraded on *The 7pm Project* and launched at a press conference where Warne answers questions about just becoming engaged to one of the world's most beautiful women. Cut-through: that is what in the middle of last year, Cricket Australia badly needed.

It is usual to say of sporting properties that they are unveiled in a 'blaze of publicity'. The KFC Big Bash League was not. When Cricket Australia revealed the new competition structure, franchise team names and colours in April 2011, there was both widespread public indifference and acute private misgivings. The BBL's purposes were twofold. Externally, the promotion of it as a fun family night out with lots of music and hoopla was CA's attempt to reconnect with young fans too impatient for longer forms of the game. Inter-nally, it was aimed at providing a new television revenue stream, weaning CA off a dependence on international cricket, where the value of bilateral series is dwindling – CA earns big dollars only when Australia play India and England. Yet the BBL was not to make money immediately. After approving minority private own-ership in the franchises, CA went cold on the idea. And because it would remain subject of the same rights agreement with Fox Sports as the old Big Bash, extending to the end of the 2012–13 season, there would be little to defray its $24 million start-up costs. At least in a cricketing sense, too, it was nothing very much: essentially the same players as in the tournament's previous iteration, spread over eight city-based teams rather than six state teams. When CA revealed that Cricket Victoria would be setting up two teams in Melbourne, the Stars at the MCG and the Renegades at Etihad Stadium, it was hard to see how it would work – not even the ubiquitous Eddie McGuire quite understood.

McGuire Media's office is upstairs in a reconditioned terrace house on East Melbourne's Jolimont Terrace. As the offices of the Melbourne Football Club, it was where the first million-dollar Australian rules football deals were done, bringing Peter Moore and Kelvin Templeton to the Demons; with McGuire officiating as president of Collingwood, it was also the setting for the 'Kiribilli House pact' which club coach Mick Malthouse struck with his heir apparent Nathan Buckley. It has one wall of bookshelves of seemingly unread books and another wall devoted to Eddie's honours including his AM, but is otherwise built for purpose, not prestige; it is the office, in fact, of someone who prefers being out of the office, shaking hands, doing deals, rationing his time, channelling his energies – being busy, always busy. And at his first encounter with representatives of Cricket Victoria offering him the presidency of the Stars, he could not immediately see why this project should detain him. Little in detail seemed to be nailed down. There was a fuzzy Asian-focused notion, for example, that putting a pentangular star on the Stars' uniform would win it the allegiance of fans from Pakistan. McGuire himself suggested calling the team 'Collingwood', leveraging his football club's brand, and his own. There seemed little common ground; the parties parted without agreement.

Curiously, given that they are often regarded as synonymous, Collingwood was involved before McGuire. The Stars started with nothing, not even an office: 35-year-old chief executive Clint Cooper, a former accountant seconded from Cricket Victoria, operated at first out of the MCG's Hugh Trumble Café, with personal assistant Megan Keating as his sole administrative support; he later rented a small suite on top of a management consultancy and a property planner, which being near Cricket Victoria had the advantage that he could pop in and use its really good photocopier. Rather than put staff on, he signed a service agreement with Collingwood's director of operations David Emerson, under which the football club provided support for membership, hospitality and backend marketing, rather as it already did for the Melbourne Vixens netball team. The deal had the side benefit of making McGuire feel involved even before he actually was – because under the influence of John Wylie, the tony investment banker who chairs the board of the MCG Trustees, he was coming round.

McGuire's lifelong loyalty to the Magpies has left him fascinated by clubs and why people follow them. He is intrigued that his sons have become fans of the Lakers, Dodgers and Celtic without the ability to watch them live; he had observed also their discovery of Warne, whom they are too young to remember playing for Australia, via the wonders of YouTube. When at last he accepted the presidency, with Wylie acting as his deputy and backstop, his strategy could be condensed to two words: Get Warne. Looking out his office window, he could see the looming bulk and soaring towers of the MCG: venue of the *first* Test match, of the *first* one-day international match and potentially of the *first* big Australian club match. He felt his sap rising. Warne could be a part of history!

Warne *was* interested. But Warne tends to be interested in everything at first; he commits more gradually. SEL prices its superstar client's services at about $100 000 a day. After fifteen years following cricket schedules, Warne prefers keeping things casual. Warne once spent nearly a day trying to choose between refrigerators. 'How much did that fridge cost you, Shane?' Erskine asked. 'Oh,' said Warne, 'about $1500.' 'No it didn't,' Erskine explained. 'It cost you $80 000. Because while you were shopping for it, that's what you could have earned.'

On 20 May 2011, Warne played what he announced as his last game of competitive cricket: for the Royals against Mumbai Indians at Wankhede Stadium. He then spent most of June, July and August in the northern hemisphere, commentating with Sky in England, recreating with Hurley in the US. He lost weight and kept losing it – the work of TaiSlim shakes, apparently, and an object of ceaseless tabloid fascination. He joined Hurley at Estee Lauder's breast cancer charity functions, and on the New York set of *Gossip Girl* in which Hurley plays vampish Diana Payne; he accompanied his friend Joe Hachem, another SEL client, to Las Vegas for the World Series of Poker; by Twitter, he organised a spontaneous fundraising auction for his Shane Warne Foundation, which began with Hurley offering a pair of her jeans for sale, and ended up with items donated by the likes of Stephen Fry, Chris Martin, Dannii Minogue, Gary Ablett Jnr and Sir Elton John all pitching in to raise $18 000. Erskine doesn't chivvy his client along under such circumstances: it's just the way Warne rolls. 'I've never really had an argument with Shane,' he says. 'I have, occasionally, been curt.'

There were some impediments to a BBL deal, too. David Gyngell wanted Warne for Channel Nine's commentary team over summer. James Packer wanted Warne to promote Crown Casino's new luxury lounge Club 23, whose name derives from Warne's lucky number, and to participate in its Aussie Millions poker tournament in January; for the preceding four years, in fact, Warne and

Hachem had held their own charity event as a precursor to the Millions. There were overlapping dates, unclear priorities and multiple potential conflicts of interest – although, of course, it was James's father who once said that if you didn't have a conflict, you didn't have an interest.

In the medium term, however, it meant that the Stars had to chug along without the figure whom McGuire envisaged as the biggest Star of all. It was a discontented winter. Stars and Renegades were essentially to split the old Victorian Bushrangers between them, a process that Bushrangers and Stars coach Greg Shipperd likened to 'dividing your children'. Worse, the players were signed on one-year contracts, guaranteeing that however much they bonded during the season, they would at the end of that time inevitably be broken up again. There was lots of kvetching about the way the 2011–12 season was to be front-ended and back-ended with first-class cricket so that the prime time of summer could be parcelled out for one T20 game per night. The answer was, of course, that in any contest between the priorities of television and the priorities of cricket, what is best for the former will almost invariability have to be sucked up by the latter – but that did not make it much more palatable.

As for developing a buzz around a new cricket competition . . . well, it was football season. Who wanted to talk cricket? The teams were called what? It would be held when? Would it be on television? Was there to be private ownership? Cooper put a marketing manager on a six-month contract at the end of August, but found sponsors non-committal at best: 'You'd spend the first half hour trying to explain what the competition was. There was nothing for anyone to see.' Wylie introduced Cooper to Richard McIndoe, chief executive of TRUenergy, which was planning an IPO in the next twelve months: green might be a bad colour in marketing, but has congenial associations in power generation. Yet McIndoe was reticent. The Stars needed star power, of the kind that the Brisbane Heat briefly generated by wooing Matthew Hayden. As if on cue, Warne returned to Melbourne to spend time with his children in September, and confided by Twitter that he was 'keen to be with a team' in the BBL, to 'play a few games–help off field'.

There was, by now, competition. Expressions of interest came from Brisbane, Adelaide and Sydney; *Footy Show* host James Brayshaw, a former Sheffield Shield rival, rang Warne directly with his own offer on behalf of the Renegades. Everyone had their pitch; everyone knew Warne was busy; everyone was prepared to be flexible. If Warne only wanted to play one game, that would be fine; what was wanted primarily, of course, was his aura. In fact, only the Stars were ever really in the race, because of their MCG home ground and because of McGuire. 'I've known Eddie McGuire since he was a journalist at Channel 10,' says Erskine. 'Nobody is wired into Melbourne like him. I promised Eddie it wouldn't be a Dutch auction.'

It became a multi-unit auction instead. After Warne's teasing tweet, Erskine spoke to Patrick Delany, newly promoted to running Fox Sports, broadcaster of the BBL. 'At Foxtel we're been right at the forefront of innovating in live and high-definition sports coverage,' Delany says. 'Where we hadn't been as good had been in innovating in our commentary, and I wanted that to change on my watch.' Delany was keen to have Warne's services in some capacity; to his surprise, Erskine volunteered that Warne was willing to be 'mic'd up' – that is, to interact with the commentators whilst actually playing, a technology that had been used in T20 coverage before, but mainly as a novelty. What Fox calls 'In-Play Insight' is seldom enough on its own. 'A really crappy movie in high-definition,' observes Delany, 'is still a really crappy movie.' Delany, though, was captivated by Warne's confidence. Warne did not have to be pushed or prodded into wearing the apparatus: he *wanted* to wear it, just like Delany wanted him to want to, in as many matches as possible.

Warne had been thinking too. Why play two games when he could play all of them? It was, again, a characteristic Warne whim. He might take time, but when he commits he commits totally: in for a penny, in for a pony. The idea of a full-fledged comeback appealed to his children, who had little recollection of him playing; the idea of appearing in a new competition probably appealed to his own inner child, to which novelty has always been an allure. This was a big deal, Erskine concluded: he could leverage it a little further still. 'Before you go off half-cocked and say yes, let me ring Cricket Australia,' Erskine told his client. 'They've invested a fortune in this.' So Erskine spoke to CA's CEO James Sutherland – something with a certain piquancy, given that for many years he had been persona non grata with the organisation because of his role in the Australian Cricketers' Association original memorandum of understanding. CA agreed to top up the sums already offered by the Stars and Fox Sports, making for a package rumoured to be worth about $650 000, plus, as was the case with Warne at the Royals, an equity component: Warne is entitled to Stars shares in the event that private ownership proceeds, and entitled to compensation if it does not.

Warne himself made two further telephone calls. Firstly, he rang David Gyngell, McGuire's successor as Nine's chief executive, and asked if the network would release him from his summer's commentary obligations, which were in any case on a casual basis. Rather as Kerry Packer's grandfather eighty years ago released Bradman from a contract to write for his newspapers in order that the Don play for Australia, so Kerry Packer's last noteworthy protégé freed Warne from calling cricket in order that he might play for the Stars. And at last Warne was in a position to telephone McGuire, who was coincidentally watching his sons play in an under-11 game for Prahran in the sylvan grove of cricket grounds that make up Melbourne's Fawkner Park. 'What would be the best result here?' Warne asked. Still reluctant to seem greedy, McGuire asked if Warne would consider playing the Stars' four games at the MCG. 'What about the lot?' Warne asked. McGuire was momentarily speechless. Having excitedly agreed, he rang Cooper. 'Are you sitting down?' he began.

Jim Stynes Room, Melbourne Cricket Ground, 8 November 2011: at one end of a long table sat McGuire and Cooper; at the other sat Shipperd and Stars captain Cameron White. 'Isn't the green slimming, ladies and gentlemen?' asked McGuire as the svelte Warne arrived to sit between them and announce his comeback for the Stars. 'It definitely wasn't the green that persuaded me,' responded Warne. 'There was a bit of green,' McGuire interposed wryly.

Warne, however, soon provided the value to go with that price. TRUenergy finally signed up as a sponsor; likewise Jeep, Antler Luggage, 2XU and Jenny Craig, whose managing director Amy Smith is a friend of McGuire's. With the exception of a pourage deal arranged by the Adelaide Strikers and the promotion of an existing state sponsor at the Hobart Hurricanes, they were the first corporate backers landed by a team in the entire league. 'Shane gave the competition credibility,' Cooper recalls. 'Suddenly there was an awareness that had been lacking before. It was "the thing that Warnie's playing in" . . . We went from cold-calling people to people cold-calling us.'

Warne was everywhere. He was photographed giving a Stars shirt to David Beckham, and to Sachin Tendulkar and Rahul Dravid; he went out to Glen Waverley Central Reserve for a coaching clinic. He conducted a lengthy private tutorial with the two youngest Stars, Alex Keath and Peter Handscomb; he rolled out the next day for a first 'official' bowl at which the Stars' sponsors were announced. He hosted a Stars function at Club 23; he became focus of the Stars' promotional campaign for 'Warnie's Bay', a core spectator group. His effect on fans, in fact, could sometimes be embarrassing. When he arrived a little late for one autograph signing session, everyone suddenly deserted the other players and lined up at Warne's end of the table. It might have caused discontent, except that Warne very obviously relished the team environment. 'When you travel round as a group with Shane, whether you're going through airports or staying in hotels, it's pretty full-on,' says George Bailey, the poised 29-year-old captain of Tasmania who joined the Stars. 'You see firsthand exactly what a celebrity he is, how people from all walks of life just want a piece of him. The good thing is that away from that, in a team environment, at training or preparing, cricket is his number-one focus, because it's what he does best. You could not find a more generous teammate.' With four seasons behind him in the IPL, Warne's knowledge of T20 was encyclopaedic, which he condensed into a two-page, twenty-paragraph dissertation on the format for the Stars' induction book. For a form of the game often thought of as crude, 'How to Win T20' was full of subtle, even Machiavellian, thinking, such as using the first and last balls of each over to keep slower-scoring batsman on strike and to isolate big-hitting opponents, the importance of taking wickets in the first six overs when you are bowling, and preserving them when you are batting. The only problem with Warne, Bailey found, was the tweeting: it was so incessant he had to unfollow @ *warne888*.

Yet the tweeting was bizarrely effective – as I observed on the morning of 12 December in the press box at Bellerive Oval for Australia's Test against New Zealand. 'Seen this?' said a colleague, holding up his iPhone to show me a photo of a disembodied hand bearing serious blisters on two fingers. It was a Warne twitpic with the explanatory legend: 'Not ideal preparation for practice match today–burning the bowling hand Get better quickly please, any suggestions–HELP.' Warne had decided to break his fast ahead of a planned warm-up game against the Renegades with a bacon roll, and managed to start a fire; the ugly lesions had resulted from his plunging his hand into cold water. The picture had already been retweeted more than a hundred times.

The press box of a morning is normally a quiet place; this day it hummed with industry. When Clint Cooper described the incident as a 'cooking mishap', it became the day's catchphrase. My colleague's iPhone rang incessantly as he tried to dash something off for *The Australian*'s website, and he recited the phrase 'cooking mishap' to each interlocutor with diminishing patience. Finally his daughter rang. 'Bet this is about Warnie too,' he harumphed. Pause. 'He's had a cooking mishap . . . ' By lunchtime, Warne's Kentucky-Fried hand was the number one story on every newspaper website in the country. *The Australian*'s version featured the warning: 'Image may offend.'

The Melbourne Stars' coup could be seen plain as day: they had recruited not so much a cricketer so much as a media event waiting to happen. Who else burns their hand so that plastic is seared into the flesh and before seeking medical assistance distributes a photograph of it and invites his fans to respond? Who else milks the moment by turning up the next day to the tournament's launch with his hand swathed in bandages? When later I asked Star coach Greg Shipperd how he had heard about the mishap, he said he had seen Warne's number flash up on his phone en route to the practice game. 'You're not going to believe this, Shippy,' Warne began. When I remarked that Warne over the years had probably used this line quite a lot and that it covered a multitude a possibilities, Shipperd, normally a rather dour man, broke into unexpectedly hearty laughter. 'We won't go there,' he said. 'No, we won't go there. Oh dear . . . '

We will go there, of course. There *is* a history – each little drama around Warne resonates with a legacy of incidents and accidents, by his surviving of which he has become the willing punchline in a kind of shared national joke, the bowler of the 'Ball of the Century' *and* the object of Sharon Strezlecki's unrequitable lust in *Kath & Kim*. For some, no doubt, he will remain the original irredeemable cashed-up bogan. But there is also to his fame a very Australian quality, of charisma without mystique, of ambition without avidity, with a tincture of absurdity as well. 'Warne gives you the impression that he is not worried about what people think, and that he will take whatever comes,' says academic David Nichols, who last year took on inner-city prejudices about outer-city life in his book *The Bogan Delusion*. 'It seems like he would be the same person whether he was famous or not.' Nicholls credits Warne with the 'relaxed erectness of carriage' that A A Phillips prescribed as an antidote to 'the cultural cringe' in his famous 1950 essay; indeed, it is hard to think of anyone who has worn renown and recognisability more lightly, and made fame look like so much fun, avoiding almost all the pathologies to which sport stars are commonly heir. He has never broken the law. He has no recorded history of violence. He has never gambled to excess, preferring the protected environs of high-end poker. He has never wrestled with alcohol or been addicted to a drug, unless you count TaiSlim shakes. If not always willingly, he has owned up variously to infidelity, to vanity, to naivety and to stupidity. His other weaknesses have been open, acknowledged and utterly prosaic: in full public view, he has worked to reverse his hair loss, battled with his weight and striven to stop smoking. The nonsense stories about him in the supermarket checkout aisles are in general harmlessly idiotic, while the true stories make for ready retelling.

Here's one. Lately, Warne has taken an interest in art and borrowed several works, including of the pioneering abstract painter Dick Watkins. He was thus receptive when approached by Sydney artist McLean Edwards, who wished to paint his portrait for the Archibald Prize. When Edwards and gallery owner Martin Browne met Warne and his personal assistant Helen Nolan at Warne's home, the painter was excited to find a Watkins in prominent position. 'Shane!' he exclaimed. 'What a wonderful big Dick you have!' Go on, laugh: you know it's funny.

As the evening approached on 17 December, and the Stars' inaugural game at the MCG, Warne was in strife. In compliance with anti-corruption codes, BBL cricketers were required to turn in their mobile phones before games – except that a security officer noticed an uninterrupted stream of tweets from *@warne888*. In fact, the redoubtable Helen Nolan was acting as Warne's social media proxy. 'I can get in trouble without even trying,' Warne laughed.

Outside, it looked like the Stars were in trouble. Crowds of up to 60 000 had been forecast for the game against the Sydney Thunder. But when Elizabeth Hurley went out to sprinkle a little magic dust on the occasion by tossing the coin, the MCG's terraces yawned emptily. Somehow, everything jarred. The Stars' opening batsmen emerged from their inflatable players' race crested in the Stars logo and enswirled with the fumes of dry ice to the strains of 'Let Me Entertain You'; the languid West Indian Chris Gayle then opened the bowling off two paces. Run out by a metre, David Hussey was off the ground by the time he was given out by the third umpire. Even the moment of Warne's actual reappearance was missed because the mid-game break had been given over to the hoary stunt of a bunch of club cricketers trying to catch tennis balls lobbed into the air by an uptilted bowling machine; never mind that the greatest bowler of this era, and perhaps of any, was warming up, a little gingerly, just off the square.

The Stars may have been proud of their sponsors, but their presence was cloying. When Warne took his turn at the crease, the public address system advised that it was 'thanks to Jenny Craig'. David Warner, no respecter of persons, came down the wicket to his fourth and ninth balls and launched them back down the ground for six, the ball bouncing round the empty seats, and coming back during a Jeep Cherokee advertisement: 'The search for the best four-wheel drive is over.' Warne came off with 2–0–19–0; the crowd figure of 23 496 made for similarly lacklustre reading.

There were, however, gladder television tidings. The official viewer number, 488 000, turned out to be the biggest pay-TV audience Australian cricket had ever attracted, being rivalled by only three other sports events (the Reds–Crusaders Super Rugby Final in July and the Rugby World Cup semi-final and final in October). 'We're thrilled by those figures,' said James Sutherland in a triumphant press release. 'It certainly sets the tournament alight.' He was wrong; that was to come.

When the Stars met the Heat three nights later at the Gabba, the occasion was just right. The ground had sold out in advance. Warne's presence was milked for every moment: his image alternating on the big screen with his family's, Warne bringing boos and his fiancée cheers from the 29 241. As the strains of the *Stars Wars* theme wafted round the Gabba, Warne came on for the eighth over and bowled six slow, teasing deliveries to New Zealander Brendon McCullum and Queenslander Peter Forrest, yielding just four runs. To the first ball of the tenth over, McCullum then came down the wicket to hit 'inside out' over cover, came up short of the pitch of the ball and miscued into space on the off side.

All the while, his former teammate turned Fox Sports commentator Brendon Julian was in his ear, and when McCullum next settled over his bat asked Warne what was next. 'Might be trying to shape to sweep one after that first one, or maybe even go inside out again a bit harder,' said Warne confidentially. 'So I might try and slide one in there . . . fast.' The ball was quicker, flatter, delivered stump-to-stump; seeking to sweep fine and rotate the strike, McCullum was defeated by the few extra kilometres per hour and bowled behind his legs.

Uproar: the cameras picked out Warne's family party clapping; through Warne's mic could be heard teammates flocking to celebrate. 'That worked well,' said Julian. 'Yeah, not bad, B J,' Warne replied nonchalantly. And it wasn't, even if in cricket terms it was not so obviously great: indeed, it was, in one sense, a pretty standard response to a batsman trying to free his arms to hit to off or leg. It was, nonetheless, a brilliant moment of television: what Fox Sports' Patrick Delany calls a 'golden nugget'; it also flashed round the world, thanks to ESPN–Star Sports throughout Asia, and to the mysterious personages who rejoice in uploading clips to YouTube – in this case 'Bashy586,' 'alexczarn', 'wazclark' and 'uuploader007', 'JainamShah9999' and 'Mrcricpaki'. At time of writing, for example, the last had had almost 200 000 views.

The print media rather strained to do the event justice. The problematic point that if you were watching the game at the Gabba, you knew nothing of Warne's wiles; you simply saw McCullum being bowled. Nobody made it: instead, reporters took the fifty-year-old advice of the editor in *The Man Who Shot Liberty Valance* that 'when the legend becomes fact, print the legend.' The account by the *Daily Telegraph*, for example, read like the description of a movie scene crossed with an advertisement for Fox Sports.

The *Star Wars* theme song blared when Shane Warne strode to the bowling crease and cricket's cagey magic man then proved he could read the stars himself.

In an audacious piece of pre-meditation which only he would be bold enough to conjure, Warne cheekily predicted how he would dismiss Brisbane Heat's globetrotting batting star Brendon McCullum last night.

'He might try to sweep me, so I'll just slide one through,' a miked-up Warne told cricket fans watching on Fox Sports.

Seconds later, that's exactly what happened as cricket's 42-year-old showman bowled the Kiwi dasher around his legs as Warne's glamour fiancée Liz Hurley flashed a million-dollar smile from a Gabba private box.

Those paying attention the night before would have noticed that the prediction made by the cagey, cheeky, audacious, bold magic showman had been subtly edited. 'He might be trying to sweep one after that first one, or go inside out a bit harder. So I'll try and slide one in there. Fast' had been simplified to 'He might try to sweep me, so I'll just slide one through' – thereby making Warne appear to have predicted the exact shot and to have explicitly stated his intention rather than more broadly expressed a desire to 'try'. Not that the *Telegraph* was alone. The quote was freely and globally adjusted, by the *Sydney Morning Herald* ('He might try to sweep me so I'll just slide one through'), by *The Australian* ('I reckon he's going to sweep me so I'll try and slide one through'), by London's *Daily Telegraph* ('I think he might be trying to sweep one after that first one. So I'll try and slide one in there . . . fast'), by Auckland's *New Zealand Herald* ('He might try to sweep me so I'll just slide one through'). Not surprisingly, the wicket got a big bash on the Big Bash League's website: 'Brendon McCullum became the latest victim in Shane

Warne's ever-expanding reel of highlights on Tuesday night at the Gabba, but the mega-star wasn't going to feel too down after being beaten to the punch by an "oracle" and a "genius".' But there was a lot of hyperbole around: the Indian website *Cricinfo* likened it to the experience of listening 'to Michelangelo talk as he painted the Sistine Chapel'.

To his credit, Warne himself shrank from making too much of the wicket. Bowlers made such plans all the time, he said afterwards: occasionally they came off; mostly they did not. But his sense of vindication must have been powerful because in the week afterwards he brooded seriously about the possibility of a return to the green and gold. Warne had flirted with the idea before, wondering if he hadn't given up too soon, watching the struggles of young epigones to fill the breach he had left. Erskine was dubious – sporting careers, like old love affairs, are seldom successfully rekindled. But he agreed to broach the possibility with Sutherland, and with CA's operations chief Michael Brown, who discussed it in turn with Australian coach Mickey Arthur. The polite but firm response came that the Australian cricket team had moved on. Not even Shane Warne, then, can step into the same river twice.

So why did he fantasise of it, however briefly, when wise heads were shaking that he had nothing to gain and hard heads were committing to the future not the past? Part of him may miss the intoxication that comes from the clutch moment, the great occasion and the biggest possible stage – and it is illuminating that he still, for all his T20 success and wealth, regards this as Test cricket. What it corroborates most of all, however, is the uncanny, irrepressible, undilutable optimism that has powered Warne through not just his cricket career but perhaps his whole life, where realism exists but only as a last resort, where first thoughts have been so rewarding that second thoughts have hardly been necessary.

With the momentum Warne lent it, the BBL became a source of encouragement, and of self-congratulation, for Cricket Australia. Just over half a million tickets were sold, with the smaller grounds, Bellerive Oval and the WACA, selling out; ratings never achieved the same level as for Warne's comeback match but were solid and consistent; membership sales were patchy, and fell short of budgets even at the Stars, but you have to start somewhere.

There was spectacular cricket, there was awful cricket, and all points between. Funnily enough, the Stars were perhaps the betweenest team of all. Their captain Cameron White had a fearful time with the bat; their bowling was inconsistent; their fielding lacked athleticism. Warne was not the only senior citizen spinner feeling his oats in the competition: the Stars succumbed to both the Sydney Sixers and to the Perth Scorchers, aided by forty-year-olds Stuart MacGill and Brad Hogg respectively. With a single win from their first four starts, the BBL's most glamorous team was briefly in danger of slipping from finals contention.

George Bailey wondered whether the glamour itself wasn't part of the problem: 'There was at the outset, I think, a huge amount of pressure to perform, particularly because in Melbourne there were the two teams, and, as somebody put it, it was like having two sets of sons playing for two different footy clubs. I think that weighed on the players quite a lot; there was so much build-up that guys were a bit in awe of what was expected of them.' The player least distracted by it all was, of course, Warne, whose only entourage was what he called 'the Foghorns' – Hurley, her son Damian (9), and his children Brooke (14), Summer (10) and Jackson (12). 'The thing I was asked about more than anything else was: what was it like to have Shane and Elizabeth round the group?' says Bailey. 'In fact, it was really not very unusual. After the game, four kids under the age of fifteen came into the dressing room and they could have been anyone's kids.'

It is Warne, in fact, whom Bailey credits with turning the Stars' season around, by a very simple expedient: he invited everyone to his mansion in Brighton's William Street on 6 January for a barbecue. 'Shane leads a very normal existence and that barbecue helped normalise the whole set-up,' says Bailey. 'It was the first time everyone had gotten together, and everyone's kids had gotten together, and it seemed to relax everyone, and after that we played good cricket, won our last three games and got into the semi-finals.' The Stars made it no further, although in the stock of memories from the competition, Warne is bound always to loom large. One suspects that in future fewer will be able to recall who won the inaugural BBL (the Sydney Sixers) than will remember the way Warne dismissed Brendon McCullum.

So what was Warne's house like? I asked Clint Cooper when we caught up one last time at the MCG – funnily enough watching the last rites of a Sheffield Shield match. 'Impressive,' he laughed. 'Ridiculous, really. Can't describe it.' I didn't ask him to, although it occurred to me that the remarks applied equally well to the house's owner, who at that moment was just tweeting that his favourite character in *Gilligan's Island* was Gilligan. We walked out via Gate 2, parting by Louis Laumen's bronze. Jason Warne was right: there *are* a fair set of cheeks on it.

The Global Mail, March 2012

Shane Warne

A LOVE OF THE LONG SHOT

Shane Warne is famously an aficionado of the films of the *American Pie* franchise, memorably invoking the Sherminator in his verbal thrust and parry with England's Ian Bell. But the ideal cinematic companion to his published comments of yesterday is surely the scene in *Dumb and Dumber*, where uberdork Jim Carrey asks the pretty girl about his chances with her, only to be told they are 'not good'.

'You mean not good like one in a 100?' Carrey asks. 'More like one in a million,' the girl replies. Carrey is undiscouraged: 'So you're telling me there's a chance.'

In many ways, the offer of his services to his 'best friend' Michael Clarke is a testimony to Warne's unquenchable spirit. 'I felt like I wanted to jump off the couch and grab the ball,' Warne told a reporter of watching the Perth Test, thereby emphasising his difference from you and me.

We sit on couches watching Test cricket and joke that we could do better; he sits there and *knows it*, and frankly it would take a brave judge to demur. The rationally impassable obstacles to it happening? Warne's 100 per cent proof self-belief simply melts them away. One in a million? Hey, the coolest chances are the longest, eh?

It's a faculty of Warne's that has hardly changed. Warne never believed a match to be lost, never experienced a cricket scenario that would not have been improved by his bowling.

Often it inspired teammates; sometimes it unsettled them. In April 1999 in Antigua, Warne was in fearful straits. Having hurried optimistically back from serious injuries, he had taken two for 268 in the first three Tests of the series and was bowling as poorly as anyone had seen him. Even his long-time spin familiar, Terry Jenner, was urging him to take some pressure off himself and agree to be rested.

Yet Warne never lapsed in his belief that he should play, even when it became clear that the other tour selectors were bent on outvoting him; he argued so persuasively for himself, in fact, that he turned one of them, Allan Border, around.

Critical observers might now impute to a Warne symptoms of that common malady of Relevance Deprivation Syndrome, the limelight of celebrity being too diffuse when compared with that of being at the centre of sport. I suspect, however, that Warne falls more properly into that category of sporting performer who never really stops playing, and continues afterwards to project themselves into the middle of any action they see.

It's one of the reasons that Warne is such a provocative and engaging commentator. He is never observing from afar; he somehow always works himself to the centre of things, wondering aloud how *he* would answer the challenge, how *he* would rise to the occasion.

Nor is this kind of individual so uncommon. Sports hooks its accomplished practitioners deeply. And so often are they asked about the great moments and their most luminous memories that it must sometimes seem as though their career is ongoing. There is a story about Geoff Boycott – probably apocryphal but utterly credible – in his commentary role at Lord's a few years ago. Absent-mindedly, the eminent Yorkshireman ventured into an area reserved for the teams. 'I'm sorry, Mr Boycott,' said a member of the security staff, 'but that's an area only for players.'

'But I *am* a player,' spluttered Boycott, and in his own mind he has remained so; he might have last played for Yorkshire in 1986, but Boycott still describes his career using the present tense.

Similar sentiments from Warne, of course, are not an affectation. It might be nearly two decades since the Ball of the Century, but tomorrow night he captains the Stars against the Renegades in the crosstown Melbourne derby at Etihad Stadium. And it is the small-scale game that now suits him best, allowing him to show off what he does best, which is to bowl brilliant individual deliveries, and relieving him of what he prefers avoiding, like batting and fielding. Last season he neither batted nor took a catch. In his superman's imagination, Warne can leap great differences in a single bound; in the mundane reality inhabited by we mortals, Test cricket is ever more demanding, ever more relentless.

What is certainly true is that there is a Warne-shaped hole in modern Australian cricket. He is the player we have never replaced – probably because he is *sui generis*. As Nathan Lyon toiled away on the last day at Adelaide Oval, dashing through over after over, one longed for a Warne to seize the day, slow the game and dictate the pace – which, incidentally, would have given the fast bowlers greater respite between overs, and perhaps improved their chances of playing in Perth.

But we also knew that that could hardly be, that Lyon would have to find his way, learn from his experience and solve the game according to his own lights. We forget that Lyon is a newcomer to cricket, let alone Test cricket, and has taken fifty Test wickets in spite of having only made his first-class debut last year.

The absence that left Australia unable to prosecute its advantage in Adelaide, furthermore, was not that of Shane Warne but of James Pattinson. Only Pattinson can know how fit he was coming into the Test; not even Shane Warne could have told us that.

That said, it is in Warne's gift to make a signal contribution to the effectiveness of Lyon, in much the same way as England's spin coach, Mushtaq Ahmed, has been a key influence on the careers of England's Graeme Swann and Monty Panesar.

Warne as Australia's spin coach? He has it in him. Nobody describes the art of slow bowling more lucidly, or more compellingly; the Stars speak glowingly of Warne's effect last season on his young teammate, Jon Holland.

What are the odds on Warne becoming the Australian team's spin coach? Probably not much. Probably a million to one. But hey, it's a chance, isn't it?

The Australian, December 2012

THE SKIPPER DECLARES

Everything about Australian cricket is changing. Now it's the farewells.

When Ricky Ponting's predecessor as Australian captain, Steve Waugh, announced his retirement seven years ago, it involved more curtain calls than Frank Sinatra.

It turns out that Australians' last sight of Ponting as a Test captain will be of him trailing off the MCG late last year, his leg stump tilted back like a fighter pilot's joystick, having lingered for two hours over 20. His spirit was not broken, but one of his fingers was, so there was no farewell – assuming, practical man that he is, he would have fantasised of it anyway.

Ponting is thirty-six, in the prime of any life save the one that he chose, of professional sport. For some time as Australia's captain, in fact, he has looked a man apart, his faded green and gold cap a contrast to the dark bottle green headgear of his younger comrades.

The successor to Allan Border as the cornerstone of Australian batsmanship has ended up leading Border's captaincy career in reverse. Where Border inherited a mediocre team and left it on the brink of greatness, Ponting took over one of the strongest XIs ever marshalled and has watched it dwindle away until he is virtually its last representative, like a much-decorated general leading a salute in front of three boy scouts sharing two catapults.

That has not been his fault, but it has transpired on his watch. Australia's giving up of the Ashes, the Border–Gavaskar Trophy and finally the World Cup have left an unfamiliar echo in the trophy cabinets at Cricket Australia.

Ponting is not *quite* finished, of course. He intends to play on as a batsman, and on the evidence of his rock-ribbed hundred in Ahmedabad last week, he can still summon great powers of concentration and adaptability. But his stepping down justifies the cliché 'end of an era', even if the new era begins as early as next week when Australia warm up in Fatullah for three one-day internationals against Bangladesh.

Only Greg Chappell and perhaps Neil Harvey among Australian batsmen can rival Ponting since Bradman, particularly because so much of his career has been spent in the vanguard batting position of number three, to which many are called but few are chosen.

His record stretches from horizon to horizon: 26 000 international runs with sixty-nine hundreds, 341 catches, ninety-nine Test victories – more than any other player in history. Ponting has also drummed out his runs at a rat-a-tat pace: 59.4 per hundred balls in Test matches; 80.5 per hundred balls in one-day internationals. At his peak, his batting was a pulse of Australian cricket – hearty, bouncy, vigorous.

Over the past two years, however, that pulse has grown thready. In his last twenty Test matches, he has averaged 35.8, and in his only hundred during that time, at Bellerive Oval, should have been caught at deep fine leg first ball by a cricketer now banned for deliberate underperformance. Before the last Australian summer, Ponting was invited to consider dropping down the order and declined it. He backed himself to perform in what he called in advance 'potentially the biggest series I'll play'. He failed – it could not be hidden.

Ponting has been a very Australian captain, in the sense once outlined by Neville Cardus: 'The Australian plays cricket to win; he has usually left it to Mr Warner to make Empire-binding speeches.' He was elevated because of his excellence as a batsman in both Test and one-day cricket rather than because of any evidence of strategic genius or flair for public relations. That didn't really change. He put on no airs, added no graces, sought no publicity, cultivated no celebrity mates, declined to tweet. Leadership remained, for him, all about effect. That being so, he has not perhaps had the same reservoir of public affection to draw on as Border, Mark Taylor or Steve Waugh.

But we're a perverse sporting public at times. It is odd that Michael Clarke has attracted criticism for being too polished, too image-conscious and a little too pleased with himself, and that Ponting has attracted criticism for the opposite. In fact, Ponting's attributes are probably better appreciated by close-up peers than distant observers. He has always been, and remains, very much a cricketer's cricketer. In his autobiography last year, Matthew Hayden penned a fond but perceptive portrait of the teammate he knew: a 'bat nuffy' who toyed obsessively with his equipment; a dressing room messpot who scattered his gear round 'like a scrub turkey sorting its nest'; a 'man of strong routine' who repeated the same incantation to every partner he joined: 'Good loud calls, mate.'

It could not be said of every holder of his office, but Ponting has always seemed like the kind of bloke with whom it would be good to play cricket, no matter the level. If you picked him in your club team, he would bat anywhere you asked and bring a decent afternoon tea. If he played for your opposition, you'd probably complain that he had 'a mouth on him', but also find that he was prepared to stick around for a beer at close of play.

When he delivered the Bradman Oration on the centenary of the Don's birth, it turned out to be a surprisingly touching speech about his own cricket upbringing. During last year's Bangalore Test match, he wore a black armband in honour of the late Ian Young, who gave nine-year-old Ponting a job as a scoreboard attendant at Launceston's Northern Tasmania Cricket Association Ground.

As an on-field captain, Ponting may not quite have fulfilled initial hopes for him. His early boosters, Shane Warne among them, talked up his 'cricket brain', promising an innovator and aggressor. But when he didn't have Warne or Glenn McGrath to whom to throw the ball, Ponting was prone to falling back on stereotyped 'plans'; in fact, if a single word was uttered by his players more than any other, it was 'plan', to the point where they might have been involved in architecture rather than sport.

Statistically, his record stands comparison with any. His teams won sixty-two per cent of their Test matches, seventy-two per cent of their one-day internationals. But the best captains have a happy knack, a Nelson touch, a capacity for spinning straw into gold – or, as Harold Rhodes once said to Richie Benaud: 'Benordy, if you stuck your head in a bucket of shit, you'd come up with a mouthful of diamonds.' Ponting was never that kind of captain. He won consecutive World Cups when Australia was in full bloom, but subsequently lost three of four Ashes series, in two of which his team had the playing resources to win. Inserting England at Edgbaston in 2005 and failing to finish them off at Cardiff in 2009 cost him dearly.

His greatest attribute as leader was the example of his

tremendous talent and professionalism, although this cut both ways. With runs under his belt, Ponting oozed authority; without them, he could look a tad forlorn. Nor did he remedy bad habits around umpires, about which he remained decidedly obdurate. 'I don't think I'm ever going to be able to stay mute, shrug my shoulders and accept bad mistakes as part of the game,' he rationalised. 'That's not me.' This meant that his final Test as captain will be remembered not only for its lacklustre result, but also for the hoo-hah over his haranguing of umpire Aleem Dar, who had given a decision that was in all likelihood perfectly correct. Although not obviously prone to the sensation, Ponting might in time come to regret the incident.

Ironically, given that his priority was always outcome rather than appearance, Ponting proved a better off-field captain than perhaps was appreciated. Ponting kept his private life private; he kept his public appearances dignified. He sold a multivitamin, but not himself. One look-see at the Indian Premier League was enough for him. He did not hang around and pretend to enjoy T20 for the sake of a few dollars.

Australian teams travelled well under him. He never lost his players' respect and affection. He never lost his temper with a crowd – booed the length and breadth of England in 2009, he took it all in good part. Ponting also gave excellent, informative, straight-talking press conferences, managing to sound neither coached and contrived, nor affectedly colloquial and matey. The television soundbites seldom reflected it, but he could be droll and funny. His predecessor once referred to a roomful of journalists as 'cockheads'. If Ponting thought that – and there were occasions on which he would have been entitled to – he kept it to himself.

At times last summer, he actually looked subtly at odds with the direction of Australian cricket, its overheated marketing, its overeager commercialism. When Ponting turned out for the announcement of the bloated seventeen-man Australian squad near the Sydney Harbour Bridge a full ten days before the First Test, he didn't bother hiding his chagrin: 'Unfortunately that's what we've got. For some reason, Cricket Australia wanted to name the squad as early as they have. We've just got to get on with it.'

His image appeared on the cover of the Test match media guide holding a replica of the Ashes urn, but with all the ease and naturalness of someone holding up a can of deodorant – of which, of course, he had some experience back in the day. When he came to retire the captaincy, there were neither tantrums, *a la* Allan Border, nor tears, *a la* Kim Hughes, *a la* Michael Vaughan. There was instead a quiet, dark-suited dignity. So while Ponting might not have had the Sinatra farewell, he can certainly claim to have done it his way.

The Australian, March 2011

Ponting as Batsman
NOT GOING GENTLE

Announcing his recent comeback for the Melbourne Stars, Shane Warne described himself as 'a young forty-two'. Next month Ricky Ponting turns a rather older thirty-seven, and whether he does so as a Test cricketer depends a good deal on the next few days in Johannesburg.

Firm, fit and preternaturally trim despite a six-month break from cricket, Warne in his green uniform did indeed have a touch of the Peter Pans. Ponting, meanwhile, than whom no batsman could be more dedicated, is suddenly looking gnarled and cramped and harried, without a Test hundred in nearly two years. Even should he make runs at Wanderers, his batting's vital signs will continue to be closely monitored. As Archie Macpherson once said of George Best: 'There aren't many last chances left for him.'

Blame the example of Steve Waugh. It's Waugh who turned raging against the dying of the light into an art form. In forty Tests after the age of thirty-five, Waugh actually improved his overall record, averaging 53.2 and adding ten centuries. Waugh could claim to have been inspired by his paterfamilias Allan Border, who played forty-one Tests after the same birthday, although Border's record tapered off slightly, averaging 42.6 in that time against a prior average ten runs greater.

Waugh is an exception that proves the rule. A comparison of pre-35 and post-35 averages among recent Australian batsman provides studies in attentuation: Hayden 53.1 versus 40.6, Langer 46 versus 39.6, Katich 46.8 versus 25.9, Gilchrist 48.3 versus 37.2 and now Ponting 55.6 versus 33.8.

Mike Hussey is an outlier, his returns having remained steady since his thirty-fifth birthday, albeit after a fallow period. But late-blooming Hussey did not win his debut cap until he was thirty, and the resurgence in his form has only followed his standing down from the accursed second-drop in the Australian order.

This being so, the question then becomes why did Waugh prosper where others have loitered palely. Possible explanations aren't far to seek. In eighty-five per cent of his Test innings, Waugh batted either number five or six; his late-career team was hugely strong; his late-career technique was an Alamo of ornery defiance.

Ponting enjoys none of these advantages, striving to get his groove back as the member of a dysfunctional top order in a mid-table Test team. Reversing the ageing process on batting is not as simple as a Botox shot and an eyebrow lift. Bowlers learn. Hunger fades. Techniques deteriorate. Simple is best. Graeme Pollock went on wellying bowlers through the covers into his forties with minimal footwork because that is what he'd always done. Complex techniques or aggressive intents, by contrast, can backfire noisily. Michael Vaughan, who had more trigger movements than Wild Bill Hickok, finished up a neurotic blur at the crease, his final Test average 10 runs off its peak. Even Viv Richards reverted to the mean, averaging a mortal 36 in his final twenty Tests.

In addressing his current batting challenges, Ponting has mentioned the inspirational example of Sachin Tendulkar – still relentless, still momentous. But Tendulkar is a more abstemious batsman than five years ago, Ponting not noticeably so. Today's Tendulkar also husbands his energies, skipping games and series where he deems it necessary. Ponting grudgingly gave up T20, which was rather like renouncing deep-fried Mars bars. Tendulkar would hardly have played with the broken finger that Ponting took, to his cost, into last year's Melbourne Test.

Ponting faces additional disadvantages too, such as cricket's increasing pervasion by video adjudication. The game is less forgiving than it used to be to the toiling batsman. In sixteen Tests since his thirty-fifth birthday, Ponting has thrice been caught short of his ground and on half a dozen occasions trapped lbw.

Twenty years ago, before recourse to the third umpire, when batsmen used to need to be at least a foot or two short for appeals to be upheld, Ponting would have been good odds to have survived the run outs. And even two years ago, the lbw decisions that befell Ponting at Cape Town as he essayed what used to be his bread-and-butter on-side push would have been interpreted as sliding down leg.

Not only has the decision review system become a court of appeal sympathetic to bowlers, but umpires are approaching lbws demanding less of a burden of proof to convict. Umpire Asad Rauf used to be unusual in granting lbws that others regarded as speculative. He's grown less so since the inference drawn from the application of Hawk-Eye that more balls are destined to hit the stumps than previously assumed: to some extent, we're all Asads now. Watching Ponting recede into the Newlands pavilion chuntering away to himself last week was like observing a fabled entrepreneur entangled by a confounding bureaucracy, old crash-through-or-crash methods no longer working.

Justin Langer has loyally enlarged on the value Ponting brings to Australia besides his runs. He has a point. To a team with a fresh captain, a preoccupied vice-captain, a relatively new manager, a locum coach and a vestigial selection panel, Ponting brings a valuable ballast of experience. But Cricket Australia has pledged to sign off on a permanent continuous management structure within weeks. The only retention argument then becomes runs, and these will be no easier to come by than they are now.

Warne made many false moves in his career, but the timing of his retirement could hardly have been better. Five years on, years as well as kilograms seem to have slipped from his shoulders. Ponting, meanwhile, deserves goodwill but not indulgence. He has been the outstanding Australian Test batsman of one generation; the game's forces are against him being the best of the next.

The Australian, November 2011

A STEP AHEAD

For a split-second at the Gabba yesterday, Ricky Ponting would have thought that he was a goner. He had sallied forth for an opportunist single, been sent back by his partner Usman Khawaja, and was marooned far from safety.

An accurate throw from Brendon McCullum at cover would have left Australia three for 25 chasing nearly 300. Perhaps more importantly, it would have left Ponting with three noughts in his last four Test innings, and added to a roll of recent run-outs at a time when some would run him out of Test cricket.

The throw was wide. The chance went begging. It didn't demoralise New Zealand, but it might conceivably have moralised Ponting. Lately he has had little luck, getting in only to get out in Sri Lanka, out before he could get in against South Africa, extending a long hiatus in production of centuries.

Was this, at last, an omen? Certainly, Ponting's batting immediately began to look ominous. To enter double figures, he stretched forward to Southee and punctured the covers with a perfectly controlled check drive, then punched straight down the ground: no sign of falling across his stumps here. Swinging Bracewell to fine leg and Martin through mid-wicket, he recalled his salad days.

For a small man, Ponting has an enormous stride, and was yesterday turning deliveries barely overpitched into mouth-watering half-volleys. He was equally comfortable going the opposite direction, reaching 50 with a delectable back-foot punch off Martin. Later he repeated the stroke off Vettori through an off-side field that a fag paper could hardly have slid through. Once the vein of luck was tapped, too, it flowed. A review of an unsuccessful lbw appeal by Dean Brownlie when Ponting was 63 also went just his way.

Ponting has been spectacular on occasions in the last thirty months, but this was his most certain batting since his 150 at Cardiff at the outset of the 2009 Ashes, when he looked as complete and immoveable as a Doric column. What could today be his fortieth Test hundred may also be one of his best.

Australia was in need of Ponting's best after faltering beginnings. Warner and Hughes might sound like an estate agency or a law firm, but as an opening partnership their names savour of everything but staidness.

Warner deserves to be judged on more evidence than his tweet of an innings yesterday, but Southee's first ball was of the sort that a Test opener should really have been capable of leaving on length, rather than propping in the en garde position then being unable to elude.

It was the kind of dismissal to keep an instinctive player like Warner awake at night wondering about the gulf between the red ball game he longs to master and the white ball game he already has. At the moment it must seem like the distance between the NFL and lingerie football.

For his part, Hughes received a better ball, deviating nearly the width of the stumps, but it remains a concern how adept he is at making good deliveries seem all-but unplayable. To fall back on, Australia was lucky to have a cricketer who has forgotten more about Test batting than either Warner or Hughes will ever know.

Inexperience was also evident in the protracted morning session, as Australia's callow pace attack struggled to maintain lines in the face of left- and right-handers, and all lengths were on the short side, which suited Vettori, who seldom ventures far forward and has long forsworn the conventional cover drive. An innings of 96 from 127 balls would normally be embellished with adjectives like 'fluent' or 'sparkling'. Vettori's was better attached to descriptions such as 'practical' and 'businesslike'. Having come into Test cricket looking like a Bloomsbury aesthete, Vettori's *Cricinfo* profile now features an image that resembles a photo ID for IBM in the 1950s. His slow bowling is still art, but his batting is free enterprise.

There was barely even a strangled appeal in the first hour, and little to disturb the serenity of the visitors' progress, although Starc's last-second hesitation turned a regulation chance from Vettori's miscued sweep into a sudden unavailing lunge. With New Zealand five for 254, Australian fielders had gone more than 400 deliveries without accepting a slip catch or even scoring a direct hit.

At last Hussey from mid-off threw out Vettori, attempting an unnecessary and overambitious single, and Clarke snaffled nicks from Young then Bracewell down by his bootlaces. Lyon's arm-ball to bamboozle the last was a collector's piece of finger spin, and again he was the most impressive Australian bowler, varying his pace adeptly, using his full height and throwing his pipe-cleaner man physique around off his own bowling. Who'd have thought that the campaign to replace Shane Warne would end up with an investment in geek chic?

A good day ended badly. At 4.45 p.m., with Brownlie bowling

to the Australians at three-fifths rat-power, umpires Aleem Dar and Asad Rauf pulled out their light meters and fussily whisked the players off, like teachers shushing schoolchildren in a museum. The sky was lightly clouded, the lights were ablaze, the match was nicely balanced and everything pointed to an intriguing last hour. Instead, pop music wafted from the public address system, advertisements played on the screen, fans began drifting towards the exits, and police and security staff moved to protective positions on the outfield to guard against incursions from empty terraces.

The new ICC playing condition regarding bad light worked in one way. The players could blame the umpires, the umpires could blame the light meters, the light meters could presumably blame their calibrations, and in the end society was perhaps to blame. But oh, one died inside. For the greatest game in the world, Test cricket can also exhibit an almost unrivalled capacity for looking ridiculous. Some think that Test cricket is a goner. It will certainly need luck to endure. Some days, as it was for Ponting today, the luck goes with you. But you don't want to depend on it.

The Australian, November 2011

BACK TO BASICS

Your best form, says an old cricket dictum, is only ever one innings away. Sometimes, all it takes is a shot – as Ricky Ponting demonstrated at the Sydney Cricket Ground yesterday.

Ponting had moved carefully to 64, about as far as he had come lately in his pursuit of the hundred that for two years had eluded him. He was facing Ishant Sharma, who had dismissed him seven times in Test cricket previously, and whose success against him four years ago first caused critics to wonder about the encroachments of age on the Australian's technique.

The fourth ball of Sharma's twelfth over was on a good length about middle, of a kind not unlike deliveries that for the last few months have been causing him to topple over to the off side – a tendency of which he has being trying to cure himself with hour upon interminable hour of practice, lining himself up with mid-on and keeping the face of the bat as open as possible.

In an instant, it all came together. Ponting's body stayed upright, and he kept, as they say these days, his shape: the ball vanished, not through mid-wicket, where Ponting used to hit naturally, but through mid-on, where the percentages are now more in his favour. Nobody bothered chasing.

This was cricket in perfect ratio: the minimum of effort, the maximum of return. Well, of course, not quite the maximum, in the sense attached to it in T20, which has made a cargo cult of The Maximum, whether a cow corner mow or a ramp over the keeper. But if you wanted to demonstrate to a lay person what in cricket is denoted 'a stroke', you could hardly have found a better example than this on-drive: a single stride, a pure swing, a fluid movement, like water flooding through a channel. To a batsman seeking corroboration that his game was in good order, this was the kind of shot to fill him with exultation, flood him with endorphins. Ponting was on his way; so, with its captain also surging ahead, was Australia.

For all the excellence of their country's bowlers this summer, Australians have awaited just such a day as this: one of crushing batting dominance, in which the promises that everyone was working hard, hitting it well in the nets and feeling a big one around the corner were honoured. And suddenly, it was on us: a long-awaited re-acquaintance with the qualities that make top-notch Test match batting, in a summer in which it has been little seen, with the personal dimensions of Ponting's rehabilitation and Michael Clarke's habilitation thrown in. There were mighty shots – like the foregoing. There was sedulous planning too.

Ponting and Clarke first scintillated through the pre-lunch session, adding 120 runs: a rate in ancient days we used to call a run-a-minute, before T20 made that seem like undue tardiness. Early on, Ponting swung the first ball of an over from Zaheer Khan for four: another resounding, heartening shot. At once, with that distinctive hand-puppetry batsmen have popularised, he matter-of-factly signalled for new gloves to come on at the end of the over.

In Ponting's hardest times staying in, the gesture would have seemed an affectation. Now it radiated intent: yes, he would be there at the end of the over; yes, he intended to be there quite some time longer; in fact, keep those gloves coming, because there were big runs in the offing.

Clarke was every bit as animated. He danced to the spinners; he marched into his drives; he stretched elastically to create half-volleys, including when he punched through extra cover to reach his century. When he played his trademark clip off his legs, he seemed to be running almost before he had connected with the ball.

Yet as attractive as it was, the stand was also measured. As Australia extended its lead, India's attack, enervated by the heat and taxed by back-to-back Tests, was beginning to look ever-so-slightly medium rare. The fast bowlers' pace fell away; Umesh Yadav bowled a telltale half-tracker, smashed for four, bracketed by apologetic wides. But Ravichandran Ashwin, on whom India rely to moderate the workloads of his colleagues, was also shrewdly picked off so that Dhoni had to keep throwing his quicker men the ball.

Ponting and Clarke were fit. Even after all these years, Ponting shows a colt's enthusiasm in the warm-ups to a day's play; on Clarke's frame hangs not an ounce of spare flesh. They were going to find out exactly how fit were their rivals. As the afternoon unfolded, captains past and present took toll. Twenty-two relief overs from Kohli and Sehwag were milked. Ishant registered the first Indian century of the series when he gave up his hundredth run, and was emulated by Ashwin and Khan.

Clarke played with immense and indissoluble discipline, passing his double hundred before he played a deliberate stroke in the air, although after a year caulking the Australian middle order he enjoyed an indulgence or two, playing his seldom-seen pull shot with gusto. Beneath his Australian cap and brandishing a cleanskin bat, he looked a sight for nostalgic eyes, his off- and cover-drives off Zaheer Khan after tea sounded as sweetly as the peal of a church bell. Because of his and Ponting's hard graft earlier, Hussey, so often the redeemer of Australian ruin, then had a rare opportunity to bat under next to no pressure and permitted himself the frivolity of a couple of straight sixes.

The day's headline event, of course, already scarcely needs reliving. Ponting's final supplicating dive to achieve his hundredth run, as if hurling himself on the mercy of the cricket gods, will be limited edition memorabilia soon enough, probably with genuine SCG dirt mixed in. Have your credit card details ready. It was a golden moment, to be sure – one of those where technique and training go out the window, and all the cricketer is left with is hope. In point of fact, Ponting almost never dives for the crease: from an old-fashioned bat slider, this was an act of palpable desperation, as revealed by the guilty grin afterwards.

As an image, Ponting's dusty shirt and joyous celebration will inevitably in time stand in for the whole of the innings, which will be poignant but also be a little misleading. Ponting's innings, and Clarke's also, were months in the making – months of dedication and determination to stave off demoralisation and doubt, months of coaching trust and selectorial faith. Some instants, it is true, are accidents. But to play as the Australians did today was not the stuff of chance.

The Australian, January 2012

Ponting in Adelaide

ROLLING BACK THE YEARS

It is sometimes said of actors that there are certain roles they are born to play. If cricket has an equivalent, Ricky Ponting was always destined to bat at the Adelaide Oval, where his sixth Test hundred at the venue, and his fourth against India in four Tests, was delivered yesterday like a command performance by an artist at the top of his form.

Heat, light, grassy embankments, fluttering flags, a hundred-year-old scoreboard, a wicket as hard and flat as an inland desert: the most traditional of Australian cricket venues suits the cricketer who still best embodies Australian cricket virtues. When he saluted all points of the ground on the achievement of his milestone yesterday, it was a little like he was taking a particularly long and heartfelt curtain call. The hundred in Sydney had been a relief; this felt closer to a real vindication.

Not quite five weeks ago, Ponting shuffled off Bellerive Oval to the sound of his own feet, in acting terms like a fading star not only forgetting his lines and missing his cues but in the habit of falling over the scenery and scalding himself on the tea urn. Somehow, though, he plumbed the depth of his resources and found runs, and his appearance at the crease with Australia two-down after ten overs of the morning had a reminiscent and reassuring quality. There he was, facing another full house, scratching around his crease, performing a preliminary reconnaissance of the pitch, looking up at a partner to utter his well-worn catchphrase: 'Nice loud calls, mate.'

This was a better innings than Sydney. It started on a firmer footing and blossomed evenly. Ponting's first straight drive from Umesh Yadav to go into double figures, upright and perfectly-balanced, imparting a kiss of momentum like a Newton's cradle, was the kind of shot, sending the ball back from whence it came, that sends a pang of affirmation through a batsman.

There followed an imperious pull, a stand-to-attention back-foot drive through point and a sweep shot that crossed the boundary before the batsman had emerged from his crouch. After each, he kicked at the loose soil round his block as though wiping his feet on the bowler. Five years ago, you would almost have pencilled Ponting in for a hundred at this point; nowadays one is more circumspect. But his game was clearly in excellent order.

Michael Clarke's game is in perhaps the best order of his career – bat straight, footwork decisive, timing like great comedy. In his first 30 runs, he acquired boundaries with a short-armed pull through square leg from Yadav, a featherlight glance from Zaheer and a goosestepping cover drive from Sharma: the hint of a tour de force to come. And as the early wickets receded into the past, a flourishing present unrolled. The most contentious runs were two just before tea taken off a rebound from Clarke's bat as he ran through to complete a single. Apparently he excused himself from a breach of cricket's politesse afterwards, but there was an avidity about it too: no run, however scrappy, was to be disdained.

In every sense Ponting's and Clarke's was a complimentary partnership. Ponting took particular toll of Yadav – 46 from 37 balls. Clarke milked Ravi Ashwin expertly – 45 from 50 balls. Both reached their fifties in 69 deliveries. Both men peppered the point boundaries. There were no real lulls in scoring, even when a period of reverse swing in mid-afternoon compelled extra diligence.

Until the very end, Clarke kept a deferential few runs in Ponting's arrears; a couple of thick edges then took him almost apologetically ahead. Ponting passed 13 000 Test runs, but this was a matter of accountancy; what mattered was the accumulating ascendancy, which by stumps was crushing.

In early despatches, Clarke's new counterpart Virender Sehwag was entitled to favourable reviews. Certainly he cut a more proactive figure than M S Dhoni – albeit that this was like the comparison between a traffic cop and a traffic cone. Turning to Ashwin's off-breaks in the fourth over with the Kookaburra embossment still visible on the ball, following the successful example Pakistan's Misbah ul-Haq has set recently with the slows of Mohammed Hafeez, paid immediate dividends.

Summing the pitch up early, Sehwag depopulated his slips quickly in favour of catchers forward of the bat, and his fields looked generally tailored: a deep mid-wicket for Ponting came ten metres finer and a little shorter for Clarke, for example, providing protection for bowlers essaying a stump-to-stump line; a leg gully wafted in when a few balls bounced encouragingly after lunch. Often it does not matter what a captain is doing or why. The sense of a mind engaged can lend a team an edge of purpose.

As the day took its desiccating course, however, the answers dried up too. Again, a large outfield exposed the limited athleticism and weaker arms in the Indian team. The ball followed Umesh Yadav all day, like a bailiff on a bankrupt's trail. Finally, Sehwag bowled thirteen overs of off-roll from three paces as though anxious the whole thing be over quickly.

Either side of tea, Ponting rolled back the years, hitting Sharma on the up through point in emulation of the front-foot square cut that Sir Donald Bradman illustrated in *The Art of Cricket*. After tea, he opened the bat face to Yadav so late and so far that the maker's name faced third man as the ball fairly flew to the boundary. There was no undue haste or flippancy. Ponting and Clarke played off each other like a great duo, turning the strike over seventy-eight times in all. But it was Ponting's day, ending when he marched briskly into the post-stumps press conference, looking as though he just walked round the corner to buy a litre of milk rather than batted five and a half hours in enervating heat. No, he wasn't retiring. He wasn't acting when he said it either.

The Australian, January 2012

LOOKING INTO THE ABYSS

He has been a great champion – one of the greatest. But the statistics tell their own story. The years, the burdens, the expectations have taken their toll. The sun is setting on a mighty career. It may already have set.

But enough about Sachin Tendulkar. Let's discuss Ricky Ponting. Or at least, let's talk about them both, for, by coincidence, the best batsmen of our generation have reached autumnal stages in their career more or less simultaneously.

Tendulkar turns 40 in April, Ponting 38 in a month. Were cricketers' ages to be gauged, theirs would appear in the red zone. Their relative travails barely compare. Tendulkar has gone twenty-eight Test innings without a hundred; Ponting only four. All the same, the manner of their recent dismissals has caught the eye. When batsmen begin getting out in the act of playing defensively, as Tendulkar and Ponting did in Mumbai and Adelaide respectively, something is amiss. Defence is meant to banish risk, not induce it.

As Ponting conceded during the Adelaide Test, he has been 'a little bit tentative' this summer; it was a candid admission from one to whom doubt has been, if not a total stranger, seldom more than a passing acquaintance.

In contemplation of a great batsman dealing with the phenomenon of 'bad form', you come to a point where rational explanation no longer suffices. Some little advantage has been lost; some indefinable aura has faded. Bowlers sense it: they attack where they used to be content to keep quiet. Fielders sense it: they crouch in the expectation of catches and relax in the confidence of accepting them. The batsman intuits this changed challenge in the middle, finds himself more often on the negative side of defensive and the reckless extreme of aggression, feels himself defending his record rather than improving it, begins comparing himself unfavourably with that past. What's most debilitating is not perhaps so much the slight decay in reflexes and the minute misfirings of technique as the steady sedimentation of frustrations, the sense of diminishing returns from the growing exertion required to maintain minimum standards.

That's the position in which both Ponting and Tendulkar now find themselves. What is keeping them going is, in part, the cognisance of how little it has previously taken for the cycle to reverse, for it to feed again on conviction rather than doubt. Nor is this mere bravado or bloviation; they will have experienced it again and again, directly and vicariously. For example, Ricky Ponting can glance across the dressing room to his fellow 37-year-old Michael Hussey, still playing all three forms of the game and probably willing to tackle a fourth or fifth.

Two years ago, having gone twenty-two Test innings with a solitary century, Hussey began the Sheffield Shield season with three runs in three innings, climaxing in a first-baller amid a West Australia score of 368 at the MCG. Hussey cut a morose and apparently doomed figure at gully as Victoria were bundled out for 141. His revival originated in a decision entirely unrelated to his predicament: WA's choice, assented to by his current coach Mickey Arthur, not to enforce the follow-on. Hussey seized the opportunity to blaze an eleventh-hour hundred, followed it with an eight-hour 195 during the Brisbane Test, and retrieved his mantle as first man picked.

Last season, of course, Ponting himself stared oblivion in the face, literally. To the second delivery he received on Boxing Day from lively Umesh Yadav, he essayed an ugly pull, the ball rebounding from forearm to grill and landing perilously near the stumps. He hurriedly kicked it away.

Inches from a sixth Test failure in eight starts, Ponting ground out the first of a couple of restorative 60s, preluding a hundred at the SCG and a double century at Adelaide Oval. No wonder even great cricketers come to believe in a kind of providence, a divinity that shapes their ends, rough hew them as bowlers sometimes will. Something that happened once can happen again. Can't it?

Sentiment plays a role more generally, too. The other dimension to the parallel stories of Tendulkar and Ponting concerns us, the fans, and the cricket systems and cultures that have nurtured and sustained them. In India, Tendulkar is off limits, an embodiment of national will and aspiration. No sooner had India lost in Mumbai with Tendulkar among the failures than Indian's minister of state Rajiv Shukla, a coming man at the Board of Control for Cricket in India, leapt pre-emptively to his defence. 'He will hang up his boots when he thinks it's time for him to go,' stated Shukla. 'He does not need any advice on this.' So much for selectors, eh? But it is fair to say that no Indian politician has ever lost a vote by standing shoulder-to-shoulder with The Little Master.

That instructive weathervane of the breezes at the BCCI, Sunil Gavaskar, went so far as to deem it an 'Indian thing', a contrast to the 'ruthless' Australian system 'because our cricketing culture is different'. Gavaskar stated proudly: 'We have a situation where we respect our senior cricketers and do not want to push them out. We want to give them a graceful exit.'

In Australia, as if to fulfil that Darwinian stereotype, there has been a contrasting exhortation of the selectors to sack Ponting, to remove matters from his hands, or at least to place him in the position of the disgraced officer of yore – shut in a room with a revolver in the desk drawer. Cricket, opined one commentator last week, is a 'performance-based industry', to put a late capitalist gloss on a frenzied threshing of straw men.

The selectors in each country must transcend these debates and evaluate the cricket issues alone. India's probably have little chance; indeed, the BCCI ousted the last selector who showed an independent mind, Mohinder Amarnath, just two months ago. There is more justification for faith in Australia's. Whatever the case, we will learn about cricket, about cricketers and about their countries in the process.

The Australian, December 2012

GOODBYE TO ALL THAT

'Catch, Ted,' said Ricky Ponting. 'Catch, Ted.'

It was late in Australia's morning training sessions ahead of the next day's Perth Test against South Africa, 29 November 2012. The small knots of onlookers had moved on; only a handful of players remained. Still wearing his pads, Ponting was seated on a bench after a long stint of facing net bowlers and throw-downs, and watching a helmeted Ed Cowan practise his short leg catching with coach Mickey Arthur. 'Catch, Ted,' he would repeat as each hit went in. 'Catch, Ted.'

Nothing so unusual about this. In his long career, Ponting had made a habit of being among the last to leave training. Except that unbeknownst to those beyond the team and its immediate circle, he had just a couple of hours earlier confided that this, his record 168th appearance, would be his farewell Test; it remained at that stage Australian cricket's best-kept secret. 'Catch, Ted,' he repeated. 'Catch, Ted.'

After one last surveillance of the practice area, Ponting

shouldered his black batting backpack, tucked two bats under his arm, and began wending his way back to the dressing room – the same dressing room from which he had emerged seventeen years earlier, a fresh-faced 21-year-old, to make his Test debut against Sri Lanka. And twenty minutes later, it was official. Amid a gathering sense of anticipation and occasion, Ponting walked into a room in the bowels of the WACA Ground, accompanied by his wife, his daughters and finally his teammates, who ringed the back wall. There had been tears earlier, Ponting admitted: 'I tried to tell them a lot, but I didn't get much out. As I said to the boys, they've never seen me emotional, but I was this morning.' Now he was more composed and there was relatively little theatre, certainly when compared to the lusty salaams that accompanied the departures of his eminent contemporaries Steve Waugh and Shane Warne. Fifteen minutes later, the journalists were composing their obsequies. It had all been disarmingly matter-of-fact – very much the Ponting vein.

And thus did an era pass that has been a long time in the fading: the era of Australian dominance of international cricket, of which Ponting, and not merely his bustling, bristling batting but his hairy-armed, spitting-in-his-hands presence, has been a personification. Australia had ceded its number-one Test ranking in August 2009, and its number-one one-day ranking three years later. Since then, all that had remained had been Ponting, and now he, too, was to go.

He had opened up in that time a sizeable gap between himself and the next highest Australian Test run-scorer, Allan Border, and even if his form had been more variable than of yore then an Australian order with his name in it could not help but bear a strong look; he drew, of course, on a massive estate of international runs in all conditions and all climes. But the clock had been running down. He had passed the captaincy on to his dauphin, Michael Clarke, with promising results. Yet the wins were coming harder, and wins were what mattered to Ponting above all else. 'Seriously,' he had said to Cowan just before the Sheffield Shield final earlier in the year, 'you don't really think I give a toss about hundreds, do you?' Cowan had joked to Ponting about the possibility he might emulate Sachin Tendulkar and score a hundred international hundreds. In reply, Ponting had enumerated all the trophies and garlands that Australia had won in his career – a lengthy list. Winning: it wasn't everything, but to Ponting it had always been the main thing.

The Test would not be kind to Ponting in either individual or collective terms. He was pushing string uphill with his batting, and made only 4 and 8. He looked on in the field as Australia gave up 569 in South Africa's second innings. The tributes flowed almost for the game's duration. One especially moving one was on the final day, when South Africa's captain Graeme Smith formed his fielders into two lines so as to applaud him to the wicket, partner Cowan joining in; when he was out, every member of the visiting team went to him individually to shake his hand as he walked off; there were further impressive displays of cricketing confraternity as the game ended. But you got the feeling that Ponting would have swapped them all for a win, even just for a few extra runs. If desire could be bottled, it would be distilled from essence of Ponting. Sometimes in his career, more of that had seeped out than even he could handle. He had a way of remonstrating with umpires that recalled the Mike Gatting school of diplomacy, although it often looked worse than it was: Ponting tended to be a barrack room lawyer rather than a pottymouth pouter. The first thing he said when he sat down at the end of the match, in the same room in which he had started it, was disappointment at the result and regret that he had not made a few more: 'It has been a hard week and we haven't got the result we were after and I haven't got the result I was after.' The desire was still there; it's just that the capabilities could no longer stretch up to the same height.

Now he *was* prepared to take questions about his career, about which he had earlier been reticent. His daughter Emmy was sitting on his knee, and, in that way little children have of objecting passively to their parents doing something when they should be available for play, stuck her fingers in her ears. Everyone else in the room was entirely spellbound. Normally, press conferences take place in a fairly formulaic fashion: they pretend to answer; we pretend to listen. Ponting's press conferences, though, were not like this. He was one cricketer who always gave straight answers to straight questions, and gave the impression of having thought about them; this was no exception. And as he spoke, there was otherwise complete silence. You could almost hear the tape recorders rolling.

In due course, he began to recite some thanks. Family. Friends. Management. Sponsors, some of whom had been with him from the very beginning, when a local bakery had sponsored his performances at Mowbray Cricket Club. He thanked that club too, with a cough and a sniff.

'It's getting a bit harder.' No – there would be no tears. 'The Mowbray Cricket Club, if they see me up here like this at the moment they'll be all over me. That's the place I learnt the game and the person I am was moulded from my background and my upbringing. What you've seen over seventeen years is a result of my early days at the Mowbray Cricket Club. Thanks to the boys back there.'

Cricket Australia. Cricket Tasmania. The pragmatist and the fantasist in Ponting showed through when he revealed that he knew when his next training was, for the Hobart Hurricanes in the Big Bash League, and that as a result he would be in the vicinity of Bellerive Oval for the next Test. 'Who knows, I might even be around for the first day of the game,' he joked. 'If I am, I might even join in the warm-up with the boys and see if there's just one more chance!'

'The boys': they came up a lot. It is funny how athletes always use that expression when they are talking about teammates. Once in a while, it's 'the guys', but usually discussion circles back to 'the boys'. I dare say that a detractor of sport would decided that this is because sport keeps athletes in a state of arrested development, of perpetual childhood, and maybe there's some truth in that. But it is perhaps also this that allows them to express themselves with such freedom and totality; when adult doubt and cynicism set in, it is time to go. Not that Ponting finished his career as anything other than an adult. His wiry frame and sun-burnished face were those of a man who had seen the world; there was knowhow and wisdom on the game he loved in his every utterance. But to see him to the very end throwing himself around at training, standing in the huddle, singing the team song, enjoying the banter was to be reminded how sport preserves in us the happiest parts of ourselves. The boys: how he would miss them. And how they would miss him: not just his run-getting, but his body-and-soul commitment to the commonweal, audible in his voice as he watched Cowan taking his catches, always upbeat, always encouraging, always urging them on. Now he was off to see them one last time as a player, with a final: 'Thanks, everyone.' It was we, of course, who should have been doing the thanking.

Wisden Cricketers' Almanack, 2013

LAST MAN STANDING

If you text a number today at Bellerive Oval, you stand a chance of winning a cricket bat signed by Michael Hussey. Meanwhile, the man himself is toiling in the middle to enhance its resale value, a patient 66 at lunch from 136 balls, a nineteenth Test century visible on the horizon.

With Ricky Ponting's retirement, Hussey has become Australian cricket's elder statesman: he will turn thirty-eight in May, after which he can be expected on present form to play in next year's full Ashes cycle. And whereas Ponting's technique in recent times has shown the passage of the years, Hussey's looks as sure and secure as ever. His statuesque figure, always crisply turned out, seems to slip naturally into established patterns and gainly attitudes. A brazen Hussey, he is not. On the contrary, he is a portrait of vigilance. Between deliveries, he studies his surrounding environment intently, examining where the ball has pitched, his guard, his gear, his attire, all brought into order with unconscious tugs and shrugs: he looks like the kind of man who would want all the pens on his desk lined up a certain way, and would straighten up any picture on the wall that looked even slightly crooked. At drinks this morning, he propped his bat on his helmet so that the handle stood off the ground; on the handle he draped his fingerless inner gloves. This miniature drying rack stood for only three minutes at most, while Hussey refreshed himself, but it sent out a little message of long-term intent and abiding meticulousness.

There has never been much to go wrong with Hussey's technique, the basics being so orthodox and grooved, although he takes no chances, rehearsing avidly, especially his vertical bat shots, which he replays pedantically in normal and slow motion. Sensible is as sensible does. When the ball is in flight, it is as though Hussey has played his shot numberless times over already.

One more attribute: Hussey is the best judge of a run in the Australian team. He has been run out twice while facing more than 12 000 deliveries in Test cricket, and in each case it was a short-range throw from a close fielder: in other words, in seventy-six Tests he has never perished while actually taking a run. Which is not to say that he eschews risk: in guiding Australia through this morning session, he helped Wade get off strike on several occasions by committing himself to short singles that ran only yards from the bat. Yet it is hard to recall him ever hurrying for his crease, let alone diving for safety.

The gilt-edged underwriting he has provided for Australian teams in recent years may in due course prove as hard to replace as Ricky Ponting. Fortunately for Australian cricket, finding his successor is not a problem it faces – yet, at any rate. When it does . . .

The Australian, December 2012

Hussey in Melbourne
A GOOD MAN GONE

One of a Test cricketer's privileges is access. Barriers that impinge on others melt away for them; they are ever on the right side of the velvet rope.

So when Mike Hussey and two of his children strolled through the security cordon guarding the arena at the MCG about an hour after the Second Test ended on Friday to play a little game of cricket just off the square, it looked no more than Mr, Master and Miss Cricket exercising an official prerogative.

In fact, Hussey was enjoying a private farewell experience. His mind was made up: after about half an hour, he re-joined his team's celebration knowing that the next Test would be his last. As the evening wore on, he quietly advised his captain and coach. They were shocked; so, now, are we all.

Usually sport finds a way to tell an athlete when their time is up. Reflex slows. Edge dulls. Error creeps in. What used to come naturally begins to take effort, what used to be shrugged off starts to nag. By telling cricket he was finished with it before cricket was finished with him, Michael Hussey has become a unique case study.

Hussey is thirty-seven years young. No player has maintained such a staggering consistency: his ICC Test ranking is exactly where it was four years ago, and has barely fluctuated in the last two. None has adapted so skilfully or completely to the trifurcation of international cricket between Test, one-day and T20 international, in all of which he was Australia's first chosen. None has continued to exhibit such an unquenchable thirst for the game – not only for batting, bowling and fielding, but for touring, training, travelling and generally contributing to the collective. 'He is the one we all look up to,' said Michael Clarke of Hussey in a recent interview.

In fact, by couching his retirement decision in terms of a loss of zeal, Hussey reveals just how long he staved off a tapering of it. 'If you're not 100 per cent in it, you shouldn't be there, you're probably just going to let the team down,' he said on Saturday, with a pleasing respect also for mathematics: notice the use of 100 per cent, rather than 110 per cent, or even a million per cent, a common going rate in these inflationary times for sporting commitment.

But then, this always seemed integral to Hussey's character. Every so often on the big screen, Cricket Australia shows film of Australian players responding to the question of what they would be doing were they not playing cricket. Most, it seems, would be either professional golfers or footballers, on TV or in rock bands. Hussey says simply that he would have been a maths or a science teacher; indeed, he studied to be one. You can tell, too, that you'd have felt blessed to be in any classroom under Mr Hussey's tutelage. The Bunsen burners and the log tables would have been immaculate.

Not that there was any ambivalence about Hussey's pursuit of his goals. He approached cricket with the fastidiousness of a man who liked to chew his food a minimum number of times and to finish each crossword down to the last clue. But his first decade as a first-class player was of a two-steps-forward/one-back variety, perhaps because he cared so much. He was well positioned to succeed Mark Taylor as opening batsman in 1999, but his form faltered, and he lost preferment, as well as his first Cricket Australia contract.

Arguably the making of Hussey was joining Northants in 2001, where he formed a close bond with coach Bob Carter, and sampled seniority for the first time: a ripening experience for every cricketer, and arguably one from which others could benefit now. He undertook mental training with a psychologist and a goal-setting consultant as determinedly as he worked physically.

The next time opportunity knocked – specifically a knock on Justin Langer's ribs in a Sheffield Shield game leaving an Australian top-order vacancy – Hussey was a seasoned thirty-year-old with forty first-class centuries behind him. No-one has then reached 1000 Test runs faster – just 165 days.

His seventy-nine Tests were played consecutively and with a remarkable continuity. Dismissed twice playing the pull shot on debut, he only once perished playing that shot again; twice thrown out from short leg, he was never run out actually taking a run. His final Test is at the SCG, where he averages a neat 100.

One last aspect of Hussey has passed strangely unremarked in the tributes to his cricket, perhaps because it now seems slightly quaint: he has been, unfailingly, a gentleman. It is impossible to remember him being drawn into a cross word or a terse exchange with anyone on a cricket field. It is impossible to remember him dissenting an umpiring decision, although his patience was tried by some absolute corkers in his time – sometimes, in fact, he seemed a faintly unlucky cricketer.

From start to finish, he has also been a master of the appropriate private gesture too. When Hussey scored a triple century for Northants, he gave his pads to Monty Panesar in token of appreciation for staying with him as he approached the milestone. When Faf du Plessis made his debut for South Africa at Adelaide a month ago, Hussey made sure to send his sometime Chennai Super Kings colleague a bottle of vintage wine. 'At Chennai we compete for spots in the batting lineup, and he was just the same nice guy towards me when I played ahead of him,' du Plessis recalled after his successful Test baptism last month. 'That's the way you judge a person's true character.'

Thus also Hussey's decision now. With Amy, whom Hussey married ten years ago, he constructed a family of four children under eight around the demands of cricket. He embarked on a tour of South Africa the day after the birth of his son Will; his daughter Molly and son Oscar were both born prematurely, respectively days after Australia's last World Cup win and during Australia's one-day international tour of England this year. Every cricketer owes a debt to his family. Some are more blithe about it than others; Hussey never seemed that sort. His retirement is both completely unexpected in cricket terms and an entirely characteristic act of basic decency.

The Australian, December 2012

THE LAST BULLION

Mike Hussey had only meant to say goodbye. Between times, it had become farewell and amen. Now a Test hung in the balance – lightly, but in the balance all the same. For a cricketer who confesses to a 'sick feeling in the stomach' every times he bats, the scenario at the Sydney Cricket Ground yesterday could have been the cue for acute mal de mer.

In the event, he was there at the end, victorious for the forty-eighth time and undefeated for the sixteenth time in his storied career, as if to draw attention to his imminent absence – its imminence that morning brought forward. For seven years, he has been the bullion in the vaults of the Australian team, the additional layer of capital to draw on in emergency. From this morning, that reserve is spent.

The selectors' decision to terminate Hussey's career with extreme prejudice is tough but has merit. Lingering goodbyes have become common practice in Australian cricket. A player retires from one form of the game then another, but remains available for this form and that, while everyone, of course, is availableamundo [sic] for the Indian Premier League.

It benefits some in particular but none in general. It also limits the ability of selectors to introduce new players to international cricket via the one-day game, which between World Cups is frankly that format's main source of interest.

This summer's one-day series is being advertised as 'Australia's Biggest Dress-Up Party', as though its target demographic is three-year-olds. That the last public sight of Hussey will be in white and wearing his baggy green in the shadow of the 127-year-old members' pavilion is all a sentimentalist could wish for. He had said goodbye, enjoyed a fine farewell, and amen to that.

With an eye on the longer-term, what does Australia lose in Mike Hussey, apart from the experience of 12 398 international runs, and his unslakeable thirst for the games, its routines and its rituals?

Many a cricket conversation has revolved around the hack-neyed and rather morbid question of who you would want to bat for your life. Another question is perhaps more interesting: who would you want to bat *with you* for your life? Hussey would not be a bad answer.

What has multiplied Hussey's value to the Australian teams he has played with has been his capacity for batting in harness. Nobody in this team has built more partnerships of at least 50: ninety-seven in seventy-nine Tests. In this respect, he rivals even his captain: ninety-three in eighty-nine Tests. He provided both a rainy-day fund of runs and a happy knack of investing them prudently along-side those of others.

Part of this was temperament, Hussey's relentless positive energy and exemplary fitness. That 'sick feeling', taken at the flood, led on to fortune. Hussey's technique meshed perfectly with others' too. With perhaps the most complete suite of scoring strokes and options in the Australian side – yesterday even a delectable reverse sweep – Hussey found gaps and rotated strike with ease, skills integral to the rhythm of successful alliances.

Above all, Hussey was a superb judge and a superb taker of a run, instant and total in his commitments. His run out in the first innings here was tantamount to the exception proving the rule – the first time he has lost his wicket taking an actual run in a Test match. Hussey responded to Clarke's errant call without hesitation, dived without heed, and was centimetres short when others would have been caught out by a metre.

This was actually an amazingly scatterbrained Test match for running between wickets, batsmen alternately coasting and capering, halting and high-tailing it. Doubt spread like a wicked rumour finding eager ears. Better fielding teams than these would have inflicted more than three run-outs.

In its way, this is a puzzle. Batsmen today train more rigorously, more ceaselessly than at any stage in the game's history. They have centres of excellence. They have batting camps. They have coaches, mentors, conditioning staff and computer analysts. With the number of bats they cart around, they will shortly have caddies too. Yet practice still takes place largely in nets, where batsmen face up to three or four bowlers then receive throwdowns from a stationary position until they have had enough.

For sure, practice regimes feature a great deal of running, but it is chiefly in the interests of fitness, rather than of fine-tuning the craft of flitting back and forth over twenty-two yards. Drills that recreate batting as a joint rather than an individual enterprise are scarce, and seldom applied concertedly.

So skills in running between wickets are acquired almost exclusively under match conditions – an anomaly in these hyper-professional times. They may actually be being neglected, given the dependence of modern batsmen on boundary flow.

In truth, everyone runs differently. Hussey's overlooked gift was that he ran brilliantly with everyone: those 50 partnerships were with twenty-three different batsmen, from Matt Hayden to Jason Gillespie, from Shane Watson to Stuart MacGill. Australia might in due course unearth another young batsman capable of averaging 50 in Test cricket. But will they be as adept at Hussey at bringing out the best in others?

Now that Nathan Lyon has been cast in Hussey's choral role, the auditioning begins in earnest at the MCG on Friday for who should take over his batting position. Optimist Hussey expressed the view yesterday that there were half a dozen quality candidates; pessimists will detect the inference that no-one really stands out; realists will not expect the selectors to get it right first time, especially given that Australia's next two Test series will involve such different batting conditions.

Hussey represented such a particular special blend of qualities, however, that he can only be succeeded – never replaced. That 'sick feeling in the stomach' may now be Michael Clarke's the next time Australia's fourth wicket falls.

The Australian, January 2013

THE CONTINUING
CRISIS

Michael Clarke

PORTRAIT OF THE CAPTAIN
AS A YOUNG SELECTOR

Steve Waugh's autobiography contains a memorable cameo of Simon Katich at a fitness session with New South Wales in the pre-season of 2002–03, when players were set a rock-climbing exercise.

Three quarters of the way up the vertical face, Katich's body seized. But rather than admit defeat, he hung there for forty minutes 'unable to progress but steadfastly refusing to back down'. Ironically, Waugh thought that such tenacity was why Katich would one day make a fine Australian captain.

It didn't work out that way. In clinging to the slippery rockface of Australian cricket now, Katich is making life awkward for the captaincy's latest office holder. The rancour is doing something else too: it is pointing up the dubious advisability of the captain doubling as a selector, as recommended in August by the Argus review.

To Katich's recent assertions that Clarke had influenced the termination of his Cricket Australia contract earlier this year, Clarke, amplified by Cricket Australia's chief executive James Sutherland, had the ready counter that he was uninvolved in the relevant selection deliberations.

It was not a resounding refutation, it being difficult to credit that the selectors did not consult their new captain at all. But having had no actual vote on Katich's position, Clarke was free to avail himself of what in politics is known as 'plausible deniability'.

Don Argus's wise men now want this to change. They have described entrusting captains with selection responsibilities as ensuring 'appropriate authority and accountability'. And to be true, there is much to be said for 'accountability'. After all, who, apart from the executive board of the International Cricket Council, believes in 'unaccountability'? In these days of cricketers cowering behind the 'bowling plan' and the 'batting group' like petty bureaucrats, there's even something quaintly refreshing about the idea. But there are also sound cultural reasons for cricket's traditional separation of powers, between leadership and selection.

Players are optimists. They have to be. They must trust their talents. They must continue believing when runs and wickets are scarce that they lurk just around the corner. 'Who ever hoped like a cricketer?' asked that most feeling of English cricket writers, R C Robertson-Glasgow.

Players collude in that optimism in others too, and captains not least of all. When the out-of-form batsman claims to still be hitting it well, no skipper retorts: 'You're fooling yourself. At the moment, you couldn't drive a dodgem and you couldn't cut a sandwich.'

Selectors transact not in hope but in expectation, in dark truths not white lies. They have their instincts too, but must exercise them disinterestedly, and in the interests of fairness to all need to temper their indulgence of the few.

A persuasive advocate of the captain joining the selection panel would almost certainly have been Clarke's predecessor. Ricky Ponting publicly coveted the role of selector. With his unrivalled reputation and uncommon sense, he would probably have made a good one. Some hunches in which he enlisted selectors paid off handsomely, Mitchell Johnson's inclusion at the WACA last summer being a case in point.

But here's the thing: Michael Clarke is not Ricky Ponting. And in certain key respects, he is very far from Ponting indeed. In succeeding Ponting with Clarke, Australia has done more than simply swap names at the top of the team sheet. They have replaced a captain who cared very little what people thought with one who cares a lot.

Ponting was the most insouciant Australian captain since Allan Border. Not that he was tactless or taciturn – well, not too often in public anyway. But in handling his team on and off the field, he was the straightest of arrows. In an era that prefers its celebrities more emollient, he retained an old-fashioned abrasive edge.

Clarke's nickname, 'Pup', was bestowed in recognition of his sunny, unfeigned, eager-to-please, happy-to-help disposition as a junior, and he remains conscious of his profile. He is good with the public. He is accessible to sponsors. He mouths agreeable nothings with the media. Thinking before he speaks, he exhibits a knack for tailoring responses to his audience.

These are not, by the way, wholly negative qualities – some are useful attributes for an Australian captain. It is impossible, for example, to imagine Clarke growing as stroppy with umpires as Ponting habitually did – perhaps his one consistent leadership shortcoming. But are Clarke's qualities those of a selector? A selector should avoid situations of needing to tell a player one thing and do another. A selector must set personal considerations aside, and on occasion bear bad tidings. And while it is pleasant handing out baggy greens, it is not so easy grabbing them back. Relations between Steve Waugh and Shane Warne, once so warm, never regained their cordiality after Waugh's part in Warne's omission from the Australian Test team at St John's in April 1999. Throwing Justin Langer then Michael Slater under the team bus in 2001 further convinced Waugh to tell CA that having players make selection calls was potentially divisive: 'The game was now a business and critical decisions such as selections needed to be based totally on clear thinking and made by those who were a step back from the coalface.'

Interestingly, Waugh was a member of the Argus review committee that advocated restoring powers he traded away. But the game is no less a business than a decade ago. With Australia now a mid-table Test team, the coalface is also a good deal grimier.

CA recently took its most positive step in years by appointing as 'National Selector' John Inverarity, one of cricket's nimblest minds. But Clarke should be acute enough to grasp that, especially at this stage in his incumbency, it is not his interests to shoulder selection responsibilities also. To set aside his ambitions in that direction would not be a confession of weakness but an indication of self-knowledge. By inducting Michael Clarke in some of the tensions involved in a dual role, then, Simon Katich might actually have done his erstwhile colleague a favour.

The Australian, November 2011

The Big Bash League 2011–12

WELCOME TO THE PLEASUREDOME

'KFC T20 Big Bash League is the most talked about event in the country. Fans love their teams and families and kids of all ages pack grounds around the country. Dressed in their team's colours, they come every week to watch the best T20 players on earth.'

'The Vision' for the Big Bash League, Cricket Australia's new-fashioned domestic T20 tournament which commenced at the SCG last night, reads like rather a lot to do with the competition, as though composed in half a minute by someone talking on the phone, watching television and listening to the radio simultaneously ('Mate, have you done that "Vision" yet?' 'Sorry mate, I've been flat out. I'll bash some crap out now.')

It does, though, encapsulate CA's sky-high hopes for what in a cricket sense is really old fast-food in a new wrapper: more or less the same players spread a little more thinly among eight city-based rather than six state-based teams, albeit sprinkled, like Colonel Sanders' herbs and spices, with New Improved Warnie.

There are some reasonable arguments for it. CA presents the

league as integral to re-winning the apparently forgone allegiance of our youth, which is an appealing sales pitch because everyone worships at the shrine of their children nowadays – myself included. And while CA won't divulge the market research on which this assertion is based, it's possible they have a point.

Of course, it's a tad less philanthropic than that. In commercial terms, the BBL is geared to developing a new television revenue stream to wean CA off its dependence on international cricket in general and India in particular.

When CA shops its broadcast rights round as the expiration of its current contracts approaches in two years, it wants a new product to sell. This is fine too, by the way. Everyone must earn a living.

There remains a quaint conviction, however, that anyone nursing any misgivings about the BBL must be one of those obdurate souls, descended from Charters and Caldicott in *The Lady Vanishes*, prone to spluttering 'It's not cricket'. Quite the contrary. T20 *is* cricket. It's CA that's pretending otherwise, by pimping the BBL as though the rest of the game does not exist.

Notice how 'The Vision', for instance, neglects that CA already promotes in the same period what are the country's most talked-about and best-patronised sporting events, the Melbourne and Sydney Test matches. Not even India, whose T20 Indian Premier League we are basically trying to imitate, dares to schedule clashing international engagements.

Nor has anyone at CA tried explaining how they see the relative rewards available for T20 not impacting on the rest of cricket. An Indian cricketer can now earn many times as much as he earns in a Test match from games a tenth the length and a fraction of the quality. If the BBL succeeds as CA wishes, that situation is perfectly foreseeable here.

Already in modern cricket, as Ed Cowan puts it succinctly in his new diary: 'You can be paid a lot more for not being as good as you used to have to be.' Has any other sport embraced this with such innocent enthusiasm?

The BBL also expresses covertly a contempt for the existing cricket fan. One of cricket's worthiest aspects is the generosity of its devotees, driven not only by local attachments but sporting ones too; they attend big games not merely to see their country win or their favourites prevail, but to be moved by the struggle.

This summer's Tests have already been little classics, from the thrilling pace of James Pattinson to the technical travails of Ricky Ponting, from the noble perseverance of Chris Martin's bowling to the slapstick comedy of his batting. One of my Kiwi colleagues during the Hobart Test fell into a reverie while describing a Martin cover drive at Basin Reserve five years ago and the ensuing standing ovation.

CA's marketing guru Mike McKenna dismisses this, arguing that cricket's future is tribal, like AFL, where he used to work, the 'club-versus-club competition' being 'where the passion is'. McKenna's notion of 'passion' clearly extends no further than ten-year-olds in face paint and replica gear aping attitudes seen in other sports, and poring over the chuckleheaded BBL websites that read like they've been written by . . . well . . . other ten-year-olds.

'His incredible pace has seen him selected to play ODI's [sic] for Australia and has him set for a hopeful future,' pants the Sydney Thunder website of Mitchell Starc in a randomly chosen example. 'A movie buff (*Shawshank Redemption* is his favourite), Mitch says he might consider a tattoo in the near future. Like most cricketers, he's hooked on PlayStation's *Call of Duty* and also spends much of his time tapping away on his iPhone: either Tweeting or Facebooking.' That makes Starc, to the Thunder website's way of thinking, 'somewhat of an overachiever'. An underachiever scarcely bears contemplation.

Doubtless some of this air of the thrown-together and thrown-up will fade now there's cricket to watch. The BBL will feature a few great and many good cricketers; T20 offers them limited scope, but quality should out, and I would watch Warnie in a Christmas pantomime if he promised to bowl a flipper. But perhaps the immediate risk is that the cricket will be drowned out by the 'booming tunes, fireworks and entertainment' that McKenna promises will 'reposition [the BBL] among the competitive environment of 3D movies, video games and music festivals'. ('Reposition . . . among the environment'?)

From its inception nearly a decade ago, T20 has been lashed to a concept called 'cricketainment' that is perhaps as naff as the word itself, involving essentially a non-stop cycle of extraneous activity meant to enrich the spectacle but actually betraying administrators' sneaking equivocation about their game's pleasures and charms. 'Cricketainment' is essentially a form of apology. Sorry for taking your time. Sorry that cricket is gradual, subtle and sometimes not utterly obvious. We know you're very busy. We know your life is replete with '3D movies, video games and music festivals'. But will you please accept this little morsel of shortened cricket if we slip it into an 'entertainment package' alongside some boy bands and dancing girls?

The trouble, of course, is that this process is potentially endless, while also subject to diminishing returns. There is only so much packaging a sport can tolerate before the inauthenticity cloys, and the activity becomes a bit of everything and a lot of nothing.

We know the T20 vision. I wonder how it will look in a few years with the benefit of T20 hindsight.

The Australian, December 2011

TV OR NOT TV?

The novelist Peter de Vries once said that his idea of success would be to have a mass audience large enough for his elite audience to look down on. But cricket's campaign to similar ends is exacerbating an abiding tension.

Given the instant gratification nature of the tournament, the rush to pronounce the Big Bash League a success or failure is unsurprising, and, according to Cricket Australia's chief executive James Sutherland, promising ratings have 'set the tournament alight'.

But at the MCG last Saturday night, the Stars v Thunder game burned rather like a damp log, all smoke and no heat, fans being underwhelmed even by a balmy evening in Melbourne and the heavenly prospect of Shane Warne. Etihad Stadium's resemblance to an aircraft hanger was then further enhanced by Thursday night's Renegades v Scorchers game.

The choicest moment of the BBL has been a televised one: Warnie talking his public through the confounding of the Heat's Brendon McCullum at the Gabba. But had you been present at the ground, this would have eluded you, because Warnie was confiding in those who had paid at the virtual box office, not the real one.

Does this matter? The pragmatic line now is that crowds are *so* twentieth century: that the TRP (television ratings point) is today's turnstile, and the couch the nation's grandstand. And in a financial sense, television audience reach is certainly a salient indicator.

Ticket sales today account for less than ten per cent of Cricket Australia's revenues. Their diminished relevance was recognised by CA's decision in April 2005 to yield to Channel Nine on the matter of broadcasting live 'against the gate', which commanded a one-off premium at unquantifiable cost to patronage of the live experience.

Grounds themselves are nowadays pervaded by a television consciousness too. Where once cricket coverage was accented to conveying to the home viewer what it was like to be at the match, now the opposite is true: the profusion of advertisements, the liberality of replays and the incessancy of music are directed to replicating the televised experience for the live spectator.

Yet is this a contributor to the emerging dynamic of a game with a large but growingly distant public? For why would I go to a cricket ground for a kind of washed-out replica of what I could see at home? Certainly, it never seems to have dawned on administrators that part of the pleasure in attending cricket is escaping the enforced passivity of over-advertisement-over-advertisement endured at home in favour of the freedom to look where one pleases and think what one chooses.

For many years, it was possible to admire the Australian commitment to the interests of the live spectator, compared, for example, to England. We charged relatively little for admission, maintained stable schedules, ran big, welcoming and characterful grounds. Then we started mucking around with the cricket calendar and with our arenas. The charming, rambling, sub-tropical Gabba was supplanted by a brutish football stadium; Adelaide Oval may be headed the same way; the jaded WACA urgently needs a facelift, but only seems able to afford Botox.

The balance between security and standover tactics, furthermore, continues to elude ground authorities, the irony being that the most intrusive presences within our arenas are not Mexican-waving members of the Beige Brigade, Barmy or Swami Armies, but those charged with running the events, with their ceaseless white noise, killjoy ordinances and pettifogging bag searches enforced by jumped-up officials in fluorescent jackets.

If you wanted to talk to your neighbour last Saturday night, for instance, you mostly had to make yourself heard over the strains of the *Addams Family* theme and the Chicken Dance. Not for a second was the crowd left to its own devices, allowed to reflect on the play or to savour a moment of excellence. 'The hunt for the perfect four-wheel drive is over,' stated the MCG ground announcer commencing a stentorian ad pitch even as David Warner's second six off Warne was being retrieved from the yawning terraces; never mind those who wished to savour the perfect straight drive.

It was like a comedy with canned laughter, a pub with noisy piped music, or a dinner party with a garrulous, attention-seeking bore – one who worked in marketing, actually. Foxtel has seldom looked so good – and the cynic might have suspected this to be the underlying idea.

In the longer term, however, the idea of a 'packed crowd' is integral to sporting theatre – on television not least of all. That is why every deed of significance during a televised game of cricket is marked with a shot of a knot of celebrating fans. That is why in the graphics of grounds that Channel Nine flashes up every so often to demonstrate scoring patterns or bowling lengths there is never a spare seat. That is why, above all, we regard the Boxing Day Test as the *sine qua non* of our summer, because in a vast, thinly populated country being in a great mass of intimate strangers partaking of a collective experience remains a compelling idea.

Those who trouble to attend big cricket in Australia, moreover, are 'sticky' fans – the thick-and-thin crowd, easily taken for granted but difficult to replace, like the core civic-minded members of a society. Standing on a street corner with its Big Bash League sandwich board offering lashings of cricketainment at the push of a remote control, Cricket Australia risks neglecting those whose commitment to it is greatest in favour of courting the fickle, promiscuous, channel-surfing sports browser.

The BBL has taken steps towards this, with its various membership drives and community initiatives to enhance the sense of ownership around the franchises. Trouble is that in the rush to ramp up the tournament's telegenia, CA reveals a different set of priorities. And the need to do more for live fans may actually best be met by doing less – a paradox marketers are apt to struggle with.

In any event, it is early days yet. The success or failure of the Big Bash League is not to be measured in the ratings or crowds of this summer, or perhaps even next. What counts will be where all cricket's forms stand in public affection in five to ten years' time.

CA is aiming, a la Peter de Vries, for the best of both worlds. Another prospect, though, is the worst.

The Australian, December 2011

THE GRAIL OF CONSISTENCY

Among the cricketing virtues, consistency is the most elusive. Players and teams are forever aiming to improve theirs, as though it is something to be honed like an outswinger or a cover drive.

Step forward the Australian XI. They are a very exciting bunch of players, in the same sense as perilous Pauline used to be an exciting silent movie heroine, except that they sometimes lose their grip on the window ledge and are not rescued from the railway tracks.

They are capable of soul-stirring victory chases and craven capitulations. They have the bounce of youth and the frailties of rawness, the wisdom of experience and the infirmities of age.

The former is incarnate in Phillip Hughes, for whom a fourth-stump line has become a corridor of lethality, lending 'Hughes c Guptill b Martin' the same idiomatic quality as 'Gooch lbw Alderman', 'Elvis has left the building' and 'Jeffrey Bernard is unwell'.

The latter is embodied by his eminence Ricky Ponting, thirty-seven on Monday and needing no reminding of it. Some great batsmen have had a knack of looking good even in getting out. David Gower's dismissals had a certain doomed poetry. Viv Richards could be beaten but never conquered. Ponting is not one of those batsmen. His forward thrust, hard hands and a batswing towards mid-on have always had a way of pushing him into positions where batsmen customarily fear to tread, and that has lately been catching up with him.

Fluctuations of output are to be expected in cricket, especially among batsmen. It's the simplest thing in the world to fetch a good one early, suffer a rough decision then maybe a sharp catch. The unpredictable player, such as Mark Waugh, can even have value when his best is truly outstanding.

But the trouble with inconsistency is that it very easily grows contagious. Through a kind of referred pressure, spasmodic performances beget others. And among players in their formative years, the effect can look like somebody falling down a spiral staircase with a six-tier wedding cake. In some respects, Hobart was a more abject failure than Capetown. Newlands was such a freak of nature that it could almost be classified as an outlier; Bellerive Oval recalled earlier systemic failures such as last year's SCG, MCG and Headingley Tests.

If our batsmen in particular suffer more from inconsistency than of yore, that may reflect a change in their upbringings. First-class cricket used to be our seedbed, here and abroad. It is often forgotten that one of the ways in which the best Australian batsmen of the last generation acquired the habits of day-in, day-out reliability was in county cricket.

Allan Border, Matthew Hayden, Justin Langer, Darren Lehmann, Tom Moody, Stuart Law, Chris Rogers, Jamie Cox, both Waughs and both Husseys ground out tens of thousands of runs in England as the go-to guys of their respective counties in four- and one-day cricket. For sure, the cricket was not sometimes of the highest quality. But there were also excellent skills to learn: the business of meeting everyday expectation, the knack of technical self-analysis, the challenge of managing motivation and workload in a new environment.

The most lucrative modern professional circuit, by contrast, is that vertiginous candy mountain, the Indian Premier League. T20 being what it is, however, consistency is not even really an expectation; rather does the emphasis fall on the occasional explosive performance, the dynamic one-off moment. Consistency: it's *so* five years ago.

All of which – season and subject – brings us to the Big Bash League. For just when it would be timely for there to be some first-class cricket in Australia to provide solid middle time for traumatised cricketers and some empirical evidence for selectors to sift, the 2011–12 season has been turned over to truckling to ten-year-olds.

There's a lot to be said for T20 – no, really there is. David Warner even suggests that some advanced pupils may in future, with an enormous amount of dedicated help and goodwill, progress to cricket's longer forms. But the way the BBL has elbowed first-class cricket in Australia out of the middle of summer bespeaks a contempt for the very qualities in cricket we are now fretting that we lack.

Cricket Australia prides itself on its excellent management. But what sort of management makes a decision as significant and irrevocable as the BBL and only *afterwards* instigates a review of Australian cricket? Aren't actions meant to *follow* reviews? And isn't marketing meant to be at the service of cricket, rather than cricket at the service of marketing?

CA has made some admirable appointments and taken some worthwhile steps in the last few months. But it also exhibits a strange predilection for hurrying into momentous decisions, like expediting plans for the BBL, and labouring over colossal trivialities, such as Simon Katich speaking his mind. How, for example, does it take days to decide whether Tasmania's Ed Cowan can captain the CA Chairman's XI? Can somebody please reintroduce Australian cricket's left hand to its right hand? They need to reacquaint.

In fact, if Australian cricket's decision-makers really want greater consistency from their cricket team, then it might be a healthy notion to set an example themselves.

The Australian, December 2011

T20

LEADERSHIP VACUUM

The captaincy of Australia, runs an exhausted cliché, is the country's second-most important job. Where does that place the captaincy of the Australian T20 side?

George Bailey's much-discussed tenure is now over after six hours' elapsed time. It remains to be seen whether he takes up the cudgels for the games at St Lucia and Barbados next month, or indeed becomes part of the overall touring party to be named towards the end of the Commonwealth Bank Series. After that, there's the World T20 in Sri Lanka in September.

Thus do the protestations about Bailey from the 'not-since-Dave-Gregory' lobby appear misguided. It seems entirely logical, given the few T20 internationals played, that one of their roles should be as a forum in which to trial players whom the selectors wish to evaluate more generally.

T20 is a high-pressure format played in front of sizeable crowds, which tests aptitude for big occasions. It is also a sharply abbreviated game in which there is little chance to grow nervous, and in which instincts can be studied – and that counts for captaincy every bit as much as batting, bowling and fielding.

What makes less sense is the limits of the experiment. If Bailey is good enough to captain his country in T20, surely he is good enough to represent it in one-day international cricket. If you wanted him to imbibe of the spirit built up around the Australian team this season, why not offer him more than a cameo? Now he drops back to the Sheffield Shield cricket, which is good news for Tasmania, but strangely ambivalent planning by a selection panel that has this summer scarcely missed a trick.

Yet Bailey's ascendant raises some more general and deeper points. How well off is Australia in reserves of leadership anyway? Who would lead this country in Test cricket were Michael Clarke unavailable? Shane Watson remains official vice-captain, but is in limbo; Brad Haddin is nominal vice-captain, but is in toils. Where are the leaders in Australian cricket? And where are they to come from?

When national selector John Inverarity was captain of Western Australia in the 1970s, the Australian team was like Napoleon's Grand Armée, in which it was said every private had a field-marshal's baton in his knapsack. Sheffield Shield captains were heavily represented: Ian Chappell (South Australia) could draw on the experience of Greg Chappell (Queensland), Ian Redpath (Victoria), Doug Walters (NSW), not to mention Inverarity's colleagues Rod Marsh and Dennis Lillee. Study the Sheffield Shield today and the scene is very different. None of Chris Hartley, Cameron White, Michael Klinger or Steve O'Keefe threaten to blossom into Test cricketers; Marcus North, a good servant, has had his time.

What has changed since the 1970s, of course, has been the advent of the national coach. Many of the responsibilities that once reposed in the skipper are now diffused among a backroom staff almost as plentiful as the team itself. Players now talk about the 'bowling plan' and the 'batting group' as though the name of the game is adherence to a checklist rather than scoring runs or taking wickets.

Interestingly, while he inherited such a set-up, coach Mickey Arthur is an avowed sceptic about over-elaborated coaching structures. As South Africa's coach, Arthur argued that 'short and sharp "refresher" courses' were more effective than 'travelling with a vast, full-time coaching squad' – an approach he applied here, for example, during the 'batting camp' ahead of the Boxing Day. Many hands may make light work, but too many leave a player and a team incapable of resolving challenges for themselves.

Remedying that situation, however, will require more concerted effort at first- and second-class level to develop cricketers capable of looking after themselves and one another. We regard the Shield and the Futures League as the test bed for Test batsmen and bowlers of the future. But is it doing enough to turn young cricketers into potential leaders, or will our next generation of players simply be made up of unthinking followers, capable of mechanically reproducing their specialist skills but lacking in any particular insight into the game itself? The trouble these days is that once a cricketer has graduated to national level, his opportunities to lead will come only sporadically if at all.

With a maximum eighty overs to look him over in action, it's not clear what Australia's selectors will have learned about Bailey from the last week or so. But that's also natural: not a lot *is* clear about leadership, which is one of the reasons why such a thriving, theoretical, contingent and contradictory literature surrounds it. Much as my colleagues and I like to pontificate from on high about 'leadership qualities', we tend to over-exaggerate the importance of evidences we can see (bowling changes, field placements) and underestimate or theorise in a vacuum about those we cannot (individual characteristics, interpersonal skills).

From what little I know of Bailey, there is much to like about him. He is an articulate young man from a family steeped in cricket. He is an attractive, free-scoring batsman who has failed only to make really huge scores; he has been part of the development of a healthy and successful culture in Tasmania, melding a disparate band of locals and imports.

More than that, Bailey has solid and continuous experience of the buck stopping with him. And as Bailey himself put it in a thoughtful interview with *Cricinfo*'s Brydon Coverdale, repeating some sage advice from his mentor Dan Marsh, captaincy is something you improve at by doing, because your experience of match situations and personality types widens with every day you put in.

All the more reason, in fact, why Bailey deserved an opportunity in the CB Series; after all, one need not be captain to take on or project oneself into a guiding role. There is more to building a cognisance of leadership in Australian cricket than filling that so-called second-most important job in the nation.

The Australian, January 2012

Cricket's Back
OR IS IT?

Last week was what Cricket Australia called 'Cricket's Back' Week. Did you notice? In Sydney, there was what is commonly called a 'media event', even if 'event' usually implies something actually happening, and nothing much at such things ever does.

Michael Clarke and a selection of his peers were put on display at the Museum of Contemporary Art, not far from a sculpture constructed of partially assembled IKEA furniture, and a performance artist dancing to music videos and eating junk food (ostensibly she was re-enacting a recent period of unemployment, although she might equally have been miming a Big Bash League game). The cricketers might almost have been involved in a piece of performance art themselves: 'Media Event 2012: The Crisis of Meaning.'

Because while there was a hashtag, a fashion shoot and a faux monumental 'Cricket's Back' sign that looked like it had been obtained from the same people who built the Stonehenge for Spinal Tap, far from being 'back', cricket remained on vacation. With less than a month until the First Test against the world's number-one

Test team, CA's only games for the week were an under-23 match in Adelaide and a women's interstate T20 match in Sydney yesterday.

Meanwhile, the core of the squad Clarke is due to lead at the Gabba against South Africa were in that country, involved in the Champions League, a tournament more widely known hereabouts as 'that T20 thing on Fox, whatever it is'. These numbered Shane Watson, David Warner, Michael Hussey, Brad Haddin, Ben Hilfenhaus, Mitchell Starc, Mitchell Johnson and Pat Cummins, not to mention Steve Smith, Moises Henriques, Doug Bollinger, Michael Beer, Brett Lee, Simon Katich, Brad Hogg and the brothers Marsh, spread among six of the teams involved.

Watson, it was then hurriedly announced, would return a tad early, to reacquaint himself with the red cricket ball he hasn't faced in a top-level game since April. But the rest remain, perhaps as late as the end of the month, impinging not simply on the preparation of the national team for the First Test against South Africa, but on the whole atmosphere of the season.

The official responses to the recall of Watson savoured likewise of left hands unaware what right hands are up to. Captain Clarke offered a mini-masterpiece of equivocation: 'I back the decision if it's in the best interests of the Australian Test team to get him prepared for that first Test match. If we think it's in the best interests of Shane to stay and play and get cricket under his belt then I back that as well.' In other words, he's in favour of the right thing to do, whatever that is.

The other Clark, Stuart of the Sydney Sixers, aired essentially an intraorganisational grievance, complaining that one part of CA, presumably at the uppermost levels of senior management, had assured him of the availability of 'Australian players' for the Champions League, but that another part, 'the high-performance team', which includes the selectors, coach and Michael

Clarke, 'don't give two hoots' about the competition.

Some might argue that Clark needs reminding of the Argus review's salient directive that 'it is the Australian Team that underwrites the appeal and financial health of the sport'. But let's be charitable: CA has pursued commercial ends with such abandon for so long that decisions for reasons to do with, y'know, your actual cricket must seem utterly disorienting. And while Clark may overestimate what national selector John Inverarity thinks of the Champions League, which I'd estimate at roughly a quarter of a hoot, the competition is in financial terms a veritable hootathon.

To explain: this supranational T20 crown was conceived by CA about six years ago as involving the winners of the world's various domestic tournaments, and successfully sold to the ruling junta at the Board of Control for Cricket in India, which then included Indian Premier League founder Lalit Modi. It became a joint venture, also involving Cricket South Africa.

The timing was exquisite. Having refrained from bidding for rights to the IPL and been embarrassed by its stark raving success, ESPN Star Sports fell over themselves in the rush to get a piece of the T20 action, paying way over the odds for the new property. In order to justify that price tag, exhaustive efforts have been made to pimp the Champions League for its biggest broadcast market. The rationale of bringing 'champions' together has faded, the number of IPL teams participating having grown to four, while the top T20 teams from West Indies, Pakistan, England and New Zealand have to 'qualify' on quite discriminatory terms. The IPL teams also enjoy first call on any players with divided loyalties – thus Mike Hussey plays for the Chennai Super Kings rather than the Perth Scorchers etc.

The competition has been endowed with a first prize ($US2.5 million) almost as big as the World Cup's ($US3 million) and bigger than that of either the IPL ($US2.3 million), the World T20

($US1 million) or, indeed, the poor old World Test Championship ($US450 000, despite a recent increase).

Trouble is that the competition makes nothing but money; otherwise it is almost entirely pointless. It has no layers or nuances. It has no rivalries or derbies. It has created no memories worth keeping and instilled little pride in the winning. It can't even keep a sponsor, being on its third in four years.

The inaugural winner, New South Wales, immediately ceased to exist as a T20 entity. The only team more than a decade old in the present tournament is the incongruous presence of Yorkshire, who have somehow escaped being rechristened the Yorkshire Puddings or the Yorkshire Rippers. The rest are cookie-cutter logos and eye-gashing uniforms straight from a marketing whiteboard.

Yet, here we are – or, to be more precise, there *they* are, the cream of our cricketers playing IPL Lite on South African cricket grounds courting Indian T20 gluttons in a tournament worth hundreds of millions of dollars, but barely worth a pub argument ('I think Faf du Plessis clears his front leg better than Michael Lumb!' – 'Does not!' – 'Does too!').

CA might yet mitigate the damage to Australia's Test preparation with some judicious fixture fiddling. But the lucrative nuisance of the Champions League levies an ongoing toll on its credibility. Because demonstrating that 'Cricket's Back' actually involves rather more than a big sign, a hashtag and a matinee of 'Media Event 2012: The Crisis of Meaning.'

The Australian, October 2012

Cricket Discipline
OF T20 BONDAGE

Does Australian cricket have an incipient discipline problem on its hands?

The evidence is fragmentary and anecdotal. One Australian player has been warned about flirting with recreational drugs; others have been penalised for playing better by night than by day; a state captain has quit citing poor form, but might not have lasted anyway.

It scarcely compares to the antics of those footballers who spend their idle time auditioning for Mötley Crüe. If anything, cricketers over the years have been exceptionally adept at avoiding strife, Shane Warne probably getting into enough trouble for all of them. But vigilance is well merited. There is money around and a rather reckless relish for Gangnam glamour. So far only the low-hanging fruit of the Argus review has been plucked. The perverse incentives and debauched values of domestic and supranational T20 are unchanged, if not worse than they were two years ago.

It's hardly surprising that the long-running shambles of

Western Australian cricket should finally have become obvious to all at the Champions League T20, global cricket's cashed-up bogan, where the Perth Scorchers were guaranteed $US200 000 merely for qualifying.

A tournament of more discrepant reward and effort would have to be called the Israel Folau Cup. Not only did the Sydney Sixers collect $US2.5 million for winning and the Highveld Lions $US1.3 million for running up, but the Nashua Titans and Delhi Daredevils collected $US500 000 each for losing their semi-finals. That's right: there is more money on offer for finishing in the final four of a ten-club T20 tournament than for a national team achieving the status of number one in Test cricket – a reverberating insult, frankly, to every young cricketer who has set his heart on representing his country.

The Argus review spotted this as an issue and recommended that the Champions League prize money be capped, and any excess be allocated to either the Sheffield Shield or some other performance incentives pool. But no progress has been made.

In the meantime, ponder this: twenty-year-old Nic Maddinson of the Sixers, a capable young cricketer who might one day go further but who has so far struggled to meet exalted early expectations, has just enjoyed comfortably the biggest pay day of his young life after a tournament in which he made 59 runs from 49 balls in five hits. What life lessons might he have learned from that, do you think? Exposed to such topsy-turvy priorities, who wouldn't think about lighting Double Coronas with $100 notes or drinking Krug out of a Manolo Blahnik?

T20 is many things, some of them even good, but it is not least of all an acute management challenge – one that cricket has scarcely come to terms with. The ratio of idle time/travel time to playing time is grossly out of whack. Players have days full of not much, training mechanically for brief and intermittent opportunities. Matches under lights encourage them to stay out late with surplus energy and cash to burn.

In two weeks in South Africa, the Perth Scorchers played 133 overs of (mostly bad) cricket in three cities. Herschelle Gibbs faced a total of 34 deliveries, leaving him to find his fun elsewhere – something at which he has exhibited some prowess.

Worst of all, growing emphasis on shorter forms of the game is lowering the bar for absolute performance. In days of yore, you asked simple questions of young cricketers. How many centuries had they scored? How many five-fors had they bagged? But you can rise these days on the basis of very limited performances, providing you exude a whiff of promise. Australia's much-lauded under-19 captain Will Bosisto, for example, has made one club hundred in his entire life. He represented WA earlier this season without having made a first-grade fifty.

Perversely, some coaches seem actually to prefer players of such limited achievements, perhaps because they offer scope for burnishing by specialist input. But here's the rub. Players recognised young for not much cannot help but develop outsized senses of expectation and entitlement, and also spread cynicism among those they achieve recognition ahead of.

The expansion from a Big Bash with six state teams to a Big Bash League with eight city teams has further enhanced opportunities for lesser players to get aboard and coast along. The West Australian Cricket Association, now determined to peer into its 'culture', has proven particularly susceptible to this malaise.

WA has a playing population a quarter the size of Victoria, but a state squad similar in number. In other words, it is that much easier both to obtain a contract and to keep it, especially if one is in favour with the ruling clique. And particularly for those still living at home, contracts make for comfortable lives.

The Warriors squad has a well-earned reputation for trying only when it suits them. Western Australia was one of the Big Bash League's most zealous converts last season, Perth Scorchers hosting the final. But afterwards the Warriors fell away, losing their last two first-class matches heavily, on their way to finishing in the bottom half of the Sheffield Shield for the sixth time in seven seasons; they won a single one-day match, narrowly, all season.

Everyone likes Mitchell Marsh, a stellar talent and a guileless young man. But he has gone a long way, and attracted some head-turning praise, for a player with a first-class record of one century and one five-wicket haul in twenty matches. One wonders whether proximity to an influential father and a prodigal brother is entirely helpful to him. One wonders whether some of the sticks waved at him haven't actually been carrot-flavoured. When Marsh trans-gressed once too often at the Centre of Excellence in August, he was simply sent back to Perth – an invitation to slump back into his comfort zone.

The buck certainly stops with players, but it doesn't start with them. If the Australian cricket system wants disciplined cricketers, then it might have to work on reconciling the values it may be instilling with those it is espousing.

The Australian, October 2012

Cricket and the Media

CONTROL FREAK SHOW

Boxing Day is Australian cricket's shop window. By the end of it, a majority of Australians, even those who don't normally follow the game, will know how the national team is doing, will have someone or something to talk about.

Runs and/or wickets here can stand a player in good stead for some time, being guaranteed exhaustive coverage and repeated reporting. It's a day Cricket Australia can relax. If not the sea, they have at least the field to themselves.

But of how many other days in the sporting calendar is that still true? Cricket at the moment emanates an uncomfortable sense of a game embattled, either trying too hard or barely at all to promote itself, hemmed in on all sides by football codes producing a non-stop cycle of news, pseudo-news and basic BS.

'The Road to Season 2013' has begun on AFL.com.au. 'The Game Never Ends' trumpets NRL.com.au, which is the obvious objective. Cricket Australia, meanwhile, blessed with one of the most internet-savvy publics of any sport, is running a website that could hardly be dowdier if you had to work it by turning a crank. While the football codes are busily powering into the digital future, CA's online profile remains as stimulating as the middle overs of a one-day international. News judgements concerning cricket might be tested if the AFL extended the draft until Christmas, or Israel Folau chose Boxing Day to foreshadow his transition to pro-celebrity waterskiing.

Editors are already doing the game few favours. The Adelaide Test might have taken Australia to the brink of number one in Test cricket, but you'd hardly have known it from the daily technicolour yawn that is the *Adelaide Advertiser*, still wallowing in Tippet Agonistes when the story had already long since passed them by.

But this concerns more than isolated editorial decisions. Part of the problem is abiding. There are a lot of footballers and they are spread around the map; there are only eleven cricketers representing Australia at any one time, they are usually all in the one place and their time is minutely rationed.

This effect is aggravated by changes in the recent media landscape caused in large measure by the dwindling profitability and value of established franchises. The football codes offer a straitened media outstanding value for investment: they are cheap to cover, rich in personalities, dynamics and rivalries, and take a robust line on comment. Cricket is growingly expensive to report in financially exigent times, generates a fair proportion of four for 300/'I'm just happy to make a contribution' kind of days, and is as primly shockable as a maiden aunt.

The Hobart Test was a case in point. A low-level smoulder of a story about ball tampering was fanned into a conflagration by complaints that weren't quite complaints and denials that weren't quite denials. Anyone who thinks Australia has a dearth of spinners hasn't dealt lately with CA's public affairs section.

Cricket was also shown again to be prickly about criticism. When the ABC had the temerity to point out the Test's crummy crowds, for example, CA director Tony Harrison took strenuous exception. 'If you don't like Tasmania, don't come,' he huffed, sounding for all the world like a local cricket poobah appeasing his constituents when he's actually the member of a newly restructured board meant to be rendering such parochialism a thing of the past.

Meanwhile, woe betide the player or coach who speaks their mind: such as the Scorchers' Simon Katich, who pointed out the obvious absurdity of the conclusion of his team's match with the Stars in Perth a fortnight ago, and the Heat's Darren Lehmann, who at the weekend drew belated attention to the 'bowling action' of the Renegades' Marlon Samuels.

You'd be forgiven for inferring that Big Bash League management is so obsessed with Facebook likes and pre-match fatuities that it's forgotten there's actual – y'know, that thing, what's it called, oh yes – cricket taking place. An effective administration would have removed the grounds for Lehmann's complaint before he needed to make it. As it is, his proscription under the code of conduct will be a further caution for any cricketer intending to speak his mind.

The episode draws attention to a larger paradox involving Cricket Australia.

Here is an organisation trying terribly hard to draw attention to its works, even as it strives simultaneously to minimise the likelihood of anyone involved saying or doing anything interesting. Here is an organisation so fixated on marketing and public relations that it has developed an aversion to actual news, which may endanger all that careful brand building.

The code under which Lehmann has been charged makes it an offence to 'denigrate or criticise another player . . . by inappropriately commenting on any aspect of his or her performance, abilities or characteristics'. It is a code that was designed to keep cricket out of a spotlight it now badly needs. Today it conduces to a climate of mechanical approbation and mealy-mouthed evasion.

CA's attitude to media, I would argue, is indicative of a general control freakiness. As often happens when bureaucracy reaches a critical mass, CA is developing a culture based on monitoring and managing everything. And the game is small enough that this almost feels within its power, in a way that the NRL and AFL will always be just that bit too large and unwieldy to come completely under centralised oversight.

Sometimes, though, good management is about giving people their heads, trusting them, allowing initiative, surrendering control, maybe making a few mistakes along the way, but being entitled to pardon where they are acting in good faith. Whatever the case, Cricket Australia badly needs a media makeover. At the moment, it performs no more than the basics competently. Otherwise, its ways are stale, sleepy and out of step with the demands of both modern sport and the modern media.

Boxing Day, eh? Marvellous. Looking forward to it. It's from the day after tomorrow that the complications recommence.

The Australian, December 2012

FANS FIRST?

The role of a selection panel is never ending, rather like painting the Sydney Harbour Bridge: no sooner do you finish at one end than you must start again at the other.

For John Inverarity and his colleagues, it's just grown harder still. Mike Hussey's retirement has committed them to working simultaneously from the middle, and the paint is suddenly very much thinner. The high-gloss enamel they have to work with, in fact, raises some disturbing questions about the whole structure they're charged with responsibility for.

In days of yore, selectors looking to replace a key batsman would have scanned the first-class cricket scene to see who was making what where, and for how long they had been doing so. The Sheffield Shield was actually a pretty reliable guide, and in some respects still is: it has been instructive in the last week or so to hear Mitchell Johnson's comments about the role interstate cricket played in his rehabilitation.

But the Sheffield Shield has been on hiatus for more than a

month while Cricket Australia dedicates itself to pimping the Big Bash League, and will not resume until just prior to the naming of the Australian touring party for India. Two Shield games are scheduled in the last week of January. Neither involves Tasmania or Queensland, with some of the best candidates to succeed Hussey and to understudy Shane Watson.

Before the dog, pony, bike and boyband show got underway, for example, Tasmania's Alex Doolan was batting as well as anyone in Australia. In the Sheffield Shield fixture at the MCG, he outshone Ricky Ponting; in the Australia A match at the SCG, he mastered the Proteas attack that later humbled Australia. Yet Doolan has not played a game of consequence since. A supernumerary for the Melbourne Renegades, he has played some club cricket for the Camberwell Magpies. Dan Harris – age thirty-three, cut from the Redbacks list in July, and with a BBL average this summer of 6.5 – is felt to be the superior T20 batsman.

Mind you, Doolan may be better off when some of his peers are considered. In the last month, Doolan's Tasmanian captain George Bailey has faced 42 deliveries, Rob Quiney 54, Peter Forrest 52, David Hussey 63. The runs they've wrung from these paltry opportunities have been virtually irrelevant, although it is odd to see so many concluding that Australia's best middle-order solution is consanguinity – simply swapping one Hussey for another. Fine player that he has been, David Hussey made 120 runs in five Sheffield Shield matches at 17.14 before his 79 runs at 19.75 in the BBL. Perhaps it does not mean much. But at thirty-five, it may mean something.

While statistics can never been definitive, they can be powerfully indicative, and what they indicate at the moment is dismaying. In July and August, Inverarity's panel showed their hand in the batsmen they picked for a tour of England with Australia A, captained by Ed Cowan: Bailey, Forrest, Joe Burns, Michael Klinger, Tim Paine, Liam Davis and Tom Cooper. In the first half of the domestic first-class summer, Burns averaged 30.8, Bailey 28.16, Klinger 26.8, Paine 25.8, Forrest 16.6, Davis 13.9 and Cooper 7.5.

Yet instead of going back to the drawing board and working on setting this to rights, they, like their colleagues and rivals, have spent the last month travelling, training and generally lolling about between games in what at times looks like cricket's attempt to pass 'Red Faces' off as *The X-Factor*. Seen the Sydney Thunder recently? They recall the line in Jimmy Breslin's famous story 'The Worst Team Ever' about the New York Mets of fifty years ago: 'With this team, nothing changes. Only the days.'

Frankly, the season is working for nobody. Consider Cowan. After the Sydney Test, he has a month to prepare for his first Test tour of India. He is scheduled to play a maximum of one BBL game for the Hurricanes and one Ryobi Cup game for the Tigers. Consider Watson. Basically we have to find a form of cricket for him in which he is not required to play any actual cricket. He is Australian cricket's equivalent of the dinnerwear your grandparents kept in the sideboard because it was too precious to use.

How, with all the expertise, talent, resources and goodwill at Australia's disposal, did we end up with this cockamamie clusterfuck? After all, it's not eighteen months since we were assured that the Argus review would fix everything, with its salutary incantation that 'it is the Australian Team that underwrites the appeal and financial health of the sport'.

The problem really lies in a parallel document, never released and seldom discussed: CA's strategic plan for 2011 to 2015. This was a curious affair, approved by the old board shortly before its dissolution, and left for the new board to implement.

The summary of the 'strategic imperatives' of the report on

CA's website contains the usual pointing at the fences, such as 'increasing the performance, efficiency and agility of Australian Cricket administration'. (I know what you're thinking. You're thinking Dave Gilbert doing Pilates). But what we're witnessing, if it was not already apparent, is the tension, almost amounting to a contradiction, between the plan's first two 'pillars'.

Pillar 1 is the injunction to 'put fans first', which CA interprets as prioritising the Big Bash League at every juncture, but which on the evidence is conducing to a surfeit of sloppy, mediocre cricket.

Pillar 2 is the directive to 'produce the best teams, players and officials in the world', which frankly Australian cricket has done for most of the last century with a vigorous and Darwinian first-class competition, but which is at odds with the new 'customer is king' mentality.

This badly needs a rethink. Put it this way. If Australia loses the Border–Gavaskar Trophy and forfeits the Ashes this year, it's hard to imagine the average fan concluding: 'Oh well, never mind; at least Cricket Australia has put me first.' After all, a selection panel can only be requested to paint the bridge. It shouldn't be expected to build the bridge itself.

The Australian, January 2013

A FIGHT WITH NO WINNER

Cricket Australia's chief executive James Sutherland believes that the incidents in the unruly 'derby' between Melbourne's Stars and Renegades at the MCG is 'a sign of where the Big Bash is at'. And he is right, but not in the way he thinks.

At the top of his press conference yesterday, Sutherland said that he had not seen the incidents, only clips – a curious distinction to draw. But then he sailed confidently onwards to effectively pay tribute to 'two teams' with 'a lot of passion' and 'a lot at stake', and an incident which 'creates greater interest in the Big Bash League'.

Did he disapprove of repeated, relentless puerile behaviour by two experienced international cricketers? Well . . . er . . . he didn't 'condone' it. Ahem, did he disapprove? Again with the 'c' word. Shane Warne? Oh, he's 'phenomenal'.

To be sure, cricket is ambivalent where on-field aggression is concerned: we affect to deplore it, yet can't look away. Many more people will search out 'Shane Warne Marlon Samuels' on YouTube than, for example, 'Kane Richardson catch', the highlight of the game the night before.

But there lies a problem. The BBL is out and proudly designed to make cricket relevant to 'new markets', which to CA's way of thinking is anyone not a white male over fifty, but which clearly accents pre-pubescent children and their parents.

In the token punishment levied on Warne and the mealy-mouthedness of Sutherland's response, the message is now out there: this is OK; this is cricket; these are acceptable bounds of aggression as calculated by the greatest superstar of our time, and an opponent with that most-lauded of modern sporting attributes, attitude. I dare say there will be twentysomething males who go 'phwoar'. But there will also be preteen boys who go 'gosh', and thirtysomething parents who go 'this doesn't happen at soccer'.

The incidents themselves will be so endlessly reviewed and anatomised that there is almost no need to elaborate on them. The dramatis personae are hardly surprising. Marlon Samuels, for all his talent, is a bit of a tit who has swanned around at the Renegades as though his teammates are privileged to be in the same postcode let alone on the same park.

His presence in the BBL has been a provocation throughout. Brisbane Heat's coach Darren Lehmann was fined for observing what is palpably obvious even to the International Cricket Council – that he borrowed the action for his quicker ball from Eric Bristow.

Shane Warne? Well, Steve Waugh once said of his most cele-brated and execrated teammate that he seemed to thrive on the chaos he precipitated. For him, this would have been a trip down memory lane: hot tempers, harsh words, umpires tut-tutting, jere-miahs pontificating, people running left and right, codes of conduct being waved.

And he'd be pardoned a sense of impunity, wouldn't he? He is best mates with his club's president; he is the fiancé of his club's most photogenic fan, Elizabeth Hurley; he is the biggest drawcard in CA's most vaunted product. It used to be Warne versus the establishment. Now Warne is part of the establishment. And they need him more than he needs them. It's just *too* delicious.

For this kind of exposure this incident has engendered is surely what he was recruited for: the tabloid grist; the television gold; the Twitter platinum; the no-such-thing-as-bad-publicity melodrama.

Warne provided last summer's BBL with the only moment anyone remembers, by nominating how he would bowl the Brisbane Heat's Brendon McCullum. He had already gifted this season with its major talking point, by heading to Blighty for Christmas with his beloved and exchanging caustic tweets with his old mucker Darren Berry. And this is actually the impression that lingers after you've watched the contretemps a few times: that, not to put too fine a point on it, it's bullshit.

In one respect, Sutherland is right. Once in a while, on-field temper is understandable, even forgivable. Cricket at its best is an exciting, intense, wholehearted, full-blooded exercise. The players are adults; they can look after themselves. Sometimes it is necessary for a player to cross a line for us to be reminded that a line exists in the first place. Mike Hussey's chivalry and deportment on the cricket field were entirely admirable, but a cricket composed only of Mr Crickets would soon lose its appeal.

But what was depressing about the incident at the MCG on Sunday night was not that it crossed the bounds of acceptable aggression, but that it crossed the bounds of acceptable artificiality. This did not feel like two great athletes strung up to concert pitch for great stakes, proving after all that they were only flesh and blood. Nor did it savour of the 'passion' and 'rivalry' of two teams, who after all in two weeks will dissolve with most of their personnel reverting to playing as teammates for Victoria.

It felt instead, like so much of the BBL, just a bit phoney: a sham clash initiated by a box-office star brought out of retirement wearing a microphone with a visiting prima donna whose remonstrations were then filmed by a camera in the umpire's hat. The antagonists were representing two made-up teams owned by the same organisation in what for the Renegades was a nine-wicket walk in the park. It's like somebody said: 'Hey Warnie, there's 46000 here to watch this piece of crap. Go pick a fight and maybe nobody will notice.'

Samuels then had his eye socket shattered by a bouncer – an ugly and unfortunate accident. But you don't reckon that won't be exploited for the purposes of somehow authenticating the finger-wagging and shirt-tugging petulance that prefigured it. Look, look: the players are trying; the players really care; I declare, it's war out there!

The irony is that I think the players *are* trying. And there's good things about the BBL too. Watching Ricky Ponting bat is cool. Watching Lasith Malinga and Muttiah Muralitharan bowl is thrilling. And following Warne is still, for the most part, fun. Sometimes, when the best cricketers are involved, the BBL is as enjoyable as the old Big Bash.

But that's not enough and this is where the BBL really 'is at': CA is so desperate to primp and plump it for sale to the highest television bidder that its chief executive sees 'passion' in what looked as contrived, and not nearly as diverting, as rock'n'roll wrestling. There is indeed at a lot at stake. But James Sutherland has more at stake than either Shane Warne or Marlon Samuels.

The Australian, January 2013

The Big Bash League 2012–13
A GAME WITH NO LOSER

Rodney Dangerfield famously went to a fight and a game of ice hockey broke out. Similarly in Perth on Wednesday night, a marketing and television property was wheeled into place and a cricket match veritably erupted – certainly the best in the Big Bash League's two seasons.

It wasn't subtle. It wasn't nuanced. Many mistakes were made, with crushing consequences. There was James Faulkner, who bottled last season's Ryobi Cup final, doing so again. There was Alex Keath, as green as his uniform, bowling. There was Shane Warne, hero of a thousand fights, *not* bowling. But, as a tweet from Alistair McDermott put it later, it was 'a serious game of cricket': the hitting, the missing, the catching – in the crowd anyway.

Did it make the BBL a success? Not really: too much of it is still dross. But it exhibited a potential that perhaps not even the BBL's promoters have grasped, so much of the tournament's epiphenomena being devoted to distracting the audience from the labour of watching an actual game.

For one obvious thing, it meant a bit. It was a semi-final. A win translated into a place in the Champions League, which might be a pile of junk as a tournament, but with $13 million in prize money is a pile of junk in an upscale neighbourhood.

It meant a bit for the antagonists too. The Scorchers beat the Stars twice in 2011–12, finally bundling them from the tournament; the Stars turned the tables in a muddy mess of a game last month. There was thus little need to build the match up as cricket's Hunger Games, and the Scorchers, of all the hosting teams, probably do this least – employing, for instance, a ground announcer, Mark Readings, who actually knows cricket, rather than the usual earbashing jackass.

BBL's impresarios envisaged that their marquee attractions would be the 'derbies' in Sydney and Melbourne, equivalent in their way to AFL blockbusters. In fact, the opportunity to stage 'derbies' was high up among rationales for replacing the contest of states with a league of franchises. But one healthy crowd aside, which only half-filled the MCG anyway, the derbies have been either forgettable, or memorable for the wrong reasons, like Warne's crime of 'passion'.

The BBL, as it was on Wednesday night, has been seen to best advantage in exploiting old-fashioned parochialism: home crowds roasting visitors from interstate, much as it was in the old Big Bash. Funny that.

The game itself? T20's virtues as a commodity entertainment are usually its limitations as cricket. To me, the players feel like captives of the format. Occasionally one breaks loose, usually a batsman; every so often a Dale Steyn or a Lasith Malinga runs amok like a fox in a henhouse, only to have to give way after four overs to someone bowling right-arm nude.

Conditions seldom impact. They don't have time. The surface doesn't wear; the ball doesn't deteriorate; set plays are executed and we all go home. In general, almost everything is contained, codified, arbitrarily organised and slicked up for sale.

But on Wednesday night . . . it rained. It rained in Perth! Just as it had rained in Perth during these teams' round one game, baffling and infuriating the locals! What a glorious cosmic joke on all the fastidious figurings. The goalposts kept shifting; the coaches kept reacting; the players kept adapting, or trying to.

The best was outstanding, and the worst became pardonable, for here was something rare at the top-level in Australia: cricket with a greasy ball. The phenomenon is more familiar in Asia, where twilight dew often complicates defending a target, although it would have been recognisable to any park cricketer who has been asked to bowl with what feels like cake of Palmolive and told: 'Just try keeping the runs down, mate.'

In big cricket in this country, rain usually entails heading for the sheds, putting your feet up, breaking out the cards, calling your manager etc. On Wednesday night, there was nowhere to hide. Or at least, you had to hide in full view, like Warne, who was perhaps reminded of the wet ball he toiled to spin during the 1996 World Cup final, and elected not to relive the experience.

That introduced another layer to the game, of pathos. The greatest bowler of his time, and he would not bowl; perhaps *could* not bowl, but wasn't he a better bet than hapless Keath? That's surely not the last we shall see of Warne, but perhaps it will be, and what an original valediction: the man who never failed to captivate us with his bowling finally transfixed us by neither bowling, nor batting, nor even (officially) captaining. He *did* shake hands quite graciously.

Anyway, the cumulative effect was that one concentrated on the cricket, dramatic and desperate, and forgot all about the artificialities – until they closed like a trap on Faulkner's final ball. No! Three inside the circle! And he overstepped anyway! Amazing scenes!

So this was not only a brilliant game, but a salutary one, because it showed how fundamentally wrong-headed from the very beginning the promotion of the BBL has been. In headlong pursuit of 'new markets', Cricket Australia has chosen to emphasise everything *except* the cricket and the cricketers. The 'It's Showtime' campaign has savoured of the work of individuals with neither affection for nor confidence in the game; indeed, who wish they were selling something else.

In a perceptive contribution to *Sports Business Insider* last week, sports branding expert Anthony Costa argued that CA have been outsmarting themselves: 'BBL presents itself as an edgy niche sport rather than a staid mainstream pastime. It's hooked on youth and is desperate not to be your dad's cricket. But by distancing itself from the game's traditions and broad spectator base the BBL risks belonging to no-one. Indeed its branding seems intent on alienating the people who should care most about the league's success.'

The media has been accused in recent times of 'talking cricket down'. But nobody has talked cricket down more resonantly than CA, who have argued in effect that the game is in crisis and desperately needs to reach out to people indifferent to cricket by pitching them a cricketainment package in which the actual cricket content is reduced if not overshadowed. A bit of distraction probably is necessary when you're sitting through a Sydney Thunder game. But Wednesday night's semi-final would have been exciting in an empty room with the sound turned down.

BBL still engenders an excess of ordinary cricket. Its duration this summer has been excessive and disruptive. Its effect on motivations and incentives will be deeply challenging. But if it can tap into the profound and abiding love for cricket that already exists, and that in the traditional season can be hard to express, it might yet achieve something worthwhile.

The Australian, January 2013

CB Series
IS IT BORING?

In a series of advertisements five years ago promoting Cricket Australia's sponsorship by the Commonwealth Bank, the Australian cricket team appeared as themselves, being presented to by two shiny spivs from an 'American ad agency' called Luke & Luke.

'Cricket,' said one of the Lukes, rolling the word round in his mouth as he looked at Mike Hussey. 'Mr Cricket.' He carried on musing: 'Is it boring? Do we need to add something to it?'

Hussey and his teammates sat stiff and stony-faced as the ad man's questions continued: 'Sweaters. What's going on with the sweaters?' The advertisement closed with the volunteering of a new slogan: 'Cricket: watch us stand.'

We were meant to laugh at this – and actually, as cricket ads go, they weren't the worst. Americans, eh? So dumb. So crass. They would never understand that cricket was complete in itself, needed no help from imported wisenheimers.

Ah, but that was then. This last month it's been hard to miss the Cricket Australia's advertising campaign promoting the

Commonwealth Bank Series as 'Summer's Biggest Dress-Up Party'. To quote from CA's own press release, it 'captures the notion that the Commonwealth Bank Series is like one big summer-house party' with 'people wearing colourful costumes from all walks of life'.

This summer's ODIs, the release explains, will feature appearances from Basement Jaxx plus Sneaky Sound System, Zoe Badwi and Sarah De Bono: 'The game provides the perfect backdrop for a summer party in a festival atmosphere with thousands of fans dressed in outrageous costumes and DJ's[sic] playing party tunes.'

Apart from being composed by someone with a rather insecure grasp of apostrophes, the release is strangely fascinating. The 'Summer's Biggest Dress-Up Party' campaign is designed by GPY&R, part of the multinational WPP, but it might as well have come straight from the drawing boards of Luke & Luke. 'Cricket. Is it boring? Do we need to add something to it?'

I would not wish to be misunderstood here. I actually enjoy the dressing up that has become part of cricket's summer pageant in the ranks of Richie Benauds and others. A cherished personal memory is walking round the back of the Wyatt Stand at Edgbaston after the Test of 2005 and coming upon a vigorous game of cricket with Queen Victoria facing Sherlock Holmes with Lord Nelson wicket-keeping to a field of Beefeaters.

But what's pleasing has been the custom's spontaneity. It arose without official sanction; it even courted official disapproval. Now it's a scheme for rounding up those all-important 'cricket consumers'. Thirty years ago, the *New Yorker's* baseball writer Roger Angell observed that Americans had evolved a way to turn 'the smallest flutter of a spontaneous incident in sports . . . into a mass-produced imitation or a slogan or an advertising gimmick'. We're all Americans now.

Frankly, too, anyone with a love for cricket should be concerned when those charged with promoting it describe it as a 'backdrop'. Because nobody can love a backdrop: they are inherently interchangeable and substitutable. There is a slope here and it is a slippery one, culminating perhaps with the crowd replying: 'Hey, can you keep that cricket down out there? We're trying to enjoy our summer party!'

Between times, there cannot help but be a confusion of messages. One-day cricket has a great many doomsayers. Shane Warne reckons it is redundant. Adam Gilchrist says it will be 'pretty much gone' within three years. Yet whenever such comments are aired, Cricket Australia noisily proclaims that fifty-over cricket is alive and well, as popular as ever.

They have to say this, of course: one-day cricket is the chief means by which we determine who leads the world, and by which the game in general is bankrolled. It is the cricket format played in the World Cup, which Australia is due to host in 2014–15, the rights for which, distributed by the International Cricket Council, keep many cricket countries alive.

In this instance, though, CA are right. The head-to-head format worked well in 2010–11; the 2011–12 tri-series was competitive and exciting all the way through. India's win over Australia and tie with Sri Lanka in Adelaide were arguably the best cricket they played last summer; I'd sooner have watched Sri Lanka's scintillating chase in the second final at the same ground than many a grim Test match.

So where exactly does one-day cricket stand? Is it in a process of managed decline, steadily being reduced to the level of house party backdrop, or of abiding popularity and ongoing rebirth? For how can CA first spruik fifty-over international cricket as 'a fantastic way to spend a glorious summer's day with friends', which makes it sound like a lazy lunch in a beer garden, then rebuild it for an event comparable with soccer's World Cup or the Olympics, which cricket likes to see itself as a peer with. It may be a mistake to expect any kind of logical coherence in marketing, but once you let Luke & Luke in, they cannot help but leave their watermark.

The predicament for one-day cricket is that it used to be the opposite of Test cricket and now it isn't: that role has been appropriated by T20. ODIs are no longer seen as short-form Test matches, but drawn-out T20s, and usually played when players are knackered, bored and indifferent.

As Graeme Swann observed in his recent autobiography, the best time to play another team in ODIs is when they have just pulped you in a Test series, because they slacken off and you have nothing to lose: which may, by the way, provide a logical underpinning for the selection of a fresh Australian squad at the weekend, as noisily peevish as Channel Nine is about it.

One-day cricket's records mean next to nothing. Who knows how many ODI hundreds Michael Clarke has scored? And who, really, cares? The rankings in the ICC's World Test Championship have actually started to mean something; the rankings in the ICC's World One-Day Championship still mean damn all.

All of which suggests that an advertising campaign that subtly derogates the actual cricket of the Commonwealth Bank Series is the very opposite of what CA should be signing off on, because it subtly derogates the cricketers also, and they deserve better. George Bailey deserves to be taken seriously as his country's captain on Friday, not dressed up in paisley on Twitter as the host of summer's biggest dress-up party.

So here's a modest, counterintuitive proposal, not because anyone in authority will take a blind bit of notice, but simply as a conversation starter. How about promoting and redesigning one-day cricket to appeal to Test match fans? After all it is traditional cricket fans who will provide the greatest support for the World Cup, not the house partygoers. Let's get Luke & Luke in, and try to explain to them what's really going on with those sweaters.

The Australian, January 2013

Channel Nine
THE BURGERMEISTERS

Kerry Packer famously said that there was nothing after death. He had been there; he knew. Yet in the last few years he has enjoyed a vibrant video afterlife, brought to the screen in the television series *Paper Giants* and *Howzat*, and to be seen later this year in *Magazine Wars*.

His shade hovered over the Sydney Test in the obsequies for the late Tony Greig, while his image will be front and centre in the World Series Cricket exhibition opening in a couple of weeks at the Bradman Museum. Packer was always larger than life. Posthumously, he seems to be getting even bigger.

But might there be more to it? This summer, of course, is the last covered by Cricket Australia's existing television arrangements with the Nine Network, Packer's former fiefdom. His heir having sold Nine into a leveraged buy-out that then collapsed last year, the network is a shadow of its former self. Yet its bluster has been vintage Packer, culminating in a breathtakingly arrogant attack on an Australian cricket captain by a Nine officer that was almost as extraordinary as the fact that Cricket Australia remained publicly mute throughout. These are not the sounds of a healthy commercial arrangement; on the contrary, they suggest one that may have run its course, and that needs to change, if not end altogether.

Brad McNamara's comments about George Bailey – that Bailey needed to 'understand where his money's coming from' and would be 'probably working in a coal mine or flipping burgers at McDonald's' but for Nine's largesse – actually almost brought cricket full circle.

In the mid-1970s, the old Australian Cricket Board had a notoriously peppery secretary Alan Barnes, who could be relied upon for a pithy comment any time players grew restless. His most famous putdown drove cricketers to fury: 'These are not professionals . . . They were all invited to play, and if they don't like the conditions there are 500 000 other cricketers in Australia who would love to take their places.' In that splendid documentary series *The Chappell Era*, Ian Chappell recounted how mild-mannered Ian Redpath pinned Barnes 'up against the wall by the bloody throat' to make his displeasure known.

Packer's World Series Cricket was partly about consigning such feudal relations between the players and their administrators to the past. But now it is Nine, Ian Chappell's long-time employer, telling cricketers to be seen, not heard and grateful for what they have, and Cricket Australia, anxious not to upset the negotiating applecart, that has let them.

Actually, Nine is nowhere near as significant to CA and cricketers as a decade ago. ESPN and other overseas rights contribute just as much to their coffers as Nine. And a cricketer such as Bailey will earn up to a third of income from non-CA sources: the Indian Premier League, county cricket and personal sponsors.

What's really significant is that Nine, vanguard of cricket's revolution, now sounds more reactionary than CA, whose citadel it stormed those many years ago. CA at last talks about venturing into 'new markets': women, the young, non-English speakers. And that being so, one must question how Nine is helping them with broadcasting so blokey, middle-aged and Anglo-Celtic?

Cricket has changed unrecognisably in the last five years, with the growing heft of India, the advent of supranational T20, the relentless spread of digital technologies, the growing hubbub of social media. But while the game has marched on, Nine has marked time. Not in a technical sense: its production is here as proficient as ever. But the voices and tone have hardly changed at all.

Individually, each caller has strengths and weaknesses; personally, I hold several in high esteem. Collectively, I fear, they are an exhibit in the case that cricket in Australia is male, pale and stale. Nine's current roster features fewer commentators under forty-five than over seventy-five. Not one of them has played T20, the IPL, the Big Bash League, or any of the last three World Cups. With three of them on duty at once, they talk incessantly, oblivious to that sage advice of their elder statesman Richie Benaud: 'Don't say anything unless you can add to the picture.' The network's idea of a fresh perspective is James Brayshaw. Mike Hussey has been temporarily retained. There has also been talk of Ricky Ponting being courted. He would be an excellent addition, but would not remedy all Nine's limitations and might compound others.

Time was when Nine made a token effort to reflect summer's changing attractions with guest commentators from the countries of the touring teams. Now there are too many many mouths to feed, too many bottoms and not enough chairs. The effect is that one summer sounds much the same as another, and the audiences reflect this.

Perhaps it's no wonder Nine is so publicly resentful of turnover of Australian players in the Commonwealth Bank Series; it counter-points the inertia in their own ranks. And perhaps it's no wonder that Nine drove so hard to wrest *Howzat* from the ABC, which fostered *Paper Giants*, as a reclamation of a foundation myth; they seem to be looking backwards rather than forwards, inwards rather than outwards.

Gen Xers can still recall the feeling of subversion and curiosity that attended changing the channel from the Test cricket on the ABC to World Series Cricket on Nine. It was a step perhaps more momentous for having to get up and cross the room to do so – there was certainly no remote control on my family's black and white Pye with rabbit ears. It was refreshing and reinvigorating for cricket generally, and the game does indeed have cause to be grateful.

But it can't remain in a posture of supplication forever. Televised cricket in Australia is overdue another such refreshment, and little about Nine at present suggests it is culturally equipped to provide it. What the network needs perhaps is more people thinking like Kerry Packer rather than simply trying to sound like him.

The Australian, February 2013

MAN OF THE PEOPLE

On Thursday morning, Cricket Australia's public affairs department circulated a 'media advisory' notice, promising that at 12.10 p.m. a 'senior member' of the Australian Test squad to tour India would be available for interview next to the statue of Dennis Lillee that has become a Melbourne Cricket Ground landmark.

A subtle juxtaposition? Cricketer, identity not clear at time of writing, terms and conditions apply, sent along to stand in the long shadow of Australia's cricket heritage. At least they didn't send what turned out to be Peter Siddle round the corner to stand beneath the outsized likeness of Shane Warne. That symbolism would have been too obvious.

Because it was that kind of week, in which old Australia, personified by Warne, cast a critical eye on new Australia, as marshalled by high-performance manager Pat Howard, national selector John Inverarity and coach Mickey Arthur, and found it wanting.

Warne burst his Twitter bonds to begin a multi-part expatiation of Australian cricket's ills, presenting a slate of handpicked candidates to take it over. One of those he would replace, Inverarity, then had the task of naming a seventeen-man squad for the forthcoming tour of India that, absent the retired Ricky Ponting and Mike Hussey, might be the weakest sent abroad in a generation.

In that sense, Warne timed his moment well, for it is not unlikely that things will get worse before they get better. And judging by the social media response, Warne clearly tapped into deep-rooted discontents about Australian cricket's direction, as well as the very human desire to hold somebody, or bodies, responsible: the 'time to get back to basics' and 'sack-this-lot-and-pick-a-bunch-of-kids' mentality that has sold many a tabloid newspaper in its time, and cost many a football coach his job.

But cricket isn't football – a fact that sometimes seems to disappoint its marketers. Football codes in this country have salary caps, drafts and other equalising measures that provide coaches with natural opportunities to rebuild. The influence of national cricket coaches and selectors is far more circumscribed: they cannot recruit from outside to remedy existing deficiencies; they cannot promote talent that does not exist. Their job is closer to Warne's other favourite game, poker, inasmuch as they must play the hand that they are dealt.

Warne has actually made this argument himself in critiquing John Buchanan. To Warne, Buchanan is a guy who was dealt flush after flush by the talent at his disposal; that view has been given some force by Buchanan's subsequent fortunes in a country, New Zealand, where the high cards are fewer.

Frankly, I suspect that Warne had it right this first time: that while they assuredly act on one another, it is chiefly cricketers who make national coaches rather than national coaches who make cricketers. So it's surprising to find him promoting the opposite view, that changing names in a management flowchart will make a world of difference.

But, then, there are some other surprising observations in Warne's manifesto, starting with the richly imagined premise. 'The current set-up is not working, as the results are showing!' Warne insists. 'What are our world rankings in all forms?' That he refrains from answering this is perhaps a giveaway that they don't serve his argument.

At the time Arthur, Inverarity and Howard took over, Australia was fifth in the world, having lost three Ashes Tests by an innings in its own backyard.

Since then it's won ten Tests and lost two and is a point shy of second on the Test ladder. But for James Pattinson's Adelaide breakdown, Australia would surely have taken a Test off the world's number-one Test nation; it might even, at a pinch, have wrested that mantle itself.

For sure, Australia has slipped to third in the ODI rankings. But South Africa, for most of the last decade Australia's most successful rival, has fallen to fourth, and nobody there seems to think this a problem.

Australia's T20 performances have been lacklustre, but, frankly, they have always lacked lustre. We were bowled out for 79 by England at Southampton in 2005. We were beaten by Zimbabwe at Cape Town in 2007. Last week, we were a boundary from beating the world's number-one ranked team, Sri Lanka, in Melbourne. On that evidence, threadbare as all evidence concerning T20Is is, we might be improving. Whatever the case, it is, again, surprising to find such an irrepressible glass half-full thinker indulging in such glass half-empty thinking.

For Warne is innately an optimist, as he confirms in remonstrating about what CA has unfortunately begun to refer to as 'informed player management'. This is certainly an expression at which the first reflex is to gag at the jarring managerialism. Nor is

Warne on his own here, for he echoes some sage judges, and the science on the subject is not definitive.

Warne wants players to send a 'very powerful and strong message' to CA: 'I do not want to be rested or rotated. I want to play every game, if I don't perform drop me.' The inference is that this is what Warne would have done had rotation or resting ever been mooted in his time.

But there is something Warne leaves out in his own case, which is that in his own career he *was* rotated – by his own body. In Warne's fifteen years' international cricket, Australia played 177 Tests and 380 ODIs. Warne played in eighty-two per cent and fifty-one per cent of these respectively. He retired from limited-overs cricket a decade ago to prolong his Test career; soon after he was sidelined for an entire year by a drug suspension, a hiatus that probably prolonged that career further.

There were also probably stages in his career that he played when he was not fit – it was part of his unconquerable spirit. But, and it's a big but, Australia then had the strength in depth that covered injured players with replacements almost as good. Now we do not. And it makes little sense to manage cricket resources in thin times the same way as in abundant times. There's the rub, really, with the manifesto. It ignores how much has changed between times, and opines that there is still a 'great Australian team now and in the future' out there just waiting to be picked, when it simply is not so.

The critique achieved traction both because of the critic, and because cricket will always have a constituency who lapse naturally into complaint. Many of those cheering Warne on were ten years ago probably bemoaning the world's inability to give Australia a decent game.

'Cricket is a simple game,' says Warne – a refrain he often

repeats. And in one sense he's right. The reason for Australia's relative decline is straightforward. It's not because the coach is a fool, or because the selectors are knaves, or because of too much rotation and too little passion, or because Howard was a Wallaby, or because Michael Clarke pals around with James Packer, or because Ed Cowan went to Cranbrook. It's chiefly because perhaps the greatest cricket generation of all has now passed. That generation now casts a long shadow. One wonders whether it will be sheltering or chilling.

The Australian, February 2013

HOW TO DO IT

India loves batsmen: big hits, big scores, big stats. Batsmen have not, however, always loved India.

Australians as fine as Ricky Ponting, Adam Gilchrist and Justin Langer averaged less than 30 on its pitches. Australia could not win for a long time there, has not since that breakthrough triumph almost nine years ago, and will need good fortune to have scoreline impact this time.

You can sum up the challenge of batting in India with a look at the recent autobiographies of Gilchrist and Matthew Hayden, and their contrasting recollections of the 2001 Chennai Test.

For Hayden, Chidabaram Stadium was where it all fell into place. Three years earlier, he had come to Chennai for a clinic on batting against spin bowling hosted by Bishen Bedi and Srinivas Venkataraghaven, and enjoyed it so much he predicted to his contemporary Matthew Elliott that he would one day make a Test century at the ground. He outdid himself with 203 in 320 balls, feeling so all-powerful it was almost as though he could 'read the bowlers' thoughts'.

For Gilchrist, Chidabaram Stadium was where it all fell to pieces, where he added scores of 1 and 1 to a peremptory pair in Kolkata. In his book, he describes it in terms like a mental breakdown: 'low and powerless'; 'mentally and physically exhausted'; 'the end of the world'; 'my tendency was to pretend nothing bad was happening'; 'inside I was terrified'; 'I felt like I was coming apart.'

India is often lumbered with that cliché of being 'the land of extremes', but in a batting sense this is not the worst description. Perhaps nowhere in the world can a batsman feel in some situations so close to impregnable, and in others so abjectly pregnable – harried, hurried, technically hemmed in, physically vulnerable.

The first fifteen minutes of every innings is disproportionately important. The transition can be disconcerting, from one-to-one conversation in an air-conditioned dressing room to being almost inaudible in a stifling and humid centre, surrounded by braying, unintelligible close fielders. The odour of urban intensity, the light from cloudless skies and the radiant heat from concrete stands flood the senses.

Yet past the first hour as the risk of the unplayable delivery abates, the battle really becomes with oneself, and the batsman who survives to persevere can go very big indeed. India's last hosting engagement, its 1–2 defeat by England, was in this respect a typical series. A third of the wickets were of batsmen dismissed in their first 20 deliveries; the average of the series' ten centuries was 186.75. England lost the First Test, but even there Alastair Cook batted more than 700 minutes, and his technique, front shoulder to mid-on, offered a model to the ten left-handers in Australia's party.

Especially in the absence of the decision review system, lbw and bat-pad catches present among batsmen's biggest risks in India. By getting his front leg out of the way and playing with his bat ahead of his pad, Cook negated both; in the event of untoward turn, he was also better placed to cope with the deviation off the back foot.

There are already those chiding the young Australians for timidity in their lead-up matches, insisting that they should assert themselves more against the slow bowlers, and both Mickey Arthur and Shane Watson have responded by flagging greater aggression in the First Test. Citing the example of England's Kevin Pietersen last year, Watson commented: 'The guys who have had the most success over here, as foreign players, are the ones who have been quite pro-active about the way they play against spin.'

Yet proactivity comes in many forms. In the main, England were actually very patient. Only Pietersen struck at better than 50 per 100 balls. Joe Root, a daring attacker as he showed on Wednesday in Napier, toiled six hours and 285 deliveries over 93 runs in Nagpur. The ideal, really, is to be positive and busy, getting off strike regularly early on and watching as much action from the non-strikers' end, eyes peeled for early signs of reverse swing and inconsistent bounce. There is seldom need to hurry in India for the sake of a result: overs lost to weather being a decided rarity, draws are few.

The essential point is this: that what works for one player will not necessarily work for another. What works for Kevin Pietersen may at a pinch suit Shane Watson or David Warner, but probably won't come naturally to Phil Hughes or Ed Cowan. The sweep shot, for example, often regarded as a default setting in India, has been a two-edged sword for tourists.

Of the record 549 runs that Hayden made in that 2001 series, fully sixty per cent were scored with the sweep. A tall man with a long stride, he seemed almost capable of sweeping the ball counter out of the umpire's hand. Gilchrist, by contrast, developed a self-destructive addiction to the stroke, his dismissal in Kolkata being of the 'don't-mention-the-war' variety: 'There were so many men around the bat, and all I can remember thinking is, "don't sweep, don't sweep, don't sweep". So the first ball, I swept.'

England's rule for sweeping in India a few months ago was to play the stroke only to deliveries outside the line of the stumps. Whatever the case, each batsman will need to have a policy and to stick to it. The only fruitless option in India, really, is having no plan at all.

It's a pity that modern Australian batsmen, with the exception of their captain, seem in general to be so creasebound. If a couple of Michael Clarke's colleagues return from India with an aptitude for using their feet to slow bowling, most of whatever other disappointments may await will be offset.

David Hookes once said to me that if there was a tour he wished he had been on, it was Australia's 1979 visit to India. It seemed an improbable source of regret, given the rather grim nature of that six-Test series, lost 0–2. But as he explained, all the batsmen returned home improved players of spin, including contemporaries such as Kim Hughes, Allan Border and Graham Yallop; in comparing himself with them, Hookes thought he had missed a crucial stage in his education. Clarke's team will shortly receive theirs.

The Australian, February 2013

Australia in India 2012–13
GROWING PAINS

Some years ago, Simon Helmot, now coach of the Melbourne Renegades, was hurling balls to a talented under-age batsman who for some reason was suddenly unable to hit it off the square. As Helmot readied himself for another round of throwdowns, the youngster emitted a grumble. 'Gee, I'm playing badly today,' he said. 'What are you doing wrong?'

Helmot tells the story as a cautionary tale of the kind of dependence on coaching and support staff that the modern game can instil. For coaches trying to nurture talent at whatever level, breaking that nexus is a constant challenge: Mickey Arthur and Michael Clarke have now publicly taken it to a drastic extreme.

The scorn and ridicule they have gotten for their trouble is to be expected. Australia now abounds in 'not-in-my-day' ex-players who will relish the opportunity to repeat that it's a simple game where you try to hit the top of off and the coach is what gets you to the ground in the morning.

But in this case they may be on the wrong side of the debate,

163

because, in effect, Arthur and Clarke have taken them at their word. What the actions of the coach and captain betoken is this: free riders are no longer welcome; contributing to the common weal is mandatory.

What's astounding is that it has reached this stage. Too much attention has already been lavished on the form of the request made of the players. When all is said and done, they were really set an almost babyishly simple task. After their abject failure in Hyderabad, a group of young men in whose development millions have been invested and who are paid hundreds of thousands of dollars were asked to consider how their team might improve in three areas.

Seriously, they should not even have needed to be asked. Rather, they should have been bursting with ideas, with vice-captain Shane Watson among those chivvying his colleagues along. Yet that Watson was among the do-nothings is not remotely surprising. Probably more coaching and management resources have been poured into him than any cricketer of his generation – for the dividend of two centuries in forty Tests.

He is a handsome player of abundant talent. He is also wealthy, pampered, immature and self-involved. That's what a life in modern professional sport can make of you. In his favour, Watson is not lazy. Indeed, Arthur went out of his way to praise the vice-captain's work ethic: 'Shane Watson prepares well. He's very professional and he goes about his business in a very professional way.' But only 'his business'; nobody else's.

Something similar applies to the other three players suspended: Mitchell Johnson, Usman Khawaja and James Pattinson. All have been have been made to feel special from youngest days. All have grown accustomed to having things done for them, to giving only of their abilities and little of themselves.

It's not impossible to break this mould. After all, twelve players went along with the exercise Arthur and Clarke had set them, some with unfeigned enthusiasm. Indeed, once they had done so, the other four were really taking the Mickey – and the Michael too. But in calling this a 'line-in-the-sand' day, coach and captain have chosen an unfortunately apt cliché: it is the fate of lines in sand to be washed away by the tide. And, in a way, a tide is what they are up against.

In the media, especially lately, young athletes are commonly presented as thriftless, feckless and heedless of moral boundaries. But their deeper problem is the opposite: they are passive, obedient and suggestible, initiate little themselves, and incline to going along with what others are doing.

It's this malleability, I think, rather than a general lawlessness or flagrancy, that leads them to indiscretion, to keep bad company, to imbibe obscure concoctions foisted on them by others, to go with the flow rather than think for themselves. They even misbehave in boring, predictable and conformist ways: getting drunk, getting violent, getting greedy.

In this respect, sport has only itself to blame, having for years demanded unthinking subservience to coaches, administrators, sponsors, broadcasters and other authority figures. Sport has grown suspicious of participants with ideas of their own; it prefers empty, porous vessels. Attempts to alter that ethic of homogeneity are usually reminiscent of the scene in *Life of Brian* where Brian tells the throng outside his window in Jerusalem that they're all different, all individuals. 'Yes!' they exult in unison. 'We're all different! We're all individuals!' 'I'm not,' says a lone voice: the Robert Murphy of his time.

Cricket should really have been different. It has only had national coaches since the mid-1980s, only made a fashion of academies and centres of excellence in the 1990s. But cricket has come to be coached in very similar fashion to other sports, with the player a kind of tabula rasa for technicians, biomechanists and others, building senses of dependence, depleting initiative and self-reliance, expressing itself in dopey mantras about 'processes', 'skills sets' and the execution thereof.

So how do you obtain, to use another vogue phrase, 'buy-in' with a new regime? When it is not offered willingly, Australia's captain and coach have obviously decided, you have to penalise non-compliance.

Coercion contains its owns risks. What the sociologist Richard Sennett has written of flexible working teams in the new economy has an application in sport as well. In making cooperation mandatory, do you encourage a participation in its substance or merely in its forms? Do you make *real* team players or simply individuals adept at feigning that role?

Management also invites consideration of its own performance. Frankly, cricketers should not have to be hectored or shamed or disciplined into wanting to contribute to the collective good. If it comes to that, and such punitive and also disruptive action is required, then management cannot avoid shouldering some blame.

The triumvirate of Arthur, Clarke and high-performance general manager Pat Howard has not just arrived and found this culture; in some ways, if unwittingly, if by omission rather than commission, they have contributed to it. However much they might now be about remedying past deficiencies, they are also complicit in them.

That's worth remembering in present circumstances. When Simon Helmot tells his little story, it is also with a note of honest self-criticism. Australian cricket could do with more such candour all round.

The Australian, March 2013

Australia in India 2012–13

ADULT CONVERSATIONS

If you're looking for it, it's section 1.5 and it starts on page 20: that is, the 650 words in last season's Argus review, that touchstone of Australian cricket administration, headed 'Improve the Australian Team's culture'.

In a week that culture came under internal and external scrutiny, it's been worth a glance. The report, if you recall, found there to be a 'lack of a strong culture' in the Australian team, and vested great faith in a '360-degree feedback process' and 'adult conversations', with individuals 'agreeing required changes to behaviour as part of an overall development plan'.

Well, that's gone swimmingly, then. How did we get from the methodical, graduated managerialism of Argus to the frantic line-in-the-sandism of Mohali? What has Cricket Australia been doing these last eighteen months?

It's possible that the suspensions of Shane Watson, Mitchell Johnson, James Pattinson and Usman Khawaja will have a salutary effect on attitudes prevalent among elite cricketers. But they are also

167

a tacit admission of management failure, because culture does not form in a vacuum. An honest appraisal of events needs an acknowledgement of the changing macro picture – something that, in hindsight, the Argus review rather neglected.

Much of the most severe commentary this week has come from distinguished ex-players such as Darren Lehmann and Mark Waugh, drawing on their own experiences. But how directly comparable are those experiences now? Lehmann left school aged sixteen to work in a car plant in Elizabeth, and took another twelve years to make his Test debut, by which time he had compiled thirty-three first-class hundreds, a number he had more than doubled by the time his career was over. When picked for *his* first Test, Waugh had compiled twenty-five first-class hundreds, a number he afterwards more than trebled.

Golden soil, wealth for toil: theirs were classic Australian careers, influenced heavily by elder statesmen in their state teams, David Hookes, Wayne Phillips and Andrew Hilditch in Lehmann's South Australia, Geoff Lawson, Greg Matthews and Mike Whitney in Waugh's New South Wales.

Yet that time-honoured culture has been steadily scaled back, marginalised and even maligned, supplanted by an accent on the hothousing of talent, elite under-age cricket, and the dogma of 'professionalism'. This year marks a decade since the commissioning of CA's Centre of Excellence – perversely commencing a period in which said excellence has been in ever shorter supply.

In some respects, the road to mediocrity has been paved with good intentions, oblivious to the possibility that primrose 'pathways', extending privileges on the basis of potential rather than in recognition of achievement, might well debauch talent, breed outsized expectations and stultify self-motivation.

The generation that is becoming the backbone of the Australian team has not, as a rule, lived and breathed cricket, or at least talked it and analysed it up hill and down dale alongside senior players. On the contrary, they have listened to coaches tell them what to do and played it alongside contemporaries in rigid age bands: under-15, under-17, under-19, etc.

It's no fluke that many seem to lose their way at around twenty, when they suddenly find themselves at the bottom of a pile, merely proficient at the game rather than being truly immersed in it.

They're of a generation not particularly confident on their own feet or of their own ideas anyway, with a limited self-awareness and a rather brittle self-worth. They certainly do not grieve defeat as did a Ponting, a Katich or a Clarke. There is, for them, always another game – and in this they are arguably right. After all, their game is run by an administration that half the time seems less involved in cricket than in staging a cricket-themed 'show'.

It's easy to look at the current Australian team and observe merely that it is 'young'. It's certainly that: its ersatz intern, teenager Ashton Agar, could be coach Mickey Arthur's son, and national selector John Inverarity's grandson. But it's more than that: it's a patchwork of vastly differing maturities. Cricketers no longer grow up at orderly rates, achieving similar milestones, experiencing regular rites of passage. Thirty-one-year-old Mitchell Johnson, for example, has played the grand total of ninety-one first-class games, fifty of them Test matches. You can criticise Johnson for his delinquency where the much-discussed 'assignment' was concerned. But, frankly, here is a cricketer who at various stages in his career has looked like he wouldn't know what to have for breakfast without consulting Troy Cooley.

Much continues to come to many quite easily, such as those on state rookie contracts while still at home, living the dream of professional sport while staving off the reality. And wealth, of course, can these days accumulate very fast indeed: you're only ever one Indian Premier League auction away from overnight millionaire status.

This brings us to perhaps a less obvious point. The challenge Arthur has set his cricketers is to be 'team players'. But what does 'team' mean any more? In a cricket world of multiple formats, cricketers are in almost constant circulation, to the point where they must wonder whether they are of a team, in a team, or merely near a team. A month or so ago, there were actually two Australian XIs playing simultaneously: one here, one in India.

Michael Clarke spoke on Tuesday of representing Australia being a 'huge honour'. But has not that sense of common purpose, and that identification between cricketer and country, been rather weakened by the squad mentality, the sense of players being autonomous and interchangeable cricketing units?

Traditionally, Australian cricketers have made linear career progressions shaped by strong allegiances and causes: club, state, country. Shane Watson, by contrast, plays for three quite different Australian sides, and has represented three different states, two BBL teams and one IPL franchise – and he is far from the most promiscuous of his generation.

In an age so abounding in teams, and so incessant in comings and goings, the bonds between cricketers are growing more superficial and contingent, the objectives of commitment and investment harder for coaches to build. And for all that this week was about 'sending a message', that message remains subtly mixed: are we *really* looking for more strong leaders in Australian cricket, or simply more disciplined followers to toe all these lines in the sand?

This week, four cricketers were made an example of. They may have had it coming. They may have needed the jolt. But the culture goes well beyond them and it will not be altered simply by management fiat. We have hardly even started the 'adult conversations' necessary.

The Australian, March 2013

Australia in India 2012–13
END OF THE CENTURY

Three–zip. Three–love. India 3, Australia yet to score. The scoreline for the Border–Gavaskar Trophy sounds drastic whichever way it's formulated. And there's another way to express it that in its way is an even greater indictment.

Six–one: that's the ratio of Indian to Australian centuries at Chennai, Hyderabad and Chadigarh. Since Michael Clarke battled his way to three figures on the first day of the series, MS Dhoni, Virat Kohli, Shikhar Dhawan, Cheteshwar Pujara and Murali Vijay have done likewise, the last named twice. Nor have they been content with the milestone: the average of their hundreds has been 174.

This is despite Australia having had the advantage of batting first in each case, while facing an attack similar to the one that in its previous series late last year conceded six hundreds to England, average 187.

In no other respect, in fact, does Australia's tailing off from its green and golden age show up more clearly than in the inability of batsmen to build big innings. Back in the day, avaricious

Australians salted away vast stockpiles of hundreds: Ricky Ponting (41), Matthew Hayden (30), Justin Langer (23), Steve Waugh (32), Mark Waugh (20), Mike Hussey (19), Mark Taylor (19) and Adam Gilchrist (17). They made them big too. Langer's average century, for example, was 173, and opponents found him harder to remove and nearly as annoying as Jonathan Holmes's smirk.

Today only Clarke (23) retains the three-figure habit, having made eight of the eighteen centuries Australian batsmen have spread over our last twenty Tests. A further six came from the now-retired Ponting and Hussey, leaving David Warner (three) and Matthew Wade (two) as the only other scorers of multiple hundreds.

Drill deeper and the picture darkens further. Twenty years ago, there were sixty hundreds scored in the Sheffield Shield; this season, there have been thirty-one. Just twenty-three of these have been by specialist batsman, only two of whom, Ponting and the perdurable Chris Rogers, have managed as many as three each. For that matter, only three other batsmen with a minimum of five games have managed to average 40. Australian representatives Rob Quiney, David Hussey, Adam Voges and Tim Paine have averaged less than 30, Shaun Marsh, George Bailey, Peter Forrest and Michael Klinger less than 20. In other words, our batsmen are not making hundreds *anywhere*; they are bringing with them to international cricket shortcomings instilled at domestic level.

Developing the concentration to bat all day and the skill to accumulate runs at different tempos, which is really what a Test century entails, are not aptitudes that can be nurtured on ProBatter or Merlyn. They are learned by doing; and we neither do them any longer, nor even seem to value them.

India, it would seem, has rediscovered these customs. The mighty partnership between Pujara and Vijay on the second day in Hyderabad, for example, was an exemplary demonstration of cricket in three moods. Before lunch, the Indians garnered 49 runs in twenty-seven overs; from lunch to tea, they collected 106 in thirty-four overs; from tea to stumps, they plundered 151 from thirty overs. Australia has players capable of batting in each of these three moods, but only Clarke has demonstrated an aptitude for all of them.

Pujara and Vijay recalled that charming French expression *reculer pour mieux sauter*, meaning to run back in order to give a better jump forwards, or to give way a little in order to take up a stronger position. By contrast, Australian batting this series has been a mixture of carte blanche and cul-de-sacs, leading to regular and profound senses of déjà vu.

But then, what precisely did anyone expect? Surrender cricket to the priorities of mass marketing and television scheduling, transform your first-class season into the hurried prelude and subdued postlude of a puffed-up T20 tournament, create a cricket system that accords greater prestige to making 20 from 10 balls than 100 from 250, then, frankly, you'll get what you deserve.

And if we're to recover some capacity to bat for the durations necessary to make big Test scores, then the first priority must be to restore some sense of proportion, coherence and continuity to our summers, rather than treating our batsmen like professional automata, somehow infinitely flexible.

Time was, if you recall, when summer was carefully scheduled in blocks on grounds that batting in five-day and one-day formats were essentially different crafts. For evidence that times have changed, consider the 2012–13 of Tasmania's George Bailey.

It runs like this: from 25 August to 3 September, four one-day internationals; from 5 September to 5 October, nine T20 internationals; from 14 October to 1 December, four Sheffield Shield four-dayers interspersed with five Ryobi Cup one-dayers; from 9 December to 5 January, seven Big Bash League T20s; from

11 January to 23 January, five ODIs; from 26 to 28 January, two T20Is; from 1 to 6 February, three ODIs; 13 February, a T20I; 19 February, a Ryobi Cup one-dayer; 21 February to today, four Sheffield Shield matches.

Fans who carp about the season's many guises should try imagining it from the perspective of Bailey, compelled to make no fewer than eighteen separate changes of format. This has been mainly at the expense of his long-form cricket: in a summer Bailey should have been challenging for an Ashes berth, he has managed a single first-class half-century. What a waste of a smart, resourceful cricketer.

For batsmen to have the opportunity to bat long, team innings also need to last. Under present circumstances, the tough love for batsmen that curators have been extending is a better idea in theory than in practice. In only a fifth of Sheffield Shield matches this season have both first innings exceeded 300; twenty-six first innings have folded up for less than 250. Pitches that psych out batsmen, flatter modest seamers and lead to games that don't last long enough to afford opportunities for spinners assist precisely nobody.

Here, then, is the line-in-the-sand we should be drawing. To be sure, Chennai, Hyderabad and Chandigarh have been shambolic failures. But it's arguable that the games were lost even before Australia arrived.

The Australian, March 2013

A WORLD GAME?

International Cricket
UNHAPPY ANNIVERSARY

For a game so minutely fastidious about its statistics, cricket can be decidedly casual about its actual history. This week, an anniversary has slipped by that is as significant as any in our annals: the sesquicentenary of the first international cricket in this country.

January 1 2012 marked 150 years since the inaugural match between English and Australian cricket teams: the Great International Challenge, played at the Melbourne Cricket Ground, pitting an XI of Surrey professionals led by H H Stephenson against an XVIII of Victoria. A century and a half ago today, the Englishmen were playing in Geelong; on Australia Day, they arrived in Sydney to take on XXII of New South Wales on the Domain.

The tour was an outcome of mass prosperity. In the preceding decade, gold worth about $40 billion in present days terms had been gouged from Victorian alluvial soil, and Melbourne's population grown six-fold, giving rise to a leisure class eager for foreign – and that meant British – attractions. So our first inbound tour was a private enterprise, bankrolled by two enterprising caterers,

Christopher Pond and Felix Spiers. Long before Kentucky Fried Cricket there was Cricket Mutton Chops in Sauce Piquante with Jellies and Gin Fizz.

There is something more to this than a straightforward bit of date spotting. The auspices of that tour tell us of the times and provide an instructive contrast with our own. The game in Australia was very young: another five years would elapse before anyone made a first-class hundred. There was a general bending over backwards to make the venture a success: Spiers & Pond were granted use of the new MCG by the Melbourne Cricket Club free of charge.

Yet commercial instincts were strong. The original memorandum of agreement, now at Lord's, is an unabashedly commercial document. Each player was offered an additional five pounds for the use of their name in team advertisements; they were free to coach for profit and also to sell photographs of themselves. Proceeds from testimonials and theatrical benefits were split 50:50 with Spiers & Pond.

What happened on the field, in fact, is actually less interesting than how lucrative it all was. The perimeter of the MCG on the first day of international cricket was taken up with hawkers, traders, sweet stalls, Aunt Sallies and a barrel organ or two: 'cricketainment' long before the term existed. There were even roulette wheels: the casino patronised the cricketers in those days, rather than the cricketers patronising the casino.

The shilling entrance fee was paid by about 20 000 – a sixth of the total population of Melbourne. For half a crown, you could sit in what was probably the world's biggest grandstand, seating 6000. Spiers & Pond, who ran their own restaurant at the game, covered the costs for the entire tour on the first fixture alone, although they were a little lucky. The curator took the money home and was so concerned about its safety that he put it in his oven; he got home just in time to stop his daughter lighting the fire to bake some bread.

What is most intriguing of all is what happened next. The interchange of cricket visits clearly had the potential to make some people a lot of money. The cricketers themselves, in Australia as well as England, extracted handsome rewards from early tours. Yet they ended up being usurped by clubs such as Marylebone and Melbourne, then by boards of control, who were keener on the diffusion of cricket rather than the grasping of every entrepreneurial opportunity.

This agreed restraint of the profit motive hit players hardest. In Australia, absolute professionalism was strenuously resisted. A cricketer who went to ply his trade with an English county, where there *was* a full-time professional system, had until the late 1960s essentially to abandon representing his country. The taboos, nonetheless, enabled international cricket to lay claim to its special status in the eyes of the public. Test matches were not about the relentless monetisation of every opportunity. Fans embraced the idea that victory was about more than eleven chosen individuals having greater skill with bat and ball on set days. They saw competition as an expression of cultural loyalty, and victory as an attestation of national nerve and willpower. They had no need or want of Aunt Sallies or roulette wheels. This was serious.

There was a financial system at work that provided for the distribution of gate takings and the maintenance of infrastructure. But because the system was at the game's service rather than vice versa, cricket, for a complicated, subtle and slow-moving game confined to the commonwealth, obtained a quite disproportionate share of mind.

The sesquicentenary falls at a time of apparent decline of the once robust system that emerged from the early Anglo-Australian interchanges and fostered a game truly multi-national, if never quite global. The world has in some respects come full circle. Entrepreneurship is again the order of the day, and commercial imperatives prevail, whether they are those of administrators raking in millions, broadcasters in pursuit of audiences, sponsors in search of exposure, players in quest of riches, or investors pursuing opportunities – for private capital is again on the march.

The biggest competition in the world is the supranational Indian Premier League, whose franchises are owned by corporations that bid for players drawn from all over the world. It is sport as light entertainment, being played in a telegenic abbreviated format and supplanting soap opera when screened in the evenings. The tournament is run by the Board of Control for Cricket in India, an aggressive monopolist, also charged with running the national team. Except that the national team has been allowed to run down from its peak by the politicians and businessmen in charge, more interested in exploiting the game for their own ends than preserving it for its own sake.

That quite a lot of international cricket does not make money is now held against it. The strong resent having to subsidise the weak. The strong resent having to do very much at all except become stronger. When there came the opportunity to act in the interests of the game recently, by investing in play-offs for the World Test Championship, everyone stood around like short-armed, long-pocketed members of a drinking school discovering they had left their wallets in the car. The weak could not afford it; the strong, Australia included, would not help. Their idea of savvy administration is another supranational tournament, the Champions League, indefensible on any level except that it makes money – for the organisers anyway, because the broadcaster is losing a bomb.

What this means is anybody's guess, but it is not a sustainable model. Now that the animal spirits of the market are abroad, everyone is beholden to them. International cricket survived to mark its sesquicentenary, but the next phase of cricket will not last 150 years; it may not even last five.

The Australian, January 2012

FEAR AND LOATHING IN DUBAI

As you approach the International Cricket Council's headquarters along Dubai's Umm Suqeim Road, the silhouettes are unmistakable: camels – wild camels, in fact – roaming freely in what a few years ago had been territory designated for the grandiose Dubailand development. Since the venture was kiboshed by the global financial crisis, they have returned.

A desert cliche, of course – but an apt one. A camel, runs the joke, is a horse designed by a committee, one of God's less congenial creatures, but also strangely fit for purpose. Could there be a better mascot for an unloved beast that is ostensibly a global governing body but too often looks like a forum in which the representatives of ten national monopolies come to split the spoils of cricket's commercial exploitation?

The ICC's personality is split too. There are the governors, personified by the presidents and chairmen of their ten full members and three associates: the headline-makers who contract the World Cup in one breath, then expand it the next; give the DRS with one hand, then withdraw it with the other; happily endorse a controversial Indian cabinet minister for a president, then draw the line at a long-serving Australian prime minister. Then there are the managers: seventy inconspicuous professionals in Dubai, plus a further sixty, including development officers, umpires and referees, around the world.

One way or another, both are set for major change. Years of debate about the ICC were brought to a head on 1 February 2012 by a sixty-page report on their governance by consultants from PricewaterhouseCoopers under the direction of the former British Lord Chief Justice Lord Woolf. So many and so far-reaching were its recommendations that further discussion was deferred until April, although the Board of Control for Cricket in India surprised no one by announcing on 13 February that the 'recommendations were not acceptable'. Chief executive Haroon Lorgat, meanwhile, was tidying his desk, his contract expiring in June, and Egon Zehnder International were searching for his replacement. Prognostications varied, the most extreme being that the ICC itself might be significantly scaled down, there being especially little love for them from their biggest member, the BCCI.

Dubai, of course, is far from the obvious place to run an ancient English pastoral game, all soaring, twisting, massing, jutting, angling towers exploring every possible variation on the theme of the tall building. The low-key and well-finished three-storey headquarters occupied by the ICC since April 2009 is at least of a rather more human scale. Televised cricket plays on two screens in the sunny atrium, and a routine experience talking to ICC personnel is the way their eyes dart away every so often to check for messages on their Blackberrys from round the world – conversation resumes with their thumbs dancing busily.

It's all very new, but then this is a young organisation. Although the ICC's antecedents extend back to 1909, their independent existence began only when they ceased to be an adjunct of the Marylebone Cricket Club in July 1993, and moved into a gutted staff canteen in the Lord's Clock Tower with inaugural chief executive David Richards from Australia, a personal assistant, receptionist and administration officer. So young is the ICC that its entire recent history can be contained in the career of that administration officer, who remains with the ICC, principally as their guru of scheduling and playing conditions. Fresh from school, Clive Hitchcock started work in MCC's ticket office in 1979, then transferred to the cricket office, which involved stints in 'The Rubble': the subterranean chamber at Lord's that contained the club archives, handwritten minutes and membership volumes.

Richards, who had met Hitchcock in Australia while organising an MCC tour, recruited him at first to handle umpire appointments, organise meetings and standardise playing conditions. The resultant slim volume was put together in a fashion more reminiscent of The Rubble than the glossy, bulging, ring-bound journal it has become. 'Dave and I sat down in a room, hung a Do Not Disturb sign on the door, took a set of playing conditions from each country, and cut and pasted the best of these into the ICC's own code,' remembers Hitchcock. 'It worked surprisingly well.'

In getting on for twenty years, the genial Hitchcock has handled just about everything there is to do at the ICC, from sorting out player eligibility to diffusing the Duckworth/Lewis system, in good times and bad, analog and digital. When the ICC's cricket committee set up a protocol for handling illegal bowling actions, for example, it was Hitchcock who organised what the accredited experts looked at. 'When a report came in, I'd book a day in the studio with an editor at a processing plant in west London,' he recalls. 'We'd go through the whole match footage, cutting and pasting on to video tapes everything from the bowling action from as many angles as possible, which we'd then mail to the individuals on the committee spread across the world. At the time, it was the best we could do.'

Hardly surprising: the ICC's revenue was then barely £100 000. A running gag was that international cricket could afford crises only on Monday, Wednesday and Friday, because those were the days the media manager worked. When the staff were augmented in June 1996 by laconic Australian Campbell Jamieson, on secondment from Australia's cricket board, it was his home board who paid him for his first five years. That state of affairs changed thanks in part to Jamieson's new role in handling the ICC's commercial arm, ICC Development International (IDI), registered in the British Virgin Islands. He helped negotiate two seminal sales of commercial rights, for the 1998 ICC Knockout, and for other ICC events, including the 2003 and 2007 World Cups. The latter deal especially, involving Global Cricket Corporation and worth $550 million when signed in July 2000, was what Jamieson calls a 'big vindication' of the council: 'It was about three times what had been projected. For countries like New Zealand, it was a breakthrough. Suddenly, they were getting $6–7 million a year.' Part was channelled into broadening the second tier of international competition, and the number of members almost doubled in the ensuing decade; part, less happily, resourced an anti-corruption unit, based at Queen Anne's Gate in London, to address player malfeasance.

Above all, the first ICC executive team was built, led by Australia's Malcolm Speed, subtly reflective of the breadth of the cricket world. Former South African wicketkeeper David Richardson, a lawyer with sports-marketing firm Octagon, ran cricket operations. New Zealander Andrew Eade was charged with encouraging ICC's associate and affiliate members. Australian Brendan McClements took over corporate affairs. Englishman Chris Kelly assumed responsibility for umpires. Urvasi Naidoo, a Briton of South African/Indian origin, came from the Salt Lake City Winter Olympics to become chief legal officer. Faisal Hasnain, a Pakistani, came from Citibank to become chief financial officer. On tax advice, Jamieson and Hasnain staffed an IDI office in Monaco. It was a worthwhile example of international cooperation – one their executive board rather failed to emulate.

For the ICC's expansion coincided with the final collapse of cricket's former set of power relations. As the BCCI were made mettlesome by their growing financial clout, their chief, Jagmohan Dalmiya, first became president of the ICC, then their main scourge. Big money created stakes worth fighting for and the expectation of privileges. Soon after arriving, Speed suggested to Dalmiya's successor, his countryman Malcolm Gray, that it might be a worthwhile economy to have directors fly business rather than first-class; Gray replied that any such proposal would ensure the briefest of chief-executive tenures.

At the board table, sovereign interests intruded more and more. A classic example was a project Speed initiated in June 2003, the *Review of the Structure of Cricket*, led by McClements with consultants from AT Kearney, including partner Phil Morgan. It was an attempt to demystify international cricket's financial model and bring order to its calendar, involving interviews with scores of stakeholders inside the game and out, and the compilation of the most comprehensive survey of the economics of bilateral arrangements yet assembled.

'Certainly the opinion of many of the non-ICC people was that there needed to be more context; that every match should count for something,' recalls Morgan. 'So the work we did reached some options for the shape of the game: how often series should happen;

what should be the minimum requirements of a series; the ideal balance of Tests and ODIs; what space should be allowed for ICC events. We had a workshop in Monaco [in September 2004], where the chief executives of the boards looked at a range of options with us. We then selected one option which a committee with representation from each country worked up into a real schedule.'

Except that the option involved less cricket for the two newest full members, Zimbabwe and Bangladesh, who would continue receiving inbound tours, but have fewer opportunities to visit other countries. After a flurry of last-minute lobbying led by Zimbabwe's wily Peter Chingoka, what had looked a done deal was noisily rejected by the ICC executive board in Lahore; some who had previously been outspoken in support of the plan, such as West Indian Teddy Griffith, were abruptly its most vociferous opponents; Chingoka even demanded that McClements be sacked.

Morgan left shell-shocked, Speed disgusted. There was similar resistance soon after, when Speed mooted replacing the board of IDI, the same as that of the ICC, with three ICC board members and three commercially expert independents: everyone heartily approved until the moment came for them to surrender any power, when they veered back towards the status quo. Speed kept his sense of humour. 'Malcolm used to say that if we sold the television rights to ICC board meetings, we would make a fortune,' recalls a former colleague. And while Speed never enjoyed good press relations, within the ICC he engendered tremendous loyalty – and still does. 'At the annual conference where he started, I remember him saying: "I'm tough but I'm fair. I'm not afraid of anybody and I treat everyone the same",' recollects Hitchcock. 'And he kept his word absolutely. I got on really well with him, and everyone here would be the same. He made a point of knowing everybody, and everybody's story, from the most senior person to the most junior.' When the ICC resolved to consolidate their administrative, anti-corruption and commercial activities in Dubai, for example, Speed made sure staff were looked after. Each member was offered a weekend in Dubai and introduced to aspects of the city by specialist consultants: parents were shown schools; singles were escorted around nightspots; development manager Matthew Kennedy, who succeeded Eade in 2004, relocated early because his wife was pregnant. The few deemed locally replaceable were generously compensated.

The rationale for the Dubai move was purely financial: the organisation was offered free land and a fifty-year tax exemption. Some wondered what they were letting themselves in for when the ICC's temporary headquarters opened on the eleventh floor of Al Thuraya Tower in Media City in fifty-degree Celsius heat on 1 August, 2005. A few never adapted to the cloistered expatriatism and headlong hypercapitalism: McClements returned to Melbourne to become chief executive of Events Victoria; Kelly took the umpire-management role at the ECB. But otherwise the move was remarkably smooth, and the heat is not so constantly oppressive as it can seem from afar: for much of the year, Dubai's climate is pleasantly Mediterranean.

The change of clime made little difference to the ICC's governance. An exquisite historical irony is that no members resisted plans for a T20 World Cup more staunchly than the BCCI and the Pakistan Cricket Board. BCCI secretary Niranjan Shah is remembered at meetings for his endless repetition of the phrase: 'India will *never* play T20.' There was a comic interlude at the decisive executive board meeting in March 2006, when the PCB's patrician elder Shaharyar Khan magisterially pronounced that T20 was not cricket, that he had personally never been to a game and never would. During the executive presentation minutes later, slides were shown of scenes from various domestic T20 competitions round the world, including one in Pakistan where the trophy was being presented by . . . just fancy that . . . Shaharyar Khan.

The BCCI and PCB agreed to participate in the inaugural World T20 only because they had failed to do any preparatory work on a bid for the 2011 World Cup, and needed to offer something in return for additional time to do so. It is the much-maligned Speed to whom international cricket owes its T20 riches, insists Hasnain, not any of its latter-day converts. 'Malcolm gave a speech at the meeting where he made the point really strongly,' Hasnain recalls. 'He said: "Gentlemen, I don't like T20. When the World T20 takes place, I will be sitting at home with my grandchildren. I can tell you I won't even watch it on television. Nothing for me can rival the long form of the game. But we have to face reality. This *has* to go through."' The world-changing India–Pakistan final – with Speed present after all – had nothing to do with those countries' administrators.

By the time it came round, the ICC badly needed the World T20 to succeed, because in the meantime there had been the big, ugly mess of the 2007 World Cup. The Cup was the ICC's attempt to recapitalise the perennially troubled West Indies Cricket Board: from this last and largest event in the GCC rights cycle, the WICB stood to benefit by more than $100 million. Ultimately responsible for the event was a local Caribbean World Cup committee, who set exorbitant ticket prices and imposed an unpopular ban on music, but the ICC were a convenient scapegoat when the tournament became a fiasco. The home team foundered, disillusioning locals; so did the teams from the biggest commercial markets, India, Pakistan and England. Tourists seethed over their cynical and exploitative reception. When the final concluded with the mother of all cock-ups by referee Jeff Crowe and the four umpires, the ICC found it couldn't even apologise properly: as Speed and Richardson said their *mea culpas* the next day, a sponsors' backdrop collapsed on top of them.

The World T20, by contrast, was a vibrant, colourful success. 'You can never say that India winning a tournament does not help the general feel-good factor round the sport,' observes events manager Chris Tetley. It inaugurated a new age in another respect too, being the first event in the new rights cycle with ESPN STAR Sports (ESS), which had succeeded GCC as the ICC's broadcast partner for, in effect, thrice the money. Cricket has seldom had a break so lucky, tided over for eight years in which other sports have been struggling to make ends meet.

Abundance, however, brought no peace round the board table – quite the opposite. The death of the president, South African Percy Sonn, resulted in the temporary appointment of his volatile and suggestible countryman Ray Mali; a succession wrangle ended in the ECB's David Morgan becoming president-elect, with the BCCI's Sharad Pawar to follow him. Few chief executives can then have arrived in such shambolic circumstances as Haroon Lorgat.

Moves to oust Speed began during an executive board meeting at Dubai's Al Maha resort at the end of October 2007, at which Chingoka demanded that the ICC issue a belligerent press release picking a fight with the British government over their refusal to issue him with a visa, and Mali ordered McClements's highly regarded successor Brian Murgatroyd to draft one. Knowing this would be an unwise provocation, Murgatroyd was reassured at the coffee break to be approached by ECB chairman Giles Clarke, attending his first meeting, who undertook to calm the necessary tempers.

Except that when discussion about Zimbabwe resumed the next day, Mali and Chingoka pressed Murgatroyd for the release; if calming had been attempted, it had failed, for Clarke said nothing. Chingoka was apoplectic, finally storming out of the meeting for a cigarette, whereupon Mali launched into a rage so empurpled that Speed intervened to protect his colleague. When Mali and David Morgan arrived early next morning in Media City for a meeting with representatives of the associates, Mali instead made a beeline for Speed's office and embarked on a tirade of abuse, culminating in his loudly and repeatedly calling Speed 'a liar', and insisting he wanted Speed out.

Morgan finally soothed tempers and later that day persuaded Mali to withdraw his demand, pointing out that terminating Speed's contract nine months early would be expensive. Mali gave Speed's assistant a handwritten three-line note in which the president said he would 'retract my offer to you to take an early retirement' – which was one way of looking at it.

From that point, however, Speed's card was marked. While his insistence on pressing for clarity about the finances of Zimbabwe Cricket was the headline cause, personality was as much the issue as principle. Nor did it matter overmuch that he was axed by a meeting in April 2008 which was probably unconstitutional, and from which several directors were absent: Speed was tired and fed up.

But the executive search for Speed's successor, recently conducted by a selection panel of Mali, Pawar, Morgan and Cricket Australia's Creagh O'Connor, had been just as divisive. Mali and Pawar favoured India's IS Bindra, Pawar's alternate director, whose adamantine convictions and booming voice had been a feature of many ICC meetings; Morgan and O'Connor were impressed by Lorgat, a chartered accountant based in Cape Town. Nobody was budging, until the Bollyline contretemps in January 2008 between Australia's Andrew Symonds and India's Harbhajan Singh. After hearing Bindra bang the table and thunder at O'Connor, Mali changed his mind: the ICC chief executive, even he could see, had to be more than an old-fashioned dictator.

Pawar, however, remained staunchly opposed to Lorgat, to the extent that Morgan countenanced a compromise candidate: Imtiaz Patel, boss of South Africa's SuperSport. Then, at the eleventh hour, bruised by their brush with the BCCI, Cricket Australia buckled: on the day the executive board was due to vote on the new chief executive, O'Connor arrived and told Morgan that CA had shifted their backing to Bindra. Morgan thought quickly, asking O'Connor not to divulge the change of mind until he absolutely had to; to his quiet pleasure, the meeting did not come to a vote, and Imtiaz Patel went through on the nod. Morgan rang Patel and told him he had the job.

Honour, then caprice, finally took a hand. Patel spoke to Lorgat: they were old friends. He modestly said he wasn't comfortable accepting a position for which he thought Lorgat better qualified. Patel then contacted Mali and withdrew his candidacy. 'It's Haroon, then,' said Morgan when Mali told him the news. 'That's right,' said Mali. 'It's Haroon.' They arranged to meet Lorgat at the Sheraton Towers in Pretoria to give him the news.

The threesome arrived and Morgan and Lorgat waited in the foyer while Mali deposited his luggage in his suite. They waited – and waited. When Morgan finally investigated, he found a dishevelled Mali evidently trying to compose himself. Pawar had telephoned and now favoured a new candidate: Prakash Wakankar, managing director of the fast-growing Indian arm of confectioner Perfetti Van Melle, who had fallen by the wayside at an earlier stage.

Bizarrely, while Morgan had rated him the second-best candidate, Wakankar had not been in Pawar's top three; Morgan suspected the hidden hand of Indian Premier League impresario Lalit Modi, then riding high as BCCI vice-president. Morgan undertook to interview Wakankar again with Mali. Fortunately the interview fortified them in their view that Lorgat was the superior candidate, and Pawar acquiesced at last in the appointment, satisfied to have Bindra accorded the status of 'adviser' – for which he still draws a fee.

Lorgat, a South African of Indian descent, was raised in Port Elizabeth. He became head boy of Woolhope High School thanks to his sporting prowess, then one of the fortunate first intake of non-white students at Rhodes University because of his knack for mathematics. He enjoyed a fruitful fifteen-year career as an all-rounder with Eastern Province and Transvaal in the Howa Bowl; his accounting credentials meant he was also roped into administrative tasks from early on. Although business became his career, cricket remained Lorgat's passion: after serving as Cricket South Africa's treasurer and on the 2003 World Cup organising committee, he held the politically sensitive role of convenor of selectors for four years.

Lorgat was less publicly tough than his predecessor, more inclined to private diplomacy. 'He's determined, he's political and he plays the angles,' says a colleague. A methodical problem-solver, he preferred fixing things before they were broken. A good example, although seldom acknowledged as such, was the spot-fixing affair, through which the ICC were guided by their two senior lawyers, South African David Becker and Scot Iain Higgins. A year before the *News of the World* expose, the ICC revised the code of conduct to include a section allowing for provisional suspensions. It was a tricky addition, given judicial traditions of presumption of innocence; the ICC rationalised it as comparable to powers enjoyed by disciplinary tribunals in such areas as medical malpractice.

'We were lucky,' admits Becker. 'Had we not had that power, those cricketers could all have played for the next six months until the end of the hearing, unless the PCB themselves had suspended them, which they showed no interest in doing. It was a very difficult environment: the allegations, the ridiculous counter-accusations, the high commissioner getting involved, the one-day matches still going ahead. Had the players continued playing, the situation would have been impossible.' As it was, Becker and Higgins worked on little else for nine months and, despite the strong prima facie case, one false move could have destroyed the whole investigation. 'The cricketers had top QCs, experienced criminal lawyers, trying to pick holes in our arguments,' observes Higgins. 'And they didn't care if they got their client off on a technicality – that's the game.'

In September 2011, Higgins set up a new anti-corruption, anti-doping and compliance unit; in February, the board received an independent review of their Anti-Corruption and Security Unit by Bertrand de Speville, Hong Kong's former solicitor-general, which included the recommendation for regular surveys of international and domestic players, and a greater investment in operational and personnel resources. Questions remain about the adequacy of cricket's ethical protections. On the game's exposed flank, domestic cricket, where the ICC have been coaxing members into their own anti-corruption measures and codes, progress has been slow. 'Only an amazingly stupid person would try fixing an element of the World Cup final,' says an ICC officer. 'But what about someone playing a domestic limited-overs game in front of fifty people where the result doesn't matter, where there are no real restrictions on using a phone in the dressing-room, and who's maybe approaching the end of his career?' With the promulgation of new T20 leagues over which the ICC have no oversight – in Australia, Zimbabwe, Bangladesh, Sri Lanka – the risks are obvious. But the ICC have dealt better with corruption this time round than last.

The ICC under Lorgat also endeavoured to prevent repeats of the Oval 2006 and Barbados 2007 by redoubling investment in umpiring and refereeing. Some good umpires have been promoted.

Some ordinary ones have gone. Referee appointment has become impressively rigorous: there were no fewer than fifty-four nominations for the most recent vacancy, filled by David Boon, who then underwent an extensive induction process with chief referee Ranjan Madugalle. Communication, argues umpires and referees manager Vince van der Bijl, is paramount, even when it's critical. 'You have to be prepared to have the tough conversation,' he says, briefly sounding like the schoolmaster he used to be. He talks to his officials wherever they are in the world every day; thanks to a multi-server mechanism maintained by his assistant Althaf Sultan, he can study every decision made; thanks to encyclopaedically detailed referee logs, he can monitor every aspect of their performance. That others are watching with a gimlet eye is attested by a note that came off the ICC fax during the World Cup, which an amused van der Bijl pinned to his wall:

> Dear sir,
> You saw how Lord Jesus Christ punished the England cricket team.
> Here after don't do any dirty tricks.
> I am watching always. Good luck,
> Lucian Perera

In general, Lorgat changed the accent of activities at the ICC to take advantage of the huge bounty of the ESS deal. A Dubai watchphrase is 'optimise rather than maximise' – that is, the quality and integrity of ICC events matter more than their immediate monetisation. 'I'm a cricket lover through and through,' says Aarti Dabas, who joined ICC in the new position of media rights and broadcast manager after working with GCC at the 2007 World Cup. 'Unless local laws in a country prevent commercialisation during broadcasts, as is the case in Britain, there is nothing to prevent broadcasters from maximising their revenues by commercialising and at times interrupting the broadcast. In India, where broadcasters derive revenues from advertising rather than subscriptions, there is huge pressure to maximise revenues to recover money spent on rights fees. This is where a rights owner like the ICC can play an important and balancing role. We think that people who watch ICC events want to watch cricket, not advertisements.'

The ICC's contract with ESS includes a 100-point checklist of expectations, including a monitored twelve-minute-per-hour maximum for advertising, zero tolerance of five-ball overs, a prohibition on pull-throughs (those lines of text or advertisements that march distractingly along the bottom of the screen superimposed on the coverage) and restrictions on squeeze-backs (reducing the size of the action to allow logos and graphics on the screen) to replays. Where the GCC deal gave the ICC little control over where their events were shown, furthermore, ESS are expected to broadcast to all participating nations as well as through North America, Africa and the Middle East. As a result, cricket's broadcasting footprint has been expanding through the last few years: Eurosport relayed the last World T20 across Europe; ESPN3 carried the most recent ICC Awards in the US; the 2011 World Cup was seen in 185 different broadcast territories.

The other word heard repeatedly is 'target' – that is, the ICC want to improve how they allocate money, rather than concentrating only on making it. As ESS's monies have increased the quantum of funds available for second-tier competitors, so they have been differently directed. 'When all this big money came in during 2008, the associate members decided among themselves to divide things up in a new way,' explains Tim Anderson, who succeeded Kennedy as global development manager in December 2010. 'Previously, distributions had been equal: Ireland $90 000, Israel $90 000, and so on. But the associates said: "Let's pool the money, *then* decide what we do." It's a much more collaborative model than applies to the full members. We could shovel $20 million out in distributions under the constitution, but the associate members prefer the central programmes and competition structures, and we're happy to invest our own money in development in order to complete that.'

It's with the nurturing of cricket's newer frontiers in mind that the ICC have also taken on the management of their Global Academy, based in part on the ECB's Loughborough facilities. Managed on behalf of Sports City, it features two picturesque, picket-fenced grounds and twenty-eight outdoor turf pitches maintained by former MCG curator Tony Hemming, and using a variety of soils and grasses from round the world. There is a $55 000 ProBatter bowling simulator; there are offices and meeting rooms, with plans to offer a university-accredited sports management course; and two accommodation blocks to cope with as many as 400 guests. It took three years longer to build than it should have, thanks to the global financial crisis, and you can almost smell the fresh paint, but it's hard to withhold admiration. So far it has played host to seven of the full members, including England during their visit to the Gulf earlier this year to play Pakistan.

Except that the executive board send conflicting messages about their commitment to broadening the game. Their abrupt decision to confine the 2015 World Cup to the ten full members provoked a storm of protest. Their volte-face, reverting to fourteen teams, coincided with a scaling back of the 2012 World T20 from sixteen to twelve for reasons ostensibly of cost that actually looked rather more like spite, and flew in the face of years of high-altitude philosophising about T20 being a vehicle for globalisation.

The jurisdiction the ICC exerts over their pennywise junior membership, moreover, tends to show up the limited authority they have over their frequently pound-foolish full members, who split three-quarters of the ICC's annual distributions ten ways without having to provide so much as a receipt. Since January 2009, associate members have in return for their distribution been expected to provide the ICC with a budget and a business plan signed off by their regional development manager; they are also retrospectively assessed by one of five support and compliance officers according to a metric known as 'The Scorecard', based not only on results but numbers of coaches, umpires, grounds and levels of non-ICC income. Attempts in Lorgat's time to strengthen the ICC's supervision of how the full members spend their money, by contrast, have been largely fruitless. 'They hate giving us their financial information,' says one ICC officer. 'They give us certain information but it's a constant struggle. In fact, we need to know. We're an international federation and custodians of the game. If a full member is in financial trouble, it impacts the health of cricket generally.'

It is the ten Test nations, rather, who keep the ICC on short rations. The organisation is funded by a quaint system of member subscriptions, based on annual costs, currently $25–30 million, three-quarters paid for by full members, a quarter by the rest; they accumulate reserves, which are capped at one and a half times annual expenses, basically by coming in under budget, although some would like the ICC to dispense with reserves altogether. Directors also bellyache constantly about the costs of operating in the Emirates. Just months after the ICC moved into their new headquarters, some on the executive board began lobbying for them to relocate either back to London or to Mumbai – at least until the potential tax impost was disclosed. Their own privileges, of course, remain untouchable. The ICC executive board spent more on their own entertainment at the 2000th Test than was at the time on offer as annual prize money for the world's No. 1 Test nation.

The BCCI in particular are a law unto themselves. It is commonly said in Dubai that every dealing with India 'starts with a no'. It can improve from there, and ground has sometimes been given with unanticipated grace. In general, however, their representatives are said to arrive at meetings ill-prepared and disdainful, having done their deals ahead of any formal discussion, rendering discussion pointless; Lalit Modi is recalled as acting as BCCI representative at one meeting with two laptops and four mobile phones in front of him, which he continued using throughout; Lorgat's attempts to stimulate debate in the general absence of it merely earned him India's ire. With their huge financial heft, the BCCI can also exert influence simply by absence of approval. Although they were not chief among the refuseniks two years ago, it was essentially the BCCI's preference for the less effectual Australian Jack Clarke over the potentially hard-headed John Howard that prevented Howard's nomination to the ICC vice-presidency – resulting in the promotion instead of the rather beige New Zealander Alan Isaac.

It was once fondly thought that an Indian president would improve relations between the ICC and the BCCI; in fact, it has probably worsened them. For all his political prestige as India's agriculture minister, Sharad Pawar had been too obviously an ally of Modi's when the IPL came unglued in May 2010, and thereby courted the distrust of the BCCI's incoming president, Narayanaswami Srinivasan. With Srinivasan's nomination to the executive board last year, in fact, the ICC inherited a new director who embodies many of their problems, already running a state association, a national board and an IPL franchise. He also holds the ICC in contempt. After one acrimonious debate at Srinivasan's first executive board meeting, New Zealand Cricket's Justin Vaughan said sympathetically to Lorgat: 'I don't know how you put up with it.'

One executive says: 'Meetings of the executive board are almost pointless. Everything has been decided by the time they take place, on the basis of who owes a favour to whom.' Another adds: 'It's honestly the biggest frustration. Preparing stuff, sending it out weeks in advance and making a presentation when I know nobody has even read it.' During an anti-corruption presentation at a recent board meeting, two directors fell asleep – nobody woke them.

Is this good enough? For some, sure: for the most powerful organisations represented on the executive board, the system works pretty well, because it is straightforwardly subverted whenever their sovereignties are challenged, because weaker boards are susceptible to influence, and because 'the ICC made me do it' is a useful line to have available in the event of unpopular decisions. But the reputation of the organisation has languished. In October 2010, the executive board received a report from consultants at Vero Communications on the ICC's image, gleaned from twenty-six in-depth interviews with commercial partners, media and member boards: even their own constituents regarded it as 'weak and confused', and lacking 'direction and strength'. That is an uncomfortable state in which to enter an uneasy phase in cricket's evolution. The ICC have until the 2015 World Cup to sell their next commercial rights cycle – the first time they have done so since the ascendancy of T20 and the advent of supranational competitions such as the IPL. There are no guarantees those rights will fetch more than they did when sold to ESS; say it soft, but they may fetch less. When the ICC executive board last year deferred play-offs for the World Test Championship from 2013 to 2017, they may well have ensured that the event never takes place – a shockingly short-sighted piece of policy making.

The ICC's future now hinges heavily on their commitment to two documents. One is an ambitious five-year strategic plan with which the board was presented in February 2011, after a consultative process again overseen by AT Kearney's Phil Morgan. It revisits themes Kearney traversed seven years earlier about context and content, with a renewed emphasis on 'more competitive teams': closing the gap between the stronger and weaker countries by means of the 'targeted cultivation of nations with performance potential' and 'development of a special fund for targeted initiatives'. Measures such as a $US12 million fund to bankroll specific national projects on a dollar-for-dollar basis imply a stronger, more creative and more interventionist ICC.

As Morgan's team gathered impressions from more than 100 cricket stakeholders, some barely hid their attitude to change. 'Peter Chingoka came to see us on a couple of occasions and walked out after five seconds,' Morgan recalls. 'We're not his favourite people.' But then, the ICC executive board don't rank high in Morgan's esteem either. 'If you look at what happens in sporting administration, people emerge, and as they emerge they acquire support and trade favours,' he observes. 'They're often not hugely experienced and with expertise in specific areas. They've simply been effective in progressing up the ranks in sports administration. When you look at the ICC board, you say: "Who is experienced? Who has expertise? Where is the continuity?"' And that, in fact, is *exactly* what he told them:

> Morgan: I thought in Dubai this is my one chance to tell them what I think. So I kind of blazed on. So much so that one of the seniors – I won't say who – asked me to stop. But I thought the importance of the work was such that I wasn't going to pull back until they got the message.
>
> Q: What were you telling them?

Morgan: I was telling them that in terms of corporate governance, there is a general view that this was one of the worst-governed sporting bodies ever seen.

Q: Surely they know that?

Morgan: No, not all of them do. Only a minority recognise how they've got there. It works for them. They wonder: 'Why do we need independence? Why should we not be able to represent our own countries? And why do we need an ICC executive at all?' I got into a bit of finger-wagging at this stage. When I talk about 'context and content', most people nod. But the implication of that, the idea that you need to redirect investment so as to enhance the competitiveness of teams and the balance of the game, means that you're redistributing wealth and there are winners and losers in that.

The same conclusions were arrived at and set down in cold, hard print, by the second seminal document: 'Cricket is a great game. It deserves to have governance, including management and ethics, worthy of the sport. This is not the position at the present time.' Presented at last to the ICC executive board in February, the Woolf review originated in the push more than a year before by the BCCI, in accord with the ECB, to change the rotation system for the ICC presidency. What appeared at the time a fait accompli attracted at the eleventh hour the opposition of Cricket South Africa, which galvanised what had until then been passive resistance at Sri Lanka Cricket and the Bangladesh Cricket Board.

Having maintained a studied distance from the issue of the presidency, Lorgat used the opportunity to press for a thorough independent review of the ICC's governance structure; somewhat surprisingly, he was licensed not only to commission it but to promise that it would be made public; quite unsurprisingly, the BCCI subsequently lobbied to restrict its terms of reference to the issue of the presidency, albeit without success. When Lorgat announced on 21 November 2011 that he would not be continuing as chief executive when his contract expired in June 2012, there was conjecture that his relations with the BCCI had soured irrevocably.

The review, however, was under way. Woolf was joined in the task of interviewing stakeholders by three officers of PwC – Richard Sykes, Alastair Tatton and Guy Higgins; as a sounding board, he also had the services of a retired Chief Justice of the Punjab, Mukul Mudgal. The last was perhaps the most intriguing appointment: Mudgal was chairman of a committee charged with drafting the Indian government's mooted National Sports Development Bill, whose advocates see it as holding the BCCI and other sporting bodies to higher standards of transparency and accountability, and which the BCCI are aggressively opposing. Maintenance of the status quo, then, was never a likely recommendation. By preserving the document's absolute confidentiality until the last moment, Lorgat then managed to promulgate a portrait of his board that was no less salutary for being what everyone knew. As the report summarised: 'The ICC reacts as though it is primarily a members club; its interest in enhancing the global development of the game is secondary.' In its view: 'The game is too big and globally important to permit continuation of full member boards using the ICC as a "club". The ICC's stakeholders are more than just its members; they include the public, players, the media, suppliers and commercial partners.'

The authors basically called on the ICC executive board to sack themselves. In the report's view, because 'self-interested or parochial decision-making' was always 'likely to predominate' under the present system, the solution was a board that had responsibility to the

ICC as their sole fiduciary duty: the configuration mooted, after an interim period, was for four directors to represent the full members plus two representing the associates (none of whom should hold any leadership or executive post with any member boards), five independents (two of whom should be chosen 'to provide greater diversity of view, with particular consideration given to experience gained from playing, officiating and commentating on the international men's and women's game') with an independent chairman and chief executive; the presidency would continue its rotation, but be reduced to a ceremonial, ribbon-cutting position. The privileged position of the full members and the subscription funding system should be abolished, they argued, to eradicate the 'culture of entitlement'; the ICC should instead be fully independent and self-funding, and distribute income on a 'needs basis', with members 'obliged to assist ICC in gaining a full understanding of the finances of global cricket'.

The home truths made for uncomfortable listening, many of them feeding back comments from members of the executive board about themselves and each other: 'There was also a widely held view expressed that meetings are poorly structured and chaired, which again adversely affects the quality of debate. The manner in which some issues are discussed amongst the ICC board members was also frequently criticised, with some referring to *"inppropriate"* or *"dysfunctional"* behaviour.'

Other sections raised more questions than answers. Whose needs take precedence in a needs-based funding system? The BCCI have no needs they cannot meet; Zimbabwe Cricket are overwhelmingly dependent on their current ICC distributions. Does that mean the BCCI will receive no money and ZC more? In the end, formal discussion of all but one measure, the creation of a chairmanship separate from the presidency, had to wait until April, despite the

BCCI's early show of displeasure; one of their high-ranking officials had already confided in an ICC director that he didn't need the advice of 'an English lawyer'. That left the ICC's balance on the precarious side of delicate. The ICC are not a camel that will ever squeeze through the eye of a needle. But the Woolf review may be a straw that breaks this camel's back.

Wisden Cricketers' Almanack, 2012

A GOVERNANCE
DREAM TEAM

Fantasy leagues and dream teams have become part of the fun of modern sport, pursued with the same fervent futility with which medieval theologians debated the number of angels who could dance on a pinhead. Cricket should now be thinking about a dream team that really matters: who should run the game.

The recommendations of Lord Woolf, Justice Mukul Mudgal and their colleagues from PwC for a new governance structure for the International Cricket Council have now been on the table, and on the worldwide web, for just over a week. They almost did not get there: but for the persuasive powers of Wally Edwards from Cricket Australia and Chris Moller from NZ Cricket, they might already have gone the way of many a report to a bunch of turkeys advocating Christmas.

Some have damned the report with faint praise. Others have praised it with faint damns. Its limitations are not far to seek. Whether the ICC likes it or not, it makes its money from its full members and loses money supporting associate members. Vague advocacy of a 'needs basis' for financial distributions arguably makes it too easy for member boards to settle on a 'devil-you-know' status quo.

A lot of comment, though, has been the kind of dead-end, closed-loop thinking that purports to be pragmatism, but is simply apathy and cynicism veiled thinly: yes, it would be great to have a majority independent ICC board; no, it will never happen because the law of the jungle is that nobody ever gives up power.

How about, just for five minutes, we pretend that we do not live in a jungle? After all, we shouldn't. How about, just for five minutes, we say that we would like cricket to be governed by principles of wisdom, prudence and expertise, rather than self-interest, self-aggrandisement and short-term expedient. After all, as was once observed by Gary Pemberton, erstwhile chairman of Brambles, Qantas and the Sydney Olympic organising committee: 'The easiest way to get good corporate governance is to get good corporate governors.'

Lord Woolf envisions a nominations committee selecting an ICC board on the following basis: four directors from candidates mooted by the present Test-playing countries, three independent non-executives, and two others 'to provide greater diversity of view, with particular consideration given to experience gained from playing, officiating and commentating on the international men's and women's game.' Arrogating to myself dictatorial powers, there are people I would like to fill these roles.

The first four should have some connection, some institutional memory, of what the ICC has been, if only to counteract the tendency of boards to reinvent the wheel when traversing similar issues. Here are half a dozen candidates with prior experience of global cricket governance from which to choose: Ehsan Mani from Pakistan and David Morgan from England, the ICC's two most effective former presidents; Mark Taylor, a current ICC cricket committee member; Michael Holding, a former ICC cricket committee member; Mike Brearley, chairman of the MCC world committee; and Chris Moller, a former chief executive of the International Rugby Board said to be the shrewdest current ICC board member.

This half-dozen seem to me to be best in class, with sufficient experience of how things have been done, and enough distance to evaluate those ways disinterestedly. Mani, for instance, helped negotiate the present ICC rights deal with ESPN STAR, which has bankrolled international cricket for the last five years, but since then has been too busy to allocate time to cricket, and perhaps too wise given the habits it has fallen into.

The next three should be chosen to address specific areas of expertise into which the ICC is required to delve: finance, marketing, media rights, game development, player welfare. Given that Asia is by far the largest market in which the ICC operates, too, commercial and political experience in the region seems almost a prerequisite.

This is my suite of candidates, with strong reputations in these areas and also abiding passions for cricket: Santosh Desai, who runs the brand consultancy Future Brands, and knows as much about Indian consumer behaviour as anyone; Piyush Pandey, the Indian advertising doyen who happens also to be a former Ranji Trophy player; Harsh Goenka, the Indian industrialist and philanthropist who sponsored the CEAT Cricket Ratings; Malaysia's HRH Tunku Imran, the new president of the Commonwealth Games Federation; Peter Hutton, now in charge of Fox International Channels, but with two decades' experience of televised cricket at IMG-TWI in India and Taj TV in the Gulf; Woolworths chairman James Strong, currently with charge of organising the next World Cup; Federation of International Cricketers' Association chief executive Tim May.

All, again, are busy people, although the best usually are. Some have existing ties that might need undoing in order to join a global cricket governing body; all the same, those who care about cricket commonly regard it as worth making sacrifices for.

In some respects, the two most interesting positions are the last, because they represent areas in which the ICC executive board has been sorely lacking. Australia's Edwards is the only individual on the executive board with Test experience: three modest games' worth in the mid-1970s. Consider, by contrast, for whom there could be places: for Anil Kumble, Mike Atherton or Steve Waugh; for Rahul Dravid, Andrew Strauss or Hashim Amla when their playing days are done; for Andy Flower or John Wright when they have finished coaching; for England's Clare Connor or Australia's Belinda Clark right now.

This governance dream team, of course, is an exercise in self-indulgence; but then, so is the counsel of despair that says nothing in cricket can possibly change. There is always scope for optimism. While cricket has its share of fools and knaves, it attracts many people of talent, intellect and love of the game. Why does it not make use of them? Why have a Bangladeshi general or a political hack from the Caribbean on the ICC board when you could have Rahul Dravid? Why have an Adelaide solicitor or a Sri Lankan spiv when you could have Michael Holding? If that's not a mandate for change, then there is no such thing.

The Australian, February 2012

THE CAPITAL OF CRICKET

Michael Clarke's Australians have this week been acclimatising to Indian conditions on a small field near a technical college in a residential area of south Chennai. Yet while it might not have felt like it, they have been playing in the closest city the world has to a modern capital of cricket.

A few cities have auditioned for this title over the years. For a long time, London, on the basis of its having two great grounds in Lord's and the Oval, would have been most people's default choice. Melbourne, having hosted the inaugural Test and one-day international, might also have had boosters, especially after becoming Cricket Australia's home base in 1980.

For various reasons, neither now fits the bill, and nor really does Dubai, despite being where the International Cricket Council is headquartered – that is less to do with a presence of cricket than an absence of tax.

Chennai, meanwhile, has the amenities of a mighty cricket city. It has fifteen first-class grounds, including historic Chidambaram

Stadium, which will host next week's First Test; it is the home of both a specialist cricket academy run by the Board of Control for Cricket in India and also the MRF Pace Academy, where Glenn McGrath is now director.

Above all, Chennai owes its eminence to a native son and an adopted one: the BCCI's hard-driving president, Narayamaswami Srinivasan, and India's hard-hitting captain, Mahendra Singh Dhoni. They have been joined at the thigh pad since 2008, when Dhoni became captain of the Chennai Super Kings, the Indian Premier League franchise acquired by Srinivasan's family company, India Cements. The pair's ties tightened further a fortnight ago when Dhoni left a long-time gig at Air India to become a vice-president of India Cements.

Srinivasan is now Dhoni's boss thrice over – with India, India Cement and the Super Kings – assuming it is sensible to conceive of a cricketer with an estimated net worth of $150 million having a boss. And Dhoni is every bit the front man for Srinivasan's BCCI administration. Cut one, the other bleeds.

Srinivasan's authority in Indian cricket is inviolable. The BCCI's headquarters remain at Mumbai's Wankhede Stadium, but cricket petitioners are as likely to converge on India Cement's offices in Chennai's Coromandel Towers. The personalities who dominated Indian cricket even five years ago – Sharad Pawar, Lalit Modi, Jagmohan Dalmiya, I S Bindra, Shashank Manohar – have all moved on from high office, of their own accord and otherwise, leaving mainly ciphers in their place. Srinivasan's reach, meanwhile, is extended by his chairmanship of the Asian Cricket Council, and his roles as the loudest voice on the executive board and the finance committee of the ICC.

Dhoni, meanwhile, seems similarly immoveable. Since his glorious six to win the 2011 World Cup, India have won six of nineteen

Tests, eighteen of thirty-three one-day internationals, eight of sixteen T20 internationals. They have hosted averagely and travelled appallingly, surrendering the Border–Gavaskar, De Mello and Pataudi Trophies. But when India's selectors apparently wanted to withdraw Dhoni's commission this time last year, Srinivasan protected him, and it was the most recalcitrant of the selectors, Mohinder Amarnath, who ended up losing his post.

In Dhoni's favour is that the Super Kings have continued to prosper, reinforced at various times by Australians Mike Hussey, Matt Hayden, Ben Hilfenhaus, Doug Bollinger and George Bailey. Australian selector Andy Bichel remains their bowling coach; Australian fielding coach Steve Rixon moonlights there too. Either side of India's World Cup win, CSK carried off a second IPL and a first Champions League. They finished narrowly second in last year's IPL and are favourites to win this year's.

Indian fans commonly gripe that Srinivasan's order of priorities ranks the Super Kings ahead of India. This may be unfair. Srinivasan has in some respects been an impressive BCCI figurehead. He is able and shrewd. His public statements are usually sensible. His public positions, like opposition to the DRS, are more than mere obstinacy. Nobody could accuse him of truckling to broadcasters or sponsors; quite the contrary. When alternative BCCI bosses are considered – self-promoting politicians such as the BJP's Arun Jaitley and the Congress Party's Rajeev Shukla – he actually starts to look quite good.

Yet there's no doubt that during Srinivasan's presidency the BCCI has become both more high-handed and more inward-looking – something somehow encapsulated in its decision last year to start producing its own television coverage, with hand-picked pundits who act more like a chorus line than a commentary team. Where the health of the rest of the cricket world is concerned, the BCCI now seems at best apathetic, at worst hostile – an irony considering that the first BCCI potentate to lead the ICC, Dalmiya, was perhaps the first great advocate of cricket's 'globalisation'.

For example, the BCCI is happy to welcome international players to the IPL, but remains implacably opposed to Indian players participating in any of the other T20 leagues springing up around the world. Lately, too, it has resisted long-running efforts by New Zealand Cricket to promote a franchise-based T20 competition in the US via its venture Cricket Holdings America – bankrolled, funnily enough, by a commendably patient Indian entrepreneur, Rajiv Podar.

When NZC representatives presented on CHA at the ICC's executive board meeting in Sri Lanka in October, the BCCI expressed adamant opposition, for seemingly no deeper reason than concern that revenues from televised cricket in the US might down the track weaken the Indian hegemony. The straitened NZC, financially dependent on a three-Test, five-ODI tour by India this time next year, had no choice but to retreat. Such is the suasion the BCCI exercises.

The Asian Cricket Council, meanwhile, has perhaps never been in shabbier shape, its senior members (Sri Lanka, Pakistan and Bangladesh) in turmoil, and its junior members no better than averagely successful in the second-tier World Cricket League (despite soaking up the bulk of the ICC's development budget).

Chennai, then, is a handsome, vibrant and vital city, but the (cricket) views are neither very far nor especially clear. They certainly don't stretch far enough beyond power to encompass responsibility. All of which might seem far away to Michael Clarke's Australians as they continue their low-key preparation for the First Test – although it's not. That little oval they've been playing on? It's the India Cements Guru Nanak College Ground. The Australians simply start a Test series on Friday. Perhaps the more profound questions concern who controls the earth beneath their feet.

The Australian, April 2013

SRINIVASAN AT BAY: FOR THE MOMENT

'The dictator is dead.'

'Who's going to tell him?'

This old joke about the two flunkies of a deceased generalissimo has been on my mind ever since the Indian Premier League was plunged into crisis ten days ago by the arrest of Chennai Super Kings' 'team principal' Gurunath Meiyappan on gambling, cheating and conspiracy charges.

The president of the Board of Control for Cricket in India, Narayamaswami Srinivasan, has long maintained that his association with the Super Kings represents no conflict, because it is not he who owns it, but his family company India Cements. But exuberant Meiyappan was swanning round the Super Kings' dug-out, and purportedly acting as both a bookmaker's client and source, for no reason other than that he was Srinivasan's son-in-law. And Srinivasan's airy response that Meiyappan was merely a 'young enthusiast' convinced no-one, being belied by virtually every known fact, including those on the Super Kings' website. That India Cements notionally stood between the BCCI president and the IPL's richest and most successful franchise could at last be seen for what it was: a distinction without a difference.

The question then became who would advise world cricket's most powerful man that even he could not brazen out this dispute. Srinivasan was taking no cues from the media, telling one television journalist who reached him: 'Shut up. Just shut up. I will fix the whole lot of you.' And 'fix' is not a word lightly bandied at the moment.

It fell to BCCI secretary Sanjay Jagdale and treasurer Ajay Shirke who by their resignations on Friday belatedly conveyed their displeasure at Srinivasan's clinging to the windowsills. Having stepped aside last night at the BCCI working committee meeting at Chennai's Park Sheraton for the duration of investigations, he finds himself with questions to which it will no longer suffice simply to repeat: 'I have done nothing wrong.'

In a blogpost yesterday, for example, the venerable former BCCI president Inderjit Bindra, who now acts as adviser to the ICC, asserted that it has been a custom in Srinivasan's time for India Cements to send an employee with the Indian team wherever it goes, home and abroad. 'Now think of this,' wrote Bindra, 'it means that these people are outsiders and are not subject to the ICC Code of Conduct. They are also out of the BCCI's purview.

'These people are privy to the Indian team's strategy meetings and dressing room deliberations and they have access to all classified information. India Cement nominees are not BCCI officials/ employees. The precedent of a private company involved in intimate cricket insider information is highly controversial and has some serious and thought-provoking implications.'

Perhaps this has a completely innocent explanation. Perhaps the 'nominee' is available in case players have any cement questions.

Perhaps he has been on hand to periodically reinforce The Wall, Rahul Dravid. But in order for a thorough investigation of these and other matters, Srinivasan really can have no connection with the BCCI, even vestigially. And, frankly, the ICC should see to it – which it would if it had any authority at all, although it doesn't, so it won't.

No, once again, cricket is confronted with the implications of having become a plaything of India's commercial, political and media elites. For Srinivasan's eclipse, which also follows Saturday's resignation of IPL chairman Rajeev Shukla, will leave a colossal power vacuum.

Srinivasan's moods and motives dominated ICC. He was able to block the governance reform urged there last year by consultant Lord Woolf, a former chief justice of England and Wales, by sniffing that he didn't need the advice of an English lawyer. He was free to foist a BCCI stooge on the ICC's cricket committee in place of the Federation of International Cricket Association's trenchant Tim May. But at least with Srinivasan ensconced, everyone knew whose sanction was needed for any major initiative, especially given his ill-concealed designs on the post of chairman of the ICC to be established next year.

Now the lines of patronage and influence will need re-establishing. Global administrators and Indian commentators alike have been on tenterhooks, waiting to learn to whom they will need to suck up. It turned out to be Jagmohan Dalmiya, the old Marwari warhorse from Kolkata, who survived his own wilderness period at the BCCI six years ago after being banned 'for life' for corruption. Turns out there *are* second acts in the lives of Indian cricket administrators – and that is a problem.

The one candidate the Indian cricket system never turns up is the fresh face from outside the Indian game's self-perpetuating ruling caste who has a passionate interest in turning the BCCI into a credible organisation where cricket's welfare is paramount. If the BCCI proves incapable of reform, however, a further possibility exists: a political appointee. In which case, we may eventually be waxing nostalgic about Srinivasan.

Even assuming Srinivasan is pure as the driven six, there is also the question of what to do with the Super Kings, bellwether of the world's evolving T20 circuit, round whom an air of malfeasance now swirls thickly. In the past, the BCCI has cut adrift two franchises, Kochi Tuskers Kerala and Deccan Chargers, for technical breaches of IPL rules (a third, Pune Warriors, has just severed the tie itself). What penalty befits these apparently far darker misdeeds, given their commission by Meiyappan, wont to refer to himself as 'owner' of the Super Kings and inclined to behave like one, whether attending team strategy meetings or bidding for players at auction?

Not only can Srinivasan have no say in the disciplinary process round the Super Kings, he cannot be suspected of a say. This will prove difficult to engineer for as long as his withdrawal is deemed temporary. That's the thing about dictators. When they purport to stand down, it's usually as a prelude to their standing up even taller.

The Australian, June 2013

THE SECRET SOCIETY

At one point in his excellent new book on the modern power-house of Indian cricket, *The Great Tamasha*, James Astill stops to wonder whether India is becoming 'an oligarchy, a democracy stage-managed by a corrupt super-elite'. One might harbour exactly the same thought about cricket.

Consider this: under the International Cricket Council's Future Tours Programme, the Board of Control for Cricket in India was scheduled to visit South Africa between November and January for three Tests, seven ODIs and two T20Is. Except that in July the BCCI began to dicker about the schedule, in the same way as six months earlier it had refused to be pinned down on the matter of a schedule for a tour of New Zealand also listed in the FTP.

Never mind that South Africa and India, first and third on the ICC Test rankings, represent probably the best cricket we've a chance of seeing in the present environment. Never mind that Cricket South Africa, like New Zealand Cricket, is an organisation whose finances depend acutely on television revenues of which the presence of an Indian cricket team would afford them a share; in fact, that was the point. Then, on, the BCCI announced that India will play two home Tests against the West Indies, not part of the FTP, partly overlapping with the time previously allotted to the South African tour. It is now possible there will be no visit to South Africa at all.

On all this, there was no elaboration whatsoever, official or unofficial. In positing nine possible explanations for *Wisden India*, Suresh Menon observed that BCCI had gone beyond its usual domineering ways and was 'functioning like a secret society'. All that seems agreed is that the BCCI and CSA have a feud. We know this because CSA's chief executive Haroon Lorgat has offered to apologise, which apparently BCCI's locum president Jagmohan Dalmiya thinks is a good idea without troubling to specify for what – something that transpired when Lorgat was running the ICC, one must assume. Dalmiya was certainly sorely grieved when Lorgat shifted the England v India match from the badly incomplete Eden Gardens during the 2011 World Cup.

The other salient fact is that the BCCI has its annual general meeting coming up on 29 September, whose overpowering presence will be its *il capo dei capi* Naryamaswami Srinivasan, temporarily restricted by the betting misadventures of his son-in-law in the Indian Premier League, but still the master string-puller. Since the May allegations about Gurunath Meiyappan, and about spot-fixing in the IPL, the BCCI has lurched about like many a debauched and embattled political regime. Quick private inquiry to exonerate all concerned – thank you, judges Chouta and Balasubramanian! Rehabilitation of former enemies it is now expedient to embrace – sorry that we once expelled you 'for life' for corruption, Mr Dalmiya! Morale boosting tributes from selected kiss-ass courtiers – congratulations, Mr Shastri, on a Sardesai Lecture that had it been delivered in North Korea would have brought a blush to the cheek of the Dear Leader!

The decision to superimpose the West Indies visit on what should have been the trip to South Africa is double the fun. There's crude populism – hey everyone, let's cheer for Sachin's 200th Test! There's gratuitous gunboat diplomacy – if you want our money, Mr Lorgat, you better beg for it! And it coincides nicely with the meteing out of 'justice' to the previous regime – that means you, Mr Lalit Modi! Because that general meeting has already been designated for imposing a life ban on the IPL's Icarus-like founder after a three-year investigation found . . . well, not as much as it wanted. After all the initial finger-pointing, the BCCI's star chamber had to work pretty hard to make the crime fit the pre-ordained punishment, because in the end he has really only been convicted of the high-handed unilateralism for which he had always been known, and in which the BCCI had previously indulged him. Perhaps his misdeeds lie elsewhere; perhaps the charges themselves achieved the desired end anyway.

To be fair to the BCCI, cricket administration is hardly to be associated with transparency and accountability anywhere. It is the domain of self-constituting national monopolies. Cricket boards have no shareholders to appease, or voters to placate. The cricket-loving public, in whose name administrators sometimes purport to govern, are diffuse, unorganised, and care little about who's running things providing they enjoy a bit of what they want every so often – whether that's semi-regular ebullitions for Sachin in India, or the maximum Ashes cricket in Australia and England. Unlike players, bound tight by codes of conduct, boards essentially police themselves, with all that that entails. What some regard as cricket's overall governing body, the ICC, has the barest powers of oversight, and receives from most of its directors only perfunctory attention: they have not visited its headquarters for nearly eighteen months, preferring to meet in a resort at colossal expense while complaining that the council costs too much.

This is actually a subtext of the present imbroglio. None hold the ICC in such conspicuous contempt as its largest member, the BCCI having declined to sign the FTP, and now setting a precedent in ignoring it altogether. The *casus belli* was the Woolf review, a thorough examination of the governance of world cricket initiated by Lorgat, which in February 2012 made high-minded, far-reaching and arguably unrealistic proposals for turning ICC into a full-fledged governing organisation with independent directors. The BCCI were having none of this. The ICC govern in the interests of cricket? Not on Srinivasan's watch. And as it happens, a tiny chink of light is available to study this by: it's this copy of the minutes of the ICC's January board meeting (www.lalitmodi. com/tiny_mce/images/ICC_Minutes.pdf), which has for many months been passing surprisingly unremarked on what we might call Modileaks – Lalit Modi's idiosyncratic but entertaining website.

For connoisseurs of shambolic governance, these minutes contain much to savour, but let's confine ourselves to two nuggets. Firstly, at section 6.2, you will find an attempt by ICC ethics officer Sean Cleary to raise Clause 3 of the council's code of ethics, which binds ICC board members to act as, amazing to say, ICC board members. Let the minutes record: 'Mr Srinivasan explained that he did not agree with that principle and that his position was that he was representing the BCCI.' Singapore's Imran Khwaja, one of three associate member representatives on the executive board, then pointed out the bleeding obvious, that 'this matter needed to be resolved one way or another in order to avoid directors technically being in perpetual breach of the Code of Ethics and for the ICC to be seen as a credible organization and an effective Board'. And, of course, everyone then stepped delicately round the multi-billion-dollar elephant in the room.

In order to convey his point, Cleary rather bravely invoked examples of ethical failures at FIFA, the International Olympic Committee and Union Cycliste Internationale: 'He emphasized that the current version of the Code of Ethics binds everybody, but that if it is flouted by all, then it becomes meaningless.' Yet rather than address what might be regarded as a pretty fundamental point, Srinivasan responded by calling on Cleary to investigate 'certain matters, which relate to the former Chief Executive, Mr Lorgat'. What this means, who is to say? Innuendo now swirls around Lorgat in much the same way as it did around Modi, with nobody showing much interest in clearing it up – not even journalists, happier these days to feed a swirl of rumour than do anything so vulgar as unearthing a fact. Anyway, precisely nobody was prepared to point out the manifest absurdity of Srinivasan's position – the board member who openly scorned the code of ethics in his own case demanding that it be applied to someone else. Because ICC president Alan Isaac is then minuted as having 'thanked the Ethics Officer for his contributions and affirmed that he believed good progress was being made in this respect'. Which respect was Isaac talking about, do you think? It certainly wasn't respect for the ICC.

Secondly, at section 9.3, ICC legal officer Iain Higgins attempts to lead a discussion of the FTP agreement, whereupon Srinivasan explains why the BCCI refuse to sign it. Let the minutes record: 'Mr Srinivasan explained that the BCCI's position was that it wished to retain the right to unilaterally terminate the FTP Agreement: a) in the event of certain financial or structural changes emanating from the implementation of certain recommendations from the Woolf Report; and b) should it be required to use DRS in any bilateral matches. In the meantime he explained that the Indian national team would continue to play the fixtures in the FTP Schedule, but he noted that it was finding it difficult to continue the commitments because there are so many events in the calendar.' Well that's jolly nice of them, then.

Incidentally, although Modi is being a little cheeky posting these minutes online, there's really no reason for them not to be freely available. They concern matters of significance to every cricket fan, and contain no information that could be described as commercial-in-confidence. An administrative class who took transparency and accountability seriously would make all such deliberations public. We are in a day and age of whistles being blown left and right. Yet we know more about the internal policies of the US's super secret National Security Agency – thanks to Ed Snowden – than we do about the attitudes and purposes of those who run cricket. So let's get it out there, shall we? The BCCI represents itself at ICC in open defiance of the council's code of ethics, and deigns to play other countries only in an unspecified 'meantime', reserving the right to set the whole of international cricket at nought if anything should happen they don't like. If they won't acknowledge it publicly, then we should spread the word ourselves.

For the moment, international cricket under the foregoing conditions quite suits the BCCI, preserving its freedom to reward those in favour, to punish those out of favour, and generally to intimidate the equivocal. Those favoured at the moment evidently include the West Indies Cricket Board, whose captain was among those who obligingly changed his vote on the ICC cricket committee away from Tim May of the Federation of International Cricketers' Associations to Srinivasan's water carrier Laxman Sivaramakrishnan. The BCCI gave the WICB a nice fat tri-series three months ago; now the WICB has returned the compliment by volunteering to provide extras for *The Tendulkar Show*. NZC now also enjoy a crumb from the rich man's table, a truncated visit from India being not only confirmed but brought forward, now that its mettlesome chairman and ICC executive board member Chris Moller is about to depart.

The out of favour obviously include CSA, despite the fact that four years ago it was CSA who made possible IPL2 at the eleventh hour. The trouble was, of course, that this abetted the BCCI's previous regime, the Modi–Pawar–Bindra alliance, rather than the present mob, the Srinivasan–Dalmiya–Sundar Raman junta; given the latter's manicheanism, that probably constitutes giving aid and comfort to the enemy. (In the annals of cricket administration, by the way, the relocation of IPL2 must now be eligible for some sort of hall of shame, given its legacies of crises and ill will at both CSA and the BCCI).

As noted, CSA is acutely beholden to the BCCI. The members of its superb Test team are in their playing and earnings prime, and understandably eager to play IPL. The country's six professional franchises depend heavily on the BCCI-led Champions League, in which CSA, with Cricket Australia, is a minority shareholder. Rightly or wrongly, some in South Africa sense that the BCCI's long-term aim is to prostrate an on-field rival, perhaps also by levering CSA out of the Champions League and replacing them with the ECB, thereby pauperising South African first-class cricket. So while the wranglings of administrators can seem as remote to the everyday fan as supersonic fighters dog-fighting in the stratosphere, they are, under the influence of an overmighty BCCI, forming part of a more worrisome pattern. And what happens when Srinivasan's unspecified 'meantime' expires?

From your more militant apologist for Indian power in cricket, response to observations like the foregoing usually condenses to:

Well, tough luck; *you* ruled, now *we* rule. Yet this misunderstands the nature of the change in cricket's patterns of governance. In the hundred years and more that authority emanated from Lord's, cricket was run along the lines of an English public school, at least as defined by Lytton Strachey: anarchy tempered by despotism. Under the economic dominion of the BCCI, the world is converging on the opposite model: despotism tempered by anarchy, the anarchy coming mainly from within India itself. For the BCCI is an organisation with many more problems than are sometimes acknowledged – full of ambitious people pulling in different directions, operating in an uncertain political, commercial and legal environment, shaped by a turbo-boosted economy that has bestowed its benefits unevenly and whose impetus is currently faltering. At an operational level, ironically, the BCCI is an increasingly impressive and efficient organisation, who probably deserve more credit for what they do and how they do it: allegations of player corruption in the IPL have been dealt with capably and expeditiously. At a governance level, however, it is an arena of self-advancement and self-aggrandisement. External fights the BCCI are inclined to pick, like the current feud with CSA, sometimes look like the phoney foreign war confected to distract from an American president's personal peccadillos in *Wag the Dog* (1997). 'The President will be a hero', says the political fixer. 'He brought peace.' Someone quibbles: 'But there was never a war.' Explains the fixer: 'All the greater accomplishment.'

Certainly the BCCI annual meeting is being treated with outsized importance. Dalmiya has deferred consideration of the dispute with CSA until afterwards: 'What we will decide we will decide only after the AGM. We are very busy with our AGM at the moment.' Hey, never let the triviality of competition between the world's two best cricket teams stand in the way of something really important like a meeting of administrators! But if we accept the BCCI at its self estimation, there is a logical conclusion to this, in which international cricket, especially Test matches, dwindles independent of its relations with India.

For some time, there have been essentially two tiers of cricket: the tier involving India (significantly lucrative) and the tier that doesn't (where, with the exception of the Ashes, the rewards are so thin that Sri Lanka can hardly afford to play Test matches any longer, and Zimbabwe and Pakistan must play consecutively at the same venue). The latter can only weaken further; the former is ripe for rationalisation. One of the most fascinating passages in Astill's book is an interview with BCCI vice-president Niranjan Shah, the board's longest-serving member, who runs cricket in the region of Saurashtra thanks to a membership populated with friends, relatives and cronies that has not changed in twenty years. From his secure vantage point, Shah regards the cricket world simply as an irritation. Why does India have to send cricket teams abroad anyway? The Indian Premier League lights the way: all should come to India as supplicants.

> At the moment we are getting money only when there is an international game. So I think IPL is the first step on this issue. Like in baseball, America is not worried whether other country is playing or not. Because cricket is a major game here, so we should not depend on whether England or South Africa come to India to get money . . .
>
> ICC is trying to control us. That's my feeling. Most of the other boards do not like that we make so much money and that their revenue depends on whether our team goes to play them. So the whole thing has been reversed. For cricket the only market in the world is India. The market is here. So we will control cricket, naturally.

Shah isn't exactly one of cricket's leading edge thinkers, being remembered at ICC for his fervent denunciations of T20 during Malcolm Speed's period as chief executive: he declared it an abomination to which India would never be reconciled. Yet Astill came away from their conversation with the feeling that Shah represented the BCCI's 'majority view'. This may or may not be true. What it more likely reflects is the prevalence of a view at BCCI that the cricket world's only proper attitude to it is one of homage.

For the time being, as it negotiates a broadcast deal for the cycle of events beyond the 2015 World Cup, the ICC is relatively secure. But is also in the throes of reviewing its group structure, specifically the use of the British Virgin Islands by its development arm, and its revenue distribution model, including how it will handle the allocation of its next lot of rights monies. Late next year, too, an option is exercisable on the ICC's headquarters under which it can be 'put' back to the building's developers, Dubai Sport City.

The council could emerge from the process a very different looking entity, most likely a smaller one, relocated to somewhere like Singapore and reduced to a kind of provider of auxiliary services, although still available to blame when things went wrong. Such a step would be unobjectionable to most cricket publics, who identify the council mainly with fiascos – overlong tournaments, unintelligible playing conditions, the DRS passim.

That would leave the way open to a long-awaited extension of the IPL season. In the IPL, the BCCI created a mighty sporting product that was also a rod for its own back, for the league at its original specifications and duration was only a marginal commercial proposition for franchisees: why invest in a sporting brand name in order to leave it inactive for nine to ten months of the year? As soon as private capital entered cricket, the rules were different – its impact has simply been deferred, not avoided. The one thing of which we can be fairly certain is that the interests of cricket will be the least concern of anyone with influence over the decision. The predominant motivations will be individual ambition, commercial advantage and potential political gain, and by the time we're told what's happened there will be nothing to do about it.

Cricinfo, September 2013

Far Pavilions

'Cricket cannot call itself a global game when one-fifth of the world's population is not aware of it,' International Cricket Council president Ehsan Mani argued not so long ago. Yet such hankerings to make cricket a global game, as distinct from one penned up in the Commonwealth past and present, extend back half a century.

It was while the Imperial Cricket Conference was an adjunct of the Marylebone Cricket Club and little more than an annual meeting at Lord's of Test-playing nations that Pakistan first mooted a category of 'junior' members. On 15 July 1965 occurred the first intake of what became known as 'associate members': countries where cricket was recognised as being 'firmly established'. The admission to the conference of Ceylon, Fiji and the United States, followed a year later by Denmark, Bermuda, East Africa and the Netherlands, also entailed the dropping of the archaic 'Imperial' in favour of more modern-sounding 'International'.

No particular urgency attended these efforts. Augmented by Canada, Gibraltar, Hong Kong, Malaysia, associate members were in 1971 granted a vote each, compared to two each for full members. Two, Ceylon (now Sri Lanka) and East Africa, were then issued invitations to take part in the first World Cup, in 1975. But there was negligible financial assistance, and not for a further four years was there any formal competition among the associates themselves.

When the inaugural fifteen-country ICC Trophy was finally held in May–June 1979 in the British midlands, the outcomes were mixed. Sri Lanka and Canada were promoted to participate in the second World Cup, where Sri Lanka's defeat of India became a key exhibit in their successful application for full membership the following year, but Canada were badly outclassed. That there were clearly huge variations in standards among cricket's wannabees would prove an abiding challenge.

Some countries had deep cricket roots. Zimbabwe, which became an associate member on independence in May 1980, had by then been competing (as Rhodesia) in the Currie Cup for fifty years, and duly won the ICC Trophies of 1982, 1986 and 1990 en route to Test status. It was naturally far more competitive than the fragmented archipelago of Fiji, rather trading on past glories, and Gibraltar, which withdrew from the first ICC Trophy because many of the players were involved in a hockey tournament, and which lost every game they played during the second. Nonetheless, the first two chairmen of the committee of associate members founded in 1979 were Fiji's Philip Snow and Gibraltar's Joe Buzaglo, and something akin to an 'old boy's club' persisted a good many years yet. A concession to the differences in ability was the establishment in 1984 of the category of 'affiliate members': countries where it was recognised that cricket was played according to official laws, starting with Switzerland and the Bahamas. But even two sizes did not fit all.

Between times, too, there were minimal opportunities for competition. When India withdrew at the eleventh hour from the second Asia Cup in March 1986, Bangladesh suddenly had opportunity thrust upon them in the form of a one-day international; they hosted the tournament two years later. But they played only twenty-two ODIs in their first dozen years of competition and lost them all.

Europe had the advantage of relatively small travel distances and financial/administrative support from Marylebone after seven nations met in Geneva in 1988 to initiate the European Cricket Federation. The following year at Meudon, France beat an MCC team led by the former Surrey captain Roger Knight; *The Cricketer* then sponsored a European Cup tournament in July 1992 at Worksop College, where Knight was headmaster, with the winner, Germany, going on to play MCC at Lord's. Germany hosted the first ECF Nations Cup in Berlin the following year, losing a closely fought final to France, and three other tournaments were held, in Oxford, Osnabrück and Zuos, before the federation was superseded by the European Cricket Council. They suffered, nonetheless, from a dependence on expatriate populations and a lack of facilities.

Cricket in Africa, meanwhile, was controlled by two conferences, rather different in quality. The East African Cricket Conference was dominated by Kenya, an ICC associate member in its own right, strong enough in the 1996 World Cup to inflict a memorable defeat on West Indies. The West African Cricket Conference, including Nigeria, Gambia, Ghana and Sierra Leone, was far weaker, and a 1994 Marylebone tour found the cricket poor.

A paradox was that the ICC's junior membership enjoyed growing voting clout. By 1989, the associates could muster more than twice the number of votes of the full members, and their support was instrumental in the campaigns by the Board of Control for Cricket in India to shift the 1996 World Cup to India and to promote their secretary Jagmohan Dalmiya as the ICC's inaugural president. The latter manoeuvre actually rather clipped the associates' wings, because the creation of the office of president also entrenched an executive board featuring only three voting members from the associates compared to nine full members. Dalmiya, however, was an avowed globalist, and a new committee for development chaired by South Africa's Ali Bacher was explicitly mandated to extend the game to new frontiers. 'Ali was excellent because he had no particular allegiance,' recalls Knight. 'He just wanted the game to grow.'

In addition to the appointment of the committee, development was for the first time to receive dedicated funding: half the profits from the first ICC Knockout between the full members in October 1998 in Bangladesh, about $US7 million, were set aside for the first two years of the programme, to be overseen by a global development manager, Australian Ross Turner, a former first-grade cricketer turned coach who had been working at the New South Wales Cricket Association. During Turner's first meeting, at Dubai's Jumeirah Beach Hotel, Bacher's committee split the globe into five regions. Arrived at in a few moments, the structure persists to this day: Europe, the Americas, Asia, East Asia-Pacific and Africa.

At the time, activities had a similarly improvised feel. The ICC's headquarters was in a reconditioned staff cafeteria in the Lord's Clock Tower, while Turner's office was in a former gents convenience. 'Oh! Oh!' spluttered an elderly Marylebone member who wandered in one day. 'This has all changed!' Yes and no. The five regional development officers had ample zeal, but found their aspirations rather greater than their budgets. Englishman Nigel Laughton had already been employed as the European Cricket Council's development officer, paid for by Marylebone. But South African Hossain Ayoub covered the entirety of sub-Saharan Africa on his own. 'They were sixteen nations covered by one missionary,' Turner remembers. New Zealander Andrew Eade, who became East-Asia Pacific development officer in April 1999, recalls visiting Vanuatu soon after and offering the local cricket association a few thousand dollars to initiate some local coaching programmes going. 'That's interesting,' said the local who doubled up running soccer in Vanuatu. 'Last year, FIFA gave us a million dollars.'

The emphasis of the development programme in its first five years was on spreading cricket's footprint: six associate members and thirty-six affiliates were recognised, requirements for the latter being far from onerous. Much still depended on the indulgence of the full members, some of whom had parallel development efforts: India, Pakistan and Sri Lanka through the Asian Cricket Council, South Africa and Zimbabwe through the African Cricket Association. Full members often deployed their own resources: in 1999, for example, a South African Academy team visited Ireland and Scotland and Pakistan Emerging Players toured Denmark and the Netherlands. That introduced somewhat of an undertone of rivalry. Under Dalmiya, the ICC agreed to an equal five-way split of funds between the regions; no sooner had Dalmiya's presidency concluded than the Asian Cricket Council insisted that half the development monies be allocated to Asia on pain of withdrawal from the second ICC Knockout. Bangladesh was also rather optimistically promoted to full membership of ICC in June 2000. Eade, who had just succeeded Turner as global development manager, had hastily to redraw his budgets.

For all this, these were exciting, trailblazing years. Cricket was found in countries undreamed of. There was discovered a thriving Japan Cricket Association initiated by Chuo University student Kenichiro Matsumura, who had discovered cricket in an encyclopaedia while in pursuit of 'a sport no-one else was playing'. Japanese cricketers, always immaculately clad in white, were technically very precise and intensely ceremonial. The passion among the cricketers of smaller countries to become national representatives, meanwhile, was brought home to young East-Asia Pacific development officer Matt Kennedy at Easter 2000 when he attended the tournament in Suva that would decide who represented Fiji in the next ICC Trophy. 'It had rained for days beforehand and the conditions were really unplayable,' he recalls. 'But a lot of the players had come from islands faraway and this was their only chance to show their abilities, so it was agreed to go ahead. Basically, they played in mud. They were coming off the ground looking like rugby players. But that's how much it meant to them.'

At that ICC Trophy, staged in Toronto in July 2001, the ICC for the first time came to grips with the differing standards of its junior membership, dividing the event into two divisions. Eade then hired Bob Woolmer, who had just retired as coach of South Africa, to design a high-performance programme for the more advanced associates. Thanks to Woolmer's input, Kenya stunned the cricket world in the 2003 World Cup by advancing to the semi-finals. It was from a chat in a Port Elizabeth coffee shop during the tournament that emerged the germ of what became the Intercontinental Cup. 'It started as a discussion about whether players could play one-day cricket without a background in playing four-day cricket,' recalls Eade. 'Bob didn't think so. From that came the idea of a four-day competition for the associate members.' After Scotland won the first instalment in 2004, Ireland won a hat-trick of titles and rather proved Woolmer's point, albeit that the pay-off had a certain poignancy: the development programme has had few better advertisements than Ireland's trouncing of Pakistan, coached by Woolmer, at the 2007 World Cup.

When Kennedy succeeded Eade the global job in January

2004, however, the ICC's development energies were now quite thinly spread and the pace of new memberships was scaled back: associate membership has been conferred on only three nations since, affiliate membership on a dozen. The need for consolidation was driven by the observable reality that lacklustre performances by 'minnows' tended to attract more criticism than good performances gained credit. At the Six-Nations Challenge in the UAE shortly after Kennedy started work, the US, a perennial underachiever, stumbled into the Champions Trophy on net run rate: 0.0276 of a run to be exact. An old team poorly led and badly managed, they were humiliated in the Champions Trophy in England a few months later, and the humiliation was contagious. 'The development programme took a hit and rightly so,' says Kennedy. 'On the other hand, it meant that we could go back to the membership and say: There are no excuses. We can't afford to be embarrassed like that again.'

As the centre of ICC operations moved from Lord's to Dubai, substantial increases in funding were now in prospect. The top five finishers in the 2005 ICC Trophy split $2.5 million in additional development monies, including privileged access to the high-performance programme now under the direction of Australian Richard Done. The ICC annual meeting in Kuala Lumpur the following year agreed to a new regime under which six per cent off the top of ICC revenues were allocated to development, in addition to the quarter share of the dividend distribution reserved for the junior membership – revenue about to expand significantly with the December 2006 sale of broadcast rights to ICC events to ESPN STAR Sports.

The rigour of competition was also about to become more Darwinian. Results over the preceding three years in the regional qualification tournaments for the 2007 World Cup became the basis of rankings for a new multi-divisional global tournament cycle, with access to top-level cricket up for grabs, including opportunities to tackle the new T20 format.

The Pepsi World Cricket League commenced in January 2007, the top two teams in the first Division One tournament, Kenya and Scotland, winning places in the inaugural World T20 in South Africa later that year. By finishing top of World T20 Qualifier in Belfast in July–August 2008, the Netherlands, Scotland and Ireland qualified for the next World T20 in England, a tournament the Netherlands turned on its head by defeating the host nation in the opening game.

At the end of the cycle in April 2009, not only did the top four of the twelve-team World Cup Qualifier graduate to the 2011 World Cup, but the top six gained official one-day-international status and the top ten obtained healthy high-performance grants on a sliding scale. Although Kenya and Canada had little impact on the big stage, England was on the receiving end of two extraordinary associate member feats: Ryan ten Doeschate's 119 off 110 balls for the Netherlands in a narrow defeat at Nagpur, and Kevin O'Brien's 113 off 63 balls for Ireland in a famous victory at Bangalore.

The promotion and relegation system of the World Cricket League introduced a tension to every contest. 'With the two-up, two-down structure, it was pretty ruthless,' says Kennedy. 'If you weren't good enough you pretty soon got knocked down. If you were good enough you could rise quite quickly.' Sometimes the tension was more than could be contained: in March 2010, the restlessness of a 10 000-strong crowd in Kirtipur when Nepal fell behind the run rate in a crucial Division 5 game against the US turned into a full-fledged riot that delayed the game by forty-five minutes. But there were exciting stories too, Afghanistan's astonishingly rapid rise becoming the subject of a hit 2010 film by Tim

Albone, *Out of the Ashes*. Unknown there not fifteen years earlier, cricket had become Afghanistan's number-one game. Having beaten Scotland in the final of the Intercontinental Cup in Dubai at the end of 2010 after an unbeaten campaign, Afghanistan played an unprecedented match against Pakistan in Sharjah in February 2012: the first time a full member had played an affiliate member in an official one-day international. Though Pakistan prevailed, Afghanistan looked anything but overawed.

The popularisation of the game took on another dimension in April 2005 when the ICC absorbed the 47-year-old International Women's Cricket Council, and made women's cricket a development priority. Here the challenges were similar to, though more marked than, those in the men's game: four nations, England, Australia, New Zealand and India, had traditionally dominated, with a pronounced falling off of standards thereafter from there. That group duly dominated the first women's World Cup under the ICC's auspices, won by England in Sydney in March 2009, and the inaugural women's World T20 staged in the West Indies fourteen months later alongside the men's event, with Australia the victor; New Zealand was the runner-up each time.

Efforts to close the gap, however, began to meet with encouraging success with the staging of the Women's Cricket Challenge in October 2010 in Potschefstrom, involving South Africa, West Indies, Pakistan, Sri Lanka, Netherlands and Ireland. A home victory in a one-day round robin and a West Indian win in a T20 leg suggested that gaps between top and bottom in global competition were beginning to close. In 2011, the ICC presented the award for Women's Cricketer of the Year for the first time to a player from outside the 'big four': the prolific twenty-year-old Stafanie Taylor, from Jamaica. The ICC women's player rankings were also becoming a more polyglot assembly.

Nearly four decades since its tentative beginnings, the promotion of cricket outside its traditional fastnesses has gone from something like missionary activity to an integral feature of cricket's administration. It is both more exciting and colourful and more competitive and demanding. As the stakes have increased, so have expectations. Because some countries are now very clearly more equal than others, for instance, no longer is money to be split within regions on an equal basis. 'The Scorecard', a funding metric introduced in January 2009 based on number of players, grounds, coaches and umpires plus levels of non-ICC income as assessed by five member support and compliance officers holds beneficiaries of funding to exacting account. 'The first time we held reviews we put six nations on notice that their status was in jeopardy, and they took steps to rectify things in the next twelve months,' Kennedy recalls. 'Over time, nobody has had their status revoked, but quite a few have been expected to come to the party.' It is also a condition of funding that every associate member provide ICC with a budget and a business plan for the year signed off by the regional manager.

Those regional managers operate from development offices in London (Europe), Melbourne (East Asia-Pacific) and Toronto (Americas), while former Sri Lankan captain Bandula Warnapura of the ACC office, based in Kuala Lumpur, and former Eastern Province batsman Cassim Suliman at the ACA, based in Benoni, double as ICC regional development managers. They report to Australian Tim Anderson, first Kennedy's offsider then his successor, based in Dubai. 'Essentially we have a $30 million annual budget,' says Anderson. 'About half is in distributions; the other half is in regional development programmes, qualifying tournaments and high performance programmes with the top associates . . . Outside football, cricket is probably the second-best funded sport, better than the International Rugby Board.'

It will need to be. At present there are estimated to be about 750 000 active cricket participants outside the ICC full members; ICC has set as its objective doubling that number by 2015. In a short space of time, it has nonetheless come a long way. If it may not yet be a world game, cricket is entitled to be considered a game of the world.

From *Building A Bigger, Better Global Game: The Story of the ICC's Development Programme* (2012)

Afghanistan

HOPE SPRINGS

Last week in Afghanistan, eight youths herding sheep were mistakenly killed in a NATO airstrike. Two ten-year-olds pardoned last year after attempting to detonate suicide bombs were rearrested trying to do the same in Kandahar. Drought wracked the northwest and heroin production was reported to have increased sixty per cent in the last year.

By the standards of life in that benighted country, however, last week constituted an exceptionally good week. The reason: the afterglow of the cricket team's one-day international match against Pakistan at Sharjah Stadium in the United Arab Emirates.

The contest was unprecedented. Afghanistan is what is called an affiliate member of the International Cricket Council, the most junior ranking. To play against a full member such as Pakistan was like a country football team being invited to play Collingwood at the MCG on Anzac Day. Yet they took 195 off the same bowling attack that had recently humiliated England, and had their opponents at one stage three for 99 in reply.

In contrast to England's recent fixtures in the Gulf, played in empty stadia, this match was attended by 15 000 fans, including Afghanistan's finance minister Dr Hazrat Omar Zakhilwal, who doubles as the chairman of the Afghanistan Cricket Board, and who was busily occupied providing prime minister Hamid Karzai with regular score updates on the phone.

If you know anything of cricket in Afghanistan, it is probably thanks to the documentary *Out of the Ashes* (2010), which told the story of the national team's progress from the perspective of its ebullient inaugural coach Taj Malik, and director Tim Albone's excellent tie-in book of the same name. As Albone relates, cricket in Afghanistan is unusual in not deriving from a colonial inheritance: the country was part of 'the Great Game' of British imperialism, but not for long enough to imbibe the great game of cricket.

Instead, cricket was discovered and adopted by Afghans languishing in refugee camps in Pakistan during the war with the Soviet Union – Taj Malik and his opening batsman brother Karim Sadiq grew up in sprawling Kacha Gari near Peshawar, as part of a family of thirteen, their father an anti-Soviet mujahideen.

Cricket was played here using improvised bats on bare earth with a tape ball, and consumed on satellite television, Pakistan's World Cup win twenty years ago causing a great spurt in interest. Television remains an inspirational influence and Australian players as a result are great favourites: Afghanistan's best young batsman Noor Ali Zadran idolises Ricky Ponting, and leg spinner Samiullah Shinwari has borrowed characteristics of Shane Warne – presumably not all of them, as this *is* Afghanistan.

The Afghanistan Cricket Federation, antecedent to the present board, was founded in 1995. And while the Taliban famously proscribed kite-flying, and prohibited any cheer at sporting events other than 'Allah Akbar' (God is great), cricket's identification with moderation and reserve appealed to their straitening instincts, as did the players' full body covering. The Taliban supported the ACF's 2001 push for ICC affiliate membership and actually sent a message of goodwill to the national team ahead of their recent big game. In general, in fact, Afghanistan's team has over time engendered widespread goodwill. Since the Taliban's fall, visitor after visitor has been staggered by their uncoached aptitude, zeal for big hitting and fast bowling, and almost swaggering dauntlessness.

It is not quite a decade since the national team's first game, against an XI put together by the International Security Assistance Force at Kabul's grandiosely named Olympic Stadium, which the Taliban had not long used for executions of adulterous women. Despite never having played with a leather ball before, the hosts routed their opponents for 56 and overhauled their target in four overs. A number of key personalities survive from that early XI, including all-rounder Nowroz Mangal, Afghanistan's calm-browed captain, and middle-order batsman Raes Ahmadzai, now chairman of selectors, who reputedly acquired the money for his kit by breaking rocks with a pickaxe.

To keep cricket going in a war zone has involved a similar kind of toil. Over the years, quite a bit of ICC money has gone into Afghanistan; not all of it has come out. Albone's book describes the situation four years ago when Afghanistan were just about to start their cricket ascent by playing a tournament in Jersey in Division 5 of the ICC's World Cricket League. Malik and the ACF accountant visited their bank in Kabul – a huge, fortified building ringed with barbed wire and overlooked by armed watchtowers. They asked politely: could they please know the ACF's bank balance? The answer came back: zero. The pair looked at each other, broke into hysterical laughter and shared a high-five. At least they didn't owe anything.

Security, meanwhile, is inevitably precarious. Cricket remains chiefly a Pashtun game, concentrated in the provinces of Kabul, Logar, Kunar, Khost, Kandahar and Logar to the east, and of Nangahar in the south, and is no stranger to tragedy. In August 2008, for example, a friend and teammate of Mangal's from the province of Khost was shot by American security forces searching for a weapons cache, almost certainly on the basis of a bogus tip-off.

Yet cricket has proven astonishingly resilient. When the Taliban fell, cricketers actually in Afghanistan, as distinct from those sheltering from fighting beyond its frontiers, probably could have been numbered in the scores; it's estimated there are now 80 000 active players, including women.

Two years ago, the Federation was reconstituted as the current board with Zakhilwal, a western-educated technocrat who is probably his country's ablest politician, as president. Chief executive Nasimullah Danesh, who oversees a staff of forty-five, was able to extend a sponsorship deal with the national telco, Etisalat, last October. An attractive new stadium in Kabul, bankrolled by USAID, was christened in December; other good quality grounds operate in Jalalabad and Mazar-e-Sharif. Perhaps most importantly, the national team has recently been reunited with Malik's highly rated successor as coach, former Pakistani Test player Kabir Khan.

Cricket in Afghanistan faces a host of challenges almost beyond our imaginings, and one challenge that is in Australia's power to solve: games. Having forged a path through the World Cricket League, been awarded one-day international status for finishing in the top six of the last World Cup qualifying tournament, and made it into the most recent World T20, Afghanistan was one of the nations whipsawed by the ICC executive board's chuckle-headed decision last year to reduce the next World T20 from sixteen countries to twelve.

Only two teams from a sixteen-team qualifying tournament in the Gulf next month will now go forward to join the full members in Sri Lanka in September. One is almost certain to be well-equipped Ireland; Afghanistan has no margin for error.

Here's a proposition – a proposition so frankly compelling that to argue against it would not be to find reasons, merely to make excuses. Australia is scheduled to play a one-day series against Pakistan from late August. Nobody is quite sure where the games will be held. Pakistan remains off limits for security reasons; the Gulf will be too hot; Sri Lanka and Malaysia are apparently possibilities.

Wherever it is, though, Australia should find a way on that journey to play an ODI against Afghanistan, a small gesture on our part here that would be received as a very great one there. Rarely does cricket find itself so exquisitely placed as to, even if only in a small way, aid understanding and to alleviate suffering.

The Australian, February 2012

DARK OF HEARTNESS

Greg Campbell's office at Cricket Haus in Boroko, Post Moresby is kept modestly habitable by three whirling ceiling fans. There is an air-conditioning unit behind him, but turning it on shorts the electricity. The landlines have not worked for twelve months, to the apathetic bemusement of a PNG Telikom technician who only came after the payment of a bribe and left without changing anything. Petitioners are coming and going. The utes need filling up. The ground staff need lunch. Campbell fishes colourful kina from a sturdy petty cash tin. He is careful, he explains, because things have a tendency to go missing round here. He estimates that in the last two years he has bought about 120 coffee cups. He reckons he is now down to about eight.

It's difficult to credit it, but we're actually in the headquarters of one of the most remarkable success stories in global cricket. At the turn of the century, despite a heritage of more than a hundred years, cricket in Papua New Guinea was in disarray, short of money, of facilities, of purpose – the same might have been said of the country, which had turned over five prime ministers in five years and was routinely ranked among the world's most unliveable places. Today PNG is ranked nineteenth in the cricket world, having joined World Cricket League Division 2 just over two years ago. It will play off in October's World T20 Qualifier in the UAE and next year's World Cup Qualifier in New Zealand; later this year it will also play in South Australia's new Premier League, alongside four teams from Adelaide and a fifth from the Northern Territory. In the last five years alone, PNG has gone from a cricket backwater into a poster country of the International Cricket Council's development programme. 'With an ever-expanding junior base, a crop of very talented national team players and a strong off-field administration, PNG is what development is all about,' says ICC's global development manager, Tim Anderson. 'Turning cricket from a game played by a traditional few countries into a genuinely global, mass-participation sport.'

To savour some of the passion for the game, you need to hit the road, which in Moresby is a memorable experience in itself, there being no speed limits, no obvious road rules and no apparent fear among pedestrians. For a few months after arriving, Campbell took the red stains on roadsides for bloodstains. They were actually expectorated splashes of the ubiquitous betel nut, but you can understand the misapprehension as you weave through the chaotic traffic. Pavements are crowded with street stalls, corners with people waiting patiently for buses that aren't exactly regular. In free use, applied to everything from mowing grass to shaving, are long-bladed machetes – 'the PNG pocket knife', as they are called by expatriates. Fences are tall and topped with generous coils of barbed wire to discourage marauding raskol gangs – after a while, in fact, the coils come to seem like a form of vegetation, growing as universally and inconspicuously as lantana does in Australia. The housing types are deliriously varied, from fibro shacks that it looks like it would take one shove to demolish to the husks of modernist houses previously occupied by the colonial administrators who began moving out after PNG's independence in September 1975.

About twenty minutes northwest of Port Moresby, a turn off the main road reveals the panorama of a village, Hanuabada. Historically, it is where Captain James Erskine of the *HMS Nelson* hoisted the union flag in November 1884 to declare Papua, the southeastern portion of the island of New Guinea, a protectorate of the Queen of England. Nowadays it is a fishing community with a population of 20 000, and a cricket community with a history of having provided over the years almost three-quarters of those who have represented Papua New Guinea – a kind of junior Barbados or south seas Pudsey.

While larger, older dwellings line the narrow foreshore, most residents occupy simple but sturdy homes on piers out over the water. Look a little closer and there is a dismaying aspect: the shore is thickly carpeted with plastic debris and other rubbish. But walk the long jetties and, strange as it may sound, you're in cricket country. My guide was PNG under-19s coach John Ovia, a native son man and boy, who lives with his wife, mother and three young children about three-quarters of the way along a jetty called Border, because it separates Hanuabada from Eleva, the village next door. They all play cricket and, after a while, it seems that everyone does. We stop to pay our respects to a cricket personage at every second house, from a Moresby quick of the 1970s, Morea Gau, to the mother of PNG's promising young opening bowler, Ray Haorda. 'And *this* man,' says Ovia proudly as he introduces a slight, white-haired, shyly smiling figure, 'he was the master of the single. By the time you looked up, he was at the other end.' I ask Pala Ura, the wicketkeeper for PNG in the 1982 ICC Trophy, the secret to good running. 'You must always run the first one hard,' Ura replies solemnly. I tell him a few Australians would benefit from the advice.

One thing, Ura adds: PNG finished that tournament in third place, with only the winner, Zimbabwe, going through to an eight-team World Cup, sans exiled South Africa, the following year. I do a quick mental calculation: this means, in effect, that thirty years ago, PNG was the tenth-strongest team competing in international cricket. And most of the players were from this village. Smiles all round. Quite something, eh? That it is, agrees Bill Leane, Campbell's predecessor at Cricket PNG, when I meet him in his home town of Melbourne – and it's also disappointing. 'No coaches, no sports science, no fitness programmes, just raw passion, and they were tenth in the world,' he says. 'It's amazing, but where did that go in between times?' So this is not so much a development story, as a redevelopment story, and also a speculative story – for where does PNG go from here?

First, though, how did it get where it is? Captain Erskine's proclamation 129 years ago completed a three-way carving of the island of New Guinea, the west forming a province of the Dutch East Indies, the east dividing British Papua to the south from German New Guinea in the north. Cricket reached Papua as part of the cultural baggage of missionaries, and among several fathers of the game one stands out: Rev. Charles Abel of the London Missionary Society, and also of the Hertfordshire County Cricket Club, who arrived in Moresby in October 1890, aged twenty-eight.

Cricket and Christ cohabited in Abel to such a degree that they had virtually fused, and he soon found the game useful. Soon after arriving, he was marooned in the village of Orokolo, 270 kilometres northwest of Moresby, surrounded by restless natives.

> There was no time to lose [wrote his son]. With his usual resourcefulness he gathered the village children together and at once began

to teach them cricket . . . The play relieved the tension considerably and soon the older people began to gather round, intrigued by the strange new game. Finally whatever the sentiments of their elders might have been, the children made friends with the white stranger. Hostility gave way to curiosity, the truculent attitude disappeared, and the danger passed.

In August 1891, Abel was posted to the LMS's easternmost head station on Kwato Island in the China Strait, a waterway growingly busy with traffic from Australia to goldfields ports to the north. This 28-hectare speck was another dicey posting. Abel's predecessor had succumbed to malaria; nearby natives had recently murdered a sea captain and only been subdued by some exemplary hangings. Encouraged by his Orokolo experience, Abel threw himself into bringing cricket to Kwato. No sooner had the church, mission station and student dormitories been completed than he enlisted his Papuan acolytes in a scheme to transform a malarial swamp into a cricket ground.

Abel's only published work, a book for Christian youth called *Savage Life in New Guinea* (1902), contains something to offend every modern sensibility. The Papuan, in his experience, occupied 'a very low position in the scale of savage peoples', being slow, lazy, dirty and base, 'guided in his conduct by nothing but his instinct and propensities, and governed by unchecked passions'; there were times, wrote Abel tremulously, when 'unbridled passion seizes and masters him, the man becomes a fiend; and then there are no limits to his barbarity'. Yet Abel wrote as much out of fear for Papuans as contempt for them. Abel, purportedly the only LMS member to read Darwin's *On the Origin of Species*, foresaw disaster if Papuans were exposed to the full onslaught of occidental ways. Only 'hard work and healthful sport', he thought, as he looked down at last on the cricket ground it took four years to complete, could fortify them.

> Their own amusements are often vicious. You cannot
> take away the pastimes of a race and give them nothing
> in their place . . . The spirit of prophecy was fulfilled when
> we transformed our spears into wickets and our shields
> into cricket bats . . . Most people will be able to appreciate
> our satisfaction as we sit in the shade of the citron trees
> sometimes after the day's work is done and watch the boys
> at cricket, with their wickets pitched on the very spot where
> a short time ago the stagnant water and oozing mud
> exuded vapours which poisoned the air.

Besides elementary subjects and Bible study, carpentry for boys and sewing for girls, the Kwato curriculum was heavily oriented to cricket, for its moral efficacy in instilling good technique, good sportsmanship and good deportment. Abel insisted that his young Papuans play in crisply laundered flannels, setting the standard with a natty bow tie, and with Victorian orthodoxy, seldom evaluating youths without an assessment of their cricket prowess ('a clever youth and a fine medium bowler'; 'nice serious lad, very clever behind the sticks'). He was no less demanding of his white colleagues, once dismissing a young teacher sent out by LMS for sporting ignorance ('Mr Hallows plays no cricket,' reads the diary entry. 'He is leaving by the next boat.'), and scorning a well-meaning government anthropologist (whom Abel dismissed as 'out of his depth' after a mild suggestion that the mission curriculum involve 'less cricket and more Christ'). The only time this incurably active man paused was when his edition of *Cricket: A Weekly Record of the Game* arrived, wrapped for appearance's sake in editions of *The Christian World*;

eyes glistening, he would pore in silent rapture over its scorecards and match reports. After a while, too, Kwato Mission began playing against outsiders. Regular games commenced with Europeans in nearby Samarai, who had built their own cricket ground, and against passengers on passing ships, including in 1910 a team from the steamer *Matunga* including Test all-rounder Frank Laver and Tasmanian keeper George Gatehouse. Only rain prevented the visitor's defeat after Kwato's star googly bowler, Aleadi, bowled Laver for nought and had Gatehouse caught for seven.

By then, cricket was no longer confined to Papua's eastern extremity. Interest was sufficient among Port Moresby's European community by Christmas 1906 to invite Samarai to send their team, while former Tasmanian leg spinner John Watt wrote *The Referee* soon after reporting that the game had a strong vogue in villages surrounding the city: 'If you visit any native village about Port Moresby, small boys can always be seen playing cricket right on the water's edge, with material of their own make. Every other hit the ball goes into the water, while the two batsmen "run them out". The Papuan is never stuck for a cricket ball, for as soon as he loses one he taps the nearest rubber tree, and makes another.' LMS evangelists here were as often Samoan as English, but preached cricket with little less enthusiasm, an Australian expeditioner recruiting bearers for a sojourn into the interior in 1910 finding the game a serious inconvenience:

> We had some trouble in getting the carriers, as all the villagers, including the Samoan missionary, were engaged in playing cricket. The craze for cricket seems to have spread from village to village all over civilized Papua. Wherever we entered a village we invariably found a cricket match in progress. The singular feature about the play was that young natives who could not speak English had most

of the English terms used in the game by heart. Thus one would hear 'Play!' 'Run!' 'Stop!' 'How's dat, umpire?' 'Out!' I must say that many of them handled a bat well and gracefully. The bowling was good and very swift, and as for the fielding it was quite up to the average. The worst of this cricket mania, my guide told me, was that if carriers were wanted and they were playing a match no inducement would make them move until the game was over. It was becoming, he said, the curse of New Guinea.

Nowhere was the vogue more ardent than Hanuabada, thanks to a Samoan representative of LMS, Fa'vae. The game was well established by the time he was succeeded by an Englishman, Rev. Robert Lister Turner. A rather more orthodox missionary than Abel, he would complete the first Motu dictionary and grammar, plus a translation of the New Testament. But he was also the brother of a Leicestershire county cricketer, and made Hanuabadan cricket famous enough by the 1920s to feature in a series of cards for 'Namo' and 'Papuan Beauties' cigarettes sponsored by the British Papuan Development Company, the prowess of its early champions Reautau Mea, Toka Gaudi, Gavera Arua and Kohu Dogoda making it a serious rival for Kwato and Samarai.

One final eastern champion, nonetheless, would outstrip all in fame. Born in Milne Bay in 1914, John Guise taught himself cricket by clipping pictures from Australian newspapers, including one treasured image of Learie Constantine hitting a six at the SCG, and imitating them in solitary drills with a tennis ball and a self-made bat on the docks at Samarai where he worked as a basket carrier. He cultivated a habit of massive scores, including a 253 in Milne Bay and a 346 in Samarai, after which he was approached by representatives of a Melbourne grade club – only, to his bitter disappointment, to be forbidden from accepting the offer by Papua's lieutenant-governor Sir Hubert Murray. His cricket thwarted, his life took different directions. Thirty-five years after Murray's death, Sir John Guise would become the inaugural governor-general of an independent Papua New Guinea under a constitution whose preamble was drafted by Rev. Charles Abel's son Sir Cecil Abel.

There actually emerged many crickets on the island of New Guinea. There were expatriate competitions, the original being a triangular in Port Moresby played for the Freezing Company Shield; expatriates began playing amongst themselves on the north coast in Lae and Madang in what the First World War had left as Australian territory as well. There were also Papuan competitions, maturing in Moresby into a league in 1937, with four of the seven teams coming from Hanuabada.

Most numerous were spontaneous local variants, one described by a correspondent in the 1928 Spring annual of *The Cricketer* as involving players wearing 'little more than is demanded by the laws of decency' using ersatz equipment in irregular numbers with elastic rules.

> There may be as many as twenty natives fielding, such is the enthusiasm for the Papuan game . . . Wearying of fielding, point, cover-point, long-stop and others betake themselves to cool groves, there to pluck the scarlet hibiscus . . . All laugh at hits and misses, for in merry Papua all is jest . . . Scoring is a strange affair, the losing side increasing its score by adding sufficient runs to the scoring book to render defeat honourable.

Yet what often looked riotous to outsiders contained strong ceremonial aspects, integral to inter- and intra-village relations. Anthropologist Cyril Belshaw documented both sixty years ago in his encyclopaedic ethnography of Hanuabada, *The Great Village*

(1954). As an example of the former he recorded the arrival of a men's team from the village of Kido to thank Hanuabada's Taoro Club for laying a pitch and performing some coaching, bringing with them a festive board of pigs, bananas and yams minutely apportioned.

> At five o'clock in the evening . . . the bananas and yams were brought out and unwrapped, the principal cricketers foregathered on the verandah of the club captain and ate the entrails and other pig tit-bits. At 6 o'clock the cricketers distributed the yams, bananas and pig cuts . . . they carried out the whole procedure with much argument and confusion and disagreement before everyone agreed that the allocation was satisfactory.

To illustrate the latter, he observed the female Laurabada Club incorporating elaborate cricket matches into their community-building activities, laced with socially approved sledging.

> Though there was much horseplay and good fun, there was a great deal of determination. Women on the sideline kept proper score and over the ground flew a large green flag embroidered with 'L.B.C.'. Regular teams developed for both cricket and evening games: women without children played women with children, married women played single women, or old women played young. As one side carried the day they would break off to dance triumphantly to a Polynesian song, or to sing a couplet of abuse, or to make humorous or obscene gestures.

These complex antecedents did not begin blending until about half a century ago, and then only little by little, after the expatriate Papua New Guinean team was invited to play its first games abroad, in north Queensland against a Cairns XI and a Tablelands XI in

January 1954 – what became an annual visit. Moresby's colour bar was a fragmentary one: some companies, like Burns Philp, distinguished between expatriates and indigenes; other, like Steamships Trading, did not. In 1958, the PNG team visiting Cairns included two Papuans: Babani Momo from Kilakila, and John Ovia's father Uduru. Nobody seems to have been overly fussed. And over the next five years, the expatriate and Papuan competitions merged as a prelude to deeper integration.

The 1960s and 1970s leading up to independence were actually a prosperous period for Papua New Guinean sport. Australian rules football produced champions such as Herea Amini and David Haro. Rugby league's Friday night competition, reinforced by quality players from Australia, was the highlight of the Moresby sporting week. Cricket kept pace. Around a thriving Sports Club in Moresby's premier expatriate suburb of Boroko were clustered three fine grounds with concrete pitches including picturesque Colts, home to a successful club team of the same name. Former Australian umpire Col Hoy, an executive with Ansett Airlines, organised the first visit from an 'Australian XI' of first-class players led by Queensland's Sam Trimble in March 1972. When a Papua New Guinea Cricket Board of Control was formed the following year with representatives from Moresby, Lae, Mt Hagen, Rabaul and Bougainville, the International Cricket Conference admitted the country as its eighth associate member. Inspired by PNG hosting its first rugby league international against a Lions team en route to fulfilling World Cup away fixtures in Australia and New Zealand, the PNGCBC invited Clive Lloyd's West Indians to play two one-day games on their way to the 1975-76 Worrell Trophy series. So it was that just five weeks after the last lowering of the Australian flag, the World Cup's inaugural winners played, confusingly, two different 'Papua & New Guinea' teams selected locally in Moresby and Lae. After the first ball from Andy Roberts soared from the concrete wicket at Moresby's Murray Stadium over the keeper's head, the visitors settled mainly for bowling part-timers. But a new cricket nation had arrived. Well, part of it had anyway.

For the teams pitted against West Indies represented the last efflorescence of expat cricket. In the first game, Richard Unsworth, a Wollongong accountant, gained a lifetime's bragging rights by dismissing Viv Richards. In the second game, Charlie Harrison, an Indian-born Australian previously resident in Pakistan, made 34, and dismissed Roy Fredericks, Alvin Kallicharran and Lawrence Rowe. But cricketers henceforward would be homegrown, if initially still led by a post-colonial elite. Brian Amini, the first Papuan to captain the national team when PNG beat Fiji by eight wickets in 1977, became chairman of the Papuan Community Development Group. His successor Nigel Agonia, a public servant from Moresby, went on to become Secretary for Minerals and Energy; Agonia's deputy Ilinome Tarua, a lawyer raised in Kwato, would later be PNG's permanent representative at the United Nations. At first, this new model prospered. Having won the gold medal for cricket at the first South Pacific Games, PNG went on to that remarkable 1982 ICC Trophy, held in Britain's Midlands. Led by Api Leka, they lost only to Zimbabwe, a class above everyone else, Kenya and Bermuda. They comfortably beat Canada, a participant in the previous World Cup, as well as Hong Kong, Israel and Gibraltar, then finally Bangladesh in a play-off for third place. They played, moreover, flamboyant cricket with a flavour of the West Indies, who whenever televisions were turned on in PNG in the 1980s to pick up the Channel 9 signal wafting across the Coral Sea seemed to be knocking lumps off Australians.

Whether PNG regressed, or the rest of the world advanced, that promise remained unfulfilled. The national team did not play another international game for a further four years, and when they did, in the next ICC Trophy, experienced a rude awakening: Netherlands cruised to 6–271 and bundled PNG out for 52. Fifth in their group, they went home early. For countries containing professionals and semi-professionals, such as Zimbabwe, the Netherlands, Bangladesh, Kenya, UAE, USA and Canada, all-amateur PNG was no match. Taking on the chairmanship of the PNG board that year, Veari Maha, a leading light in local Australian Rules football, did little to change that. A word you hear much of in PNG is *wantok* – pidgin for 'one talk', it conveys the idea of reciprocal obligation based on shared blood, shared clan or shared language. Maha was the patriarch of a large sporting family: in due course, his cousin William would become coach, his son Navu become captain, his other son James and nephew Rod key players. It was not a family one offended lightly.

There were still glory days. The South Pacific Games came to Moresby in September 1991, and PNG again secured cricket gold. Victoria, led by Matthew Elliott, came to Moresby in April 1995 and lost to PNG by six wickets. The PNGCBC rolled out an adaptation of Kwik Cricket, called Liklik Cricket, promoted by Dean Jones. But the peculiar difficulties of PNG now made themselves felt: the distance between cricket centres, the distance from the rest of the cricket world, the growing heft of rugby league exemplified by the Australian achievements of Adrian Lam, Arnold Krewanty and Elias Paiyo, and such infrastructural shortcomings as the continued absence of turf wickets. 'Wherever the English went round the world, they left behind beautiful turf wickets,' PNGCBC's long-time secretary Wayne Satchell would lament. 'The Australians in Papua New Guinea left behind only concrete.'

Wayne Satchell was one continuous thread throughout this time. His father Bruce had arrived in PNG in 1956 to set up local

operations for Trans Australia Airways; his mother Daphne was an
ebullient cricket lover; he married a girl from Hanuabada. A patient
opening batsman for Lae's successful Morobe Cricket Club, he was
the epitome of the dedicated amateur administrator: his office was
the boot of his car, and his office hours when he was not required as
a general manager of Gibson Chemicals. For a time, Satchell and
the board were so indivisible that he slipped into the habit of covering expenses of the national team at the ICC Trophy himself: some
of them in 1990 and 1994; nearly all of them, which involved mort-
gaging his home, when the tournament came to Kuala Lumpur in
1997. 'We'd always sent a team to ICC events,' he says. 'I wanted us
to maintain that record.'

Ask about this period in PNG's cricket history, however, and
the answers all get a little vague, perhaps not surprisingly given what
was happening elsewhere, with the collapse of the resources economy, the deterioration of security in Moresby, Lae and worst of all
on Bougainville, and a succession of chaotic and violent elections.
For some, it was not an entirely bad time to be away, including
PNG's two best players at the 1997 ICC Trophy. John Ovia accepted
the opportunity to train at the AIS Cricket Academy in Adelaide,
where among other things he enjoyed the thrill of batting to Brett
Lee in the nets and became a lifelong Australian cricket supporter.
'My father, he always supported West Indies,' says Ovia. 'But I
couldn't support anyone but Australia. It would be stealing.' Charles
Amini, whose family rivals the Mahas as Papuan cricket's most
fecund, spent the late 1990s in Melbourne on a posting with Shell,
becoming indispensable to St Barnabas CC. Charles and son Chris
played in the 2nds, wife Kune in the 5ths, sons C J and Colin in the
under-12s and under-14s; all would represent PNG. For Chris, now
national captain, it was an invaluable first exposure to two-day
cricket. 'I learned how to bat in Australia,' he says.

Local efforts, however, to raise standards were fitful. Veari Maha and Wayne Satchell promoted a plan to upgrade Amini Park, welcoming Allan Border to Boroko in September 1999 to turn the first sod. It was a prestigious, high-visibility event: Border was presented to the prime minister, governor-general and local dignitaries, providing the focus for days of media coverage. Yet disappointingly little happened afterwards; indeed, the ground started slipping into disrepair. Any shelter in Moresby will over time attract squatters. Cricket's precinct offered a number of instant accommodation opportunities including the old Boroko Sports Club and a curator's house. Squabbles broke out among local administrators chafing at the long Maha ascendancy, a lack of information around finances and a want of resources for teams. PNG players arrived for the under-19s World Cup in New Zealand in January 2002, for instance, with neither equipment nor footwear nor uniforms. Cricket PNG, as the board was now known, even lost its patron, which since Sir John Guise's time had been the governor-general, when the country went for six months without a vice-regal representative because of two politicians wrangling over the job.

Yet it was out of this chaos that came the first important step to reviving cricket in PNG: the appointment as patron of Sir Brian Bell. Bell, born in the Darling Downs township of Chinchilla in 1928, would in earlier time have been a South Seas merchant adventurer. Reading a magazine story about the infamous 'Telefolmin incident' in November 1953, when four Australian patrol officers were bloodthirstily killed by tribesmen in the northern province of Sanduan, Bell decided PNG must be 'an exciting place', and moved there. Over the next half a century, he built a vast family retail conglomerate, sealing everything with a handshake. He brought a similar goodwill to the role of patron, available to endow senior tournaments, under-19 tournaments, women's cricket challenges alike.

Things, though, would get worse before they got better. Bell's deputy on the board of Moresby's general hospital was Mick Nades, a savvy Sri Lankan-born accountant who had come from Sydney with Steamships Trading in 1976. When Nades was drafted to provide Cricket PNG with an overdue and thorough audit, troubles started emerging. Satchell was claiming to be owed tens of thousands of dollars for personal contributions to Cricket PNG; Bank of PNG was expressing concerns about K250 000 borrowed to redevelop Amini Park, whose title itself was unclear, being vested in a trust on which Veari Maha sat with a crony called Numa Alu. Unfathomable liabilities; uncertain assets: Cricket PNG was on a financial brink. It pulled back thanks to Bell, who quietly retired the bank debt, and Nades, who succeeded to the chairmanship and watched every cheque for the next few years until the finances stabilised.

The macro prospects were also suddenly improved. In July 2006, the ICC's development programme finally obtained significant secure funding, the full members agreeing to allocate associate members six per cent off the top of revenues, in addition to their quarter share of dividend distributions. A new multi-divisional global tournament cycle, the World Cricket League, provided an avenue to more money and improved opposition. 'All of a sudden there was something to play for,' recalls Ravua Dikana, then PNG's captain, who was appointed its first high-performance manager. To accord with this new dispensation, Nades decided, it would be necessary to succeed Satchell with an outsider – someone free of the history, personal and familial ties in which Cricket PNG was trussed. His choice was a bright and personable Australian youth ambassador, Andrew Knott, who had been working as a volunteer in Samoa at the South Pacific Games in September 2007. With money from the Brian Bell Company and in-kind support from

Hebou Constructions, a new headquarters, Cricket Haus, was erected at Amini Park for Knott and a small staff.

Yet nothing could have prepared Knott for the challenges of PNG. The Amini Park and Colts grounds were in poor shape, strewn with garbage, from broken glass to used condoms; neighbouring Ken Lifu Reserve was worse, having been churned into a bog by locals using it for driving practice. The precincts by now were also seething with squatters: Knott retained one named Luke at K50 a month to act as an intermediary with the rest, and found him very helpful, even inviting him to the staff Christmas Party at a Chinese restaurant. 'You have never seen a man pile his plate so high with food,' Knott recalls. 'Then he tells us very proudly that he's a Seventh Day Adventist and doesn't eat pork. We didn't have the heart to tell him that he had about half a pig on his plate.' But a day at Cricket Haus could be scary, especially the three hours without electricity because of the local utility's practice of 'load shedding', and throw up startling problems. On one occasion, Luke visited Knott about a personal matter. In the course of an altercation, his mother had killed a man by hitting him with a watering can; this man's wantoks were now threatening to descend on Cricket Haus to raise hell unless he could raise the compensatory 'payback'. Unsure if the ICC had intended its annual grant be spent this way, Knott made the restitution anyway.

Knott drew on the laconicism and resilience of his staff: then Dikana and his two development officers, Lakani Oaha and John Ovia. Nothing much fazed them. One afternoon, Knott and Dikana were talking at Cricket Haus when gunshots rang out, and a group of felons began sprinting across Amini Park with police in hot pursuit. They watched in fascinated silence as the police caught their quarry up and began absolutely leathering them with their batons. Knott paled at the brutality, but found his colleague unmoved.

'They'll cop it worse at the station,' said Dikana simply, and resumed reviewing the high-performance programme. This, Knott realised, was what you had to do – just get on with things. He introduced policies for training, selection and touring. He implemented a rebranding with a competition to devise new names for the national teams, and persuaded South Pacific Breweries to sponsor a new domestic competition, the SP Supa Series. The Brian Bell Company paid for two young players, Assad Vala and Willie Gavera, to play in Townsville in 2007–08 with Wanderers, the club best known for discovering Mitchell Johnson.

There was a limit, however, and Knott encountered one in December 2008, when PNG was rocked by a shocking crime. Sir George Constantinou, principal of Hebou Constructions, was carjacked in the Moresby suburb of Gerehu and stoned to death. As the PNG government exacted bloody reprisals and the Australian government issued travel warnings recommending 'a high degree of caution' in view of 'high levels of serious crime', Knott felt the ever-present 'mood of paranoia' in the expatriate community intensify. 'It [Constantinou's death] was one of the reasons why I felt it was time to move on,' Knott recalls. 'You can't help but feel as though you're playing a game of chance and your number will come up at some stage.' The replacement he helped recruit, Australian Bill Leane, remembers his introductory visit for its atmosphere of lockdown: 'Knotty had done a great job, and a ton of groundwork that gave the ICC confidence in dealing with us. But he was shit-scared. I could see it. He was surrounded by squatters, and it had gotten to the point where he couldn't even walk the facility.' Leane wasn't going to put up with that, and he didn't.

Few conversations with anyone involved in cricket in Papua New Guinea last five minutes without mention of Bill Leane. He is a divisive figure, although rather than causing some to love him and some to hate him, he usually leaves people doing both. That was probably bound to happen. For all its sanguinary eruptions of violence, PNG is bound by social structures of suffocating tightness: there is always a reason not to do something, because it has always been done some other way, or because of who might be offended by a change. Leane had no patience with these customs. The standard exchange about Leane will begin with a complaint, that Bill didn't understand this, or didn't listen to that, or that he was rude, or impetuous, or cavalier. Equally you never leave a conversation without the admission he accomplished what had hitherto appeared impossible.

Leane came to Cricket PNG from the Australian Cricketers' Association, where he'd been commercial manager for two years, after a long career in retail, and an even longer one as a fierce competitor in grassroots cricket and football. His most conspicuous work at the ACA had been building its Masters cricket tour for past players: as a result, he had a Filofax full of cricket contacts all over the world. First priority was a proper coach, as near to full-time as possible. 'I could see that the players weren't lazy; they worked hard,' he recalls. 'But they only worked hard so far as they could see. They were visual learners. They followed examples. It was pretty clear written programmes and processes were a bit pointless for them; they needed leadership and mentoring.' One candidate stood out: 'Andy Bichel was perfect. He's just a great bloke. He engages people. He shows you how. He also had a story: he'd been Australia's twelfth man more often than anyone else. He was all about the team. Plus he had a profile, which was something you could sell.' Already bowling coach at the Chennai Super Kings and only available sixty-five days a year, Bichel was an expensive investment; Leane paid him more than he paid himself. But he proved worth every Kina, making friends everywhere. He stayed while in Moresby in Hebou's Airways Hotel, PNG's finest, where the restaurant maitre'd still wears the national shirt that Bichel gave him.

Over the years, the experiences of John Ovia and Chris Amini notwithstanding, PNG had benefited relatively little from its proximity to Australia. Leane was resolved that that should change. In December 2009, Bichel welcomed Michael Kasprowicz, Damien Martyn, Greg Matthews, Greg Blewett, Andrew Symonds and Jimmy Maher for the inaugural Legends Bash, sponsored in the name of the 'Don't Drink and Drive' campaign by Pacific MMI Insurance. Cricket PNG had not known such publicity for ten years, since Allan Border's flying visit. The games were covered by EMTV locally, by Foxtel in Australia, and won an ICC award for best marketing and media event outside the full members. Leane was also adamant that the traffic should be two ways. He expanded the Brian Bell-sponsored scholarship programme, placing a score of young hopefuls with Melbourne clubs where he had contacts: they were billeted with families, paid in modest allowances and public transport vouchers enabling them to practise twice a week amongst themselves at the Maddocks Indoor Cricket Centre in Blackburn. He then tapped the same clubs to donate gear, which Maddocks staff loaded into one and a half containers for shipment by freight forwarder from Brisbane.

Leane's greatest coup, however, was to introduce a turf wicket table to Amini Park – a task in which he enlisted an invaluable ally. From Wellington in NSW, Mitch Lutschini opened the bowling in early 1980s for Sydney in NSW grade cricket; his sister Marie also played eight Tests for Australia. Thirty years ago he accepted a diesel engineering apprenticeship in PNG, and joined Hebou, where he grew ever more senior and ever more adept at getting things done. Asked to describe himself, he says simply: 'I fix things.' As Leane had cricket contacts in Australia, Lutschini had professional and political contacts in PNG, in abundance. Lutschini is too full of bonhomie to muse aloud on his motives, but his passion for cricket in PNG, to provide an opportunity for cricketers to make something of themselves, seems to come from a deeply personal place. Sir George Constantinou's murder hit him doubly hard. Not only had Lutschini regarded the Hebou patriarch as a surrogate father, but his own life had been scarred many years earlier by the carjacking death of his first wife, pregnant with their third child. In the last five years, Hebou has turned into Cricket PNG's first KI million sponsor, including backing for the national championships, the Hebou Shield, held from May to July. But Lutschini's support has been deeper and broader. He has been the solicitous voice on the phone in times of trouble; he has been the shrewd interpreter of local customs; one senses he has been a secret source of authority too. Joining Lutschini in the Airways' private Havanaba one evening, I found him deep in conversation with a nuggety figure in an open-neck shirt who looked vaguely familiar. 'Meet the prime minister of PNG,' said Lutschini casually.

The challenge of finally introducing turf cricket to PNG more than a decade after it had been promised required that Amini Park at last be secured. First, the title had to be sorted out, by a byzantine legal process that finally brought a halt to opportunist petitioners at Cricket Haus claiming to be traditional owners of the land. Second, the area needed to be purged of its unruly inhabitants, whose drinking sessions and pitched battles with improvised weapons on the oval had now reached epic proportions: one, reported in the 2012 edition of *Wisden*, involved as many as 400 combatants. Again, Leane explored legal remedies, this time to no avail. At last, Lutschini suggested the old-fashioned remedy of 'smoking them out'. In short, this involved Hebou setting fire to the derelict Boroko Sports

Club where most of the squatters were congregated, having them arrested as they emerged, then bulldozing the charred remains into the ground. As soon as this process was complete, Lutschini deployed earthmoving equipment to ring the ground with two-metre moats and two-metre fences topped with barbed wire. The ubiquitous Luke was offered the run of the old curator's house in return for becoming the resident security chief, a duty he performs to this day with utmost vigilance.

Early in 2010, Leane and Lutschini then flew to Brisbane to learn about turf wickets. They met former Gabba curator Kevin Mitchell Snr for tuition. They visited Jimboomba Turf to discuss grasses, choosing a couch known to flourish in tropical Darwin. Cultivated in Beaudesert, the turf was moistened, palletised and flown to Moresby by Air Niugini, where a former golf course designer, Josh Hanrahan, supervised its installation. Hebou provided a road roller to roll the surface, and dammed the nearby creek so that water could be drawn by a bore pump. The donation of a ride-on mower allowed them to retire the old Victas they had previously used on the outfield; within twelve weeks, Papua New Guinea was playing an Australian Indigenous team on a wicket that visiting umpire Bruce Oxenford deemed 'world class'. 'We never dreamed of having turf,' says Chris Amini. 'Bill just bulldozed through. He was a bulldozer. A big one.'

A year after Leane's arriving, Cricket Haus was a busy place, utes constantly coming and going, disgorging cricketers for regular practices, dispersing cricketers to run a fast-growing programme of junior cricket instruction, Schools Kriket, sponsored by BSP Bank. Many of these cricketers were now employees of Cricket PNG itself, and thus lifted a little above the ruck in a country where paid employment is exceptional. Nobody would be busier than Leane, one minute descending from the ride-on mower to oversee fielding drills, next minute putting on a tie to meet a sponsor or conferring with the five regional managers he appointed to begin covering the country beyond Moresby and the south-east coast. He could be a hard man to work with; stories are legion of his expletive-laced temper. He had limited patience with administrative chores like reports, budgets, paperwork and board relations, and ever-diminishing time – which is why he hired Greg Campbell.

A bustling and bouncy right-arm quick, Greg Campbell would have played more than five Tests for Australia in 1989–90 but for incurable damage to his left knee. He narrates the end of his career wryly. He and his Tasmanian teammate David Boon were admitted for operations by the same surgeon, and were in adjacent beds when they received their post-operative prognoses. 'You're fine,' the surgeon said to Boon, then turned to Campbell. 'You, I couldn't do anything for.' And that, in those days, was that. Campbell relocated to the Gold Coast, drifted in and out of coaching, then into a series of mid-level managerial jobs to which he struggled to warm, finally running one of a chain of café cum carwashes owned by Ian Healy. He missed cricket, still felt he had something to offer, and his wife urged him to offer it, but he faced a common dilemma. 'When I applied for jobs, I'd be rejected for lacking experience,' he recalls. 'But how was I to get experience if I couldn't get a job?' Leane's invitation to become Cricket PNG's operations manager seemed to offer that experience; it almost lasted one day.

On the morning Campbell arrived, he found Leane typically consumed by his daily tasks. There was nothing for him to do, nowhere even for him to sit. Leane looked up long enough to foreshadow dinner at the Port Moresby Yacht Club, then disappeared again; Campbell stood there in Cricket Haus, sweating, self-conscious. Dinner was late, terse, tense, and ended with Leane throwing him the keys to a unit, with the blithe advice that, oh, by the way, it had neither electricity nor bed linen. Campbell lay on the couch in the darkness brooding on how he might convey his dissatisfaction, but no sooner had he opened his mouth the next morning than Leane jumped down his throat. 'What are you worried about?' he railed. 'I can't be running around making your fuckin' bed for you. You're a fuckin' big boy. You can fuckin' sort it out.' It was, he learned, a pretty standard Leane tirade, although at the time only the fact that he had so coveted a job in cricket kept Campbell from leaving by the next flight.

Over the next year, Campbell developed great admiration for his boss, who worked the clock around for little reward or recognition. PNG, there were regular reminders, was a dangerous place: in August 2011 another senior sports administrator, PNG football team manager Peter Meli, was stabbed to death. It wore one down, thought Campbell: it could make you cautious, but also impetuous, determined to plough on round, over and sometimes through obstacles. Things, including a big fenced court of artificial practice pitches, were inclined to cost too much – a problem exacerbated by escalating rates of inflation, fed by a new mining boom. But otherwise they took too long, and cricket in PNG had already done too much waiting. 'Bill's got a big heart, he's passionate, and he gets the job done,' says Campbell now. 'He just wanted to succeed so badly . . . It's true that he overspent, but the money was always coming. It just got spent before it arrived.' For the last few months of Leane's time in PNG, leading up to his departure not quite two years ago, his relations with chairman Nades were tense – entrepreneur Leane feeling restricted, accountant Nades feeling neglected. But by PNG standards, tensions in cricket were mild indeed. Still by far the country's biggest sport, rugby league has been rocked in recent years by crisis after crisis: feuds, scandals, governance splits, legal battles, corruption allegations. In less than three years, cricket had come further than any other sport in PNG – further, in fact, than most institutions. Its reputation is now for professional management and positive thinking. 'There are bigger sports in this country,' says John Mogih, a teacher at Jubilee Secondary, a school in the BSP Cricket for Schools programme, which has now reached 125 000 students. 'But apart from cricket, no other sport has been interested in us. And cricket is a sport I admire, because it is very well run. It is putting our country on the map.'

How great a place it eventually occupies on the map is now interestingly poised. Sound administration, generous sponsors, growing participation numbers: these are necessary conditions of success but not sufficient. Strategic dilemmas loom for cricket in PNG. Two are simply geographic. Cricket is still concentrated to New Guinea's south and east, in the province encompassing Hanuabada known as Central. The day I visited John Mogih at Jubilee Secondary, he was still chuffed about a recent classroom discussion during a BSP Cricket for Schools session when a boy answered correctly a question about the name of England's captain: the boy who answered Alastair Cook and who turned out to like watching cricket on television was from PNG's remote Highlands, not traditionally a cricket stronghold. Cricket's identification with the coast, says Mogih, remains a handicap. 'Children will still say to you: "I'm not from Central so I don't play cricket." They see it as a different culture.' PNG Cricket now has ten regional managers, but they have huge territories to cover, and there is a way to go before the game can truly be regarded as national.

PNG also suffers from where it sits in the world, grouped in with associate members of ICC's East-Asia Pacific region, where it is by far the strongest. Trivia question: which country has made the highest international one-day score? Answer: PNG in making 7/572 in fifty overs against New Caledonia in the 2007 South Pacific Games, breaking their own record of 9/502 in the corresponding fixture four years earlier. An established solution to the dearth of quality competition has been to place players with Australian clubs: ten spent last summer spread among four clubs on Queensland's Gold Coast, so as to be near new national coach Peter Anderson. Another possibility has just emerged almost by accident, because of a conversation between two former Tasmanian teammates of Campbell's, Jamie Cox and Michael Dighton. Cox, now the South Australian Cricket Association's director of cricket, was talking about an idea he had for a premier league pooling the talents of local grade cricket into four zonal teams, also involving a team from the Northern Territory; he was negotiating with the Australian Capital Territory to be the sixth team. Dighton, a well-travelled international coach with stints behind him in Canada and the Netherlands, had just been in PNG for the fourth Legends Bash, and been impressed by the talent on display. When the ACT decided against joining the premier league, Cox revisited the conversation. 'We wanted a team of players who weren't in our talent pool; weren't in any Australian talent pool,' says Cox. 'And PNG certainly weren't.' The league opens the possibility of a PNG player being picked up in the Big Bash League by the Adelaide Strikers, and being followed with the enthusiasm PNG sports lovers showed for their star export to Australia's National Rugby League, Melbourne Storm's Marcus Bai: likeliest candidate is Vala, a 26-year-old left-hander, who trained last summer with the Brisbane Heat.

That still leaves international competition, just adequate for present purposes, but really of insufficient frequency and intensity to advance players to the next level. PNG last played anything other than T20 against another country more than a year ago. With Amini Park still their country's only turf wicket table, PNG's cricketers still grow up with hard-wicket habits; fearless horizontal bat hitters flourish; aspiring spinners do not. Fielding is a strong suit: uneven, unkempt outfields hone quicksilver reflexes. But PNG's aspirations to play more in Asia, and perhaps even join the ICC's Asia development region, will be restricted by their home conditions. Amini Park, moreover, is in constant demand, not only for cricket but for Australian Rules, and where their seasons overlap the custom is simply to roll the pitch as soon as football ceases to rub out the stop marks for cricket the next day – a rather more relaxed attitude to curation than other countries are used to.

And attitude generally is what it will probably all come down to. Ultimately, PNG's future will be shaped by its national players. And that in its way is the missing piece of the puzzle. To repeat, PNG is a country of many different crickets. What Cricket PNG and the ICC are seeking to foster is *another* form of the game – the cricket that aspires to being a truly global sport, with an expanding elite level and healthy commercial undergirding. They are like the missionaries of a century ago, evangelists for an imported sporting culture remote from previous experience which may or may not take root.

Life amid the pre-existing culture for Leane and Campbell has been both frustrating and fascinating. Leane recalls a comment made to him by another local sports administrator soon after he arrived – that in PNG, what mattered was being picked and 'getting on the plane', not any success that might follow. That had a host of entailments. Selection had always been a vexed issue in PNG. 'It was one thing I could never unpick,' admits Andrew Knott. 'I couldn't speak motu or pidgin. There was never a lot of expertise around choosing teams: they had really been picking their *wantoks* forever and a day.' Leane tried. When he learned that selectors usually made their choices from information they received from others, he sacked them, appointing a new panel led by former captain Api Leka which he bound to attend games. That had its own implications, for Leka's daughter Lisa is a national player and married to Chris Amini. But it did introduce a more robust sense of competition for places.

Leane wanted also to regularise behaviour on tours. Just before he arrived, PNG participated in the World Cricket League Division 3 in Buenos Aires. Reviewing the visit, Leane learned that the majority of the players were in the habit of gorging themselves at breakfast and lunch, which were provided, and eating nothing in the evening so as to save their modest allowances for distribution among their *wantoks*. If it satisfied their familial obligations, it was detrimental to their cricket, and in this event tiny differences had counted: a single heavy defeat by Afghanistan cost PNG their chance to advance to the ICC World Cup Qualifier. That was it, said Leane: allowances were out and communal evening meals were in, the message being that good cricket required good preparation.

Another step followed a chance glimpse in the street of a woman wearing a PNG national team uniform, evidently borrowed from a player. That was it, said Leane again: uniforms were to be returned to Cricket PNG after use. Respect for and pride in the colours was not negotiable. To instil it further, he traversed the annals of the national team allocating numbers to all past and present players, who each received a specially made 'baggy black'. Sometimes Leane's determination to professionalise PNG was carried to a fault. When PNG visited Dubai to tackle World Cricket League Division 2, it brought Leane, Campbell, Bichel, batting coach Andrew Cavill, bowling coach Ray Bright and a strength and conditioning coach. It was more attention than the players ever had and at first left them feeling overwhelmed. 'There was information coming from everywhere,' recalls Chris Amini. 'It was too much for some players to absorb.' The team redeemed a poor start by winning a third-place play-off, thereby qualifying for a $US700 000 two-year high-performance grant from the ICC, but gaining no additional fixtures – a good result just short of great. And in some respects, PNG remains in search of its breakthrough win.

Running Cricket PNG, Campbell reports, has pastoral as well as professional elements. Nineteen senior men, ten rookies and ten senior women are contracted on sums between K120 and K250 a month. But the choice between the calls of sport and of family is no contest. A year ago, Campbell lost one of his squad's most valuable batsmen, Kila Pala, who top-scored in that aforementioned record score against New Caledonia, because his father had decided it was time for him to return to Hanuabada to work. Campbell visited the father to plead for the young man's cricket career, but to no avail. Sport? What kind of 'job' was that? *Wantok* networks impose heavy and ineluctable obligations. Not so long ago, Campbell wanted to give one of his staff a raise. The man pleaded otherwise: if it was known he had more money, *wantoks* would materialise to importune their share.

The fluidity of property extends further, to a mainly harmless, scarcely malicious but little changing problem with petty theft, from petrol being siphoned from cars to blades being detached from the ride-on mower. 'One thing you have to understand about PNG, Campbo,' Dikana told Campbell when he arrived. 'Daytime is for sleeping; nighttime is for stealing.' Individuals tend not to think through the implications of taking something because in their daily lives there usually aren't. PNG still has a law criminalising sorcery; somewhat different concepts of personal property should not perhaps surprise us. And, well, we have a few strange habits ourselves. Ovia and I were chatting in the ute one day when he turned to me with great earnestness. 'You know, I read that the man in charge of the Australian cricket team, he is a rugby player,' he said. 'Why is that?' Trying to explain Pat Howard to John Ovia: some of cricket's cultural gaps are simply unbridgeable.

When we returned to Cricket Haus, I took in again its most striking feature, which is a doorway on the first floor, perhaps five metres in the air, that simply leads into space. 'There was a fire escape there,' Campbell explains. 'But we decided it would simply be quicker to jump.' Nobody had bothered to cordon it off or post a warning sign; instead it yawned, almost inviting you to walk through it. A metaphor for its cricketers' steps into the unknown, perhaps? While the development programme has provided them with a beckoning doorway, the leap still requires courage.

The Nightwatchman, July 2013

Tendulkar's 100th Hundred
THE PURSUIT

The Indian novelist R K Narayanan once said that his country lived permanently in the eleventh hour.

Perhaps Sachin Tendulkar's great achievement has been to defy that endless cycle of crisis and catastrophe characteristic of India's history, and to tackle about his cricket with such a sense of such soothing certainty. But he finds himself at the Sydney Cricket Ground on a personal brink growing ever more vertiginous, 290 days having elapsed since his ninety-ninth international hundred.

For a mighty continent of cricket fans, Tendulkar's century of centuries has become a grand consuming passion, a painfully delayed gratification. Never, perhaps, has a cricketer experienced such an incessant bombardment of goodwill and gratuitous advice – heard, unheard, thought and felt.

Indian news outlets have prepared so long and so lavishly for the feat that when it finally occurs it will almost seem like old news. Electronic files full of stories with only places and names remaining to be filled have already been written and await only the order to print.

Numberless other specials will already have been cancelled. During the recent Mumbai Test, I received an email request from an Indian magazine requesting 1000 words of appreciation immediately, Tendulkar being 85 not out at the time. The piece had progressed no further than an opening paragraph when a supplementary email arrived cancelling the commission, Tendulkar having been dismissed for 94.

For those who savour a little synchronicity with their statistics, the prospect of a Tendulkar hundred in Sydney's hundredth Test could hardly be more exquisite. It was at the SCG against the first Indian team to tour Australia that Bradman, whom Indians generously rank alongside Tendulkar among cricket's divinities, scored his hundredth first-class hundred in November 1947.

The visitors were then so excited by the prospect of being part of such a wondrous record that their captain Lala Amarnath entrusted the ball for the ultimate over to Googamul Kishenchand, a bowler so part-time he did not trouble to remove his cap, and whose amiable full toss Bradman pushed gratefully to mid-on for a single. No similar charity, it need hardly be said, will be extended Tendulkar's way in this match. Yet very few cricketers are unmoved by the event of a great landmark, and cricket is a rare game in that individual statistical achievement has a transcendent popularity among its public.

Like other sports, cricket is sewn with salutes for spectacles and ovations for champions. But it also takes a peculiar and ecumenical joy in the milestone, both the visible, from the old-fashioned applause for the batsman's fifty and hundred and the new vogue for celebrating the bowler's five-for, and the invisible, captured in the perpetual scoreboard of the record book of each player, team and ground. There is particular satisfaction to be found in the feat requiring time, effort, perseverance, scope and, not least of all, luck.

And what feat could express that better than the one on whose brink Tendulkar stands, twenty-three years and five continents in the making?

The extremes of attention lavished on Tendulkar's quest have been paid the compliment of huffy disdain. Test hundreds and one-day hundreds put together? Preposterous, say a self-appointed cognoscenti. On *Cricinfo* recently, the essayist Mukul Kesevan scoffed that the record was a 'half-wit's holy grail'. He insisted: 'The real cricketing illiterates are the people who believe that adding ODI centuries to Test centuries and arriving at a hundred gives you a heroic landmark. It doesn't. This isn't just a meaningless statistic, it's a pernicious one, because it equalises two different orders of achievement.'

Well, d'uh. Statistics are *always* equalising different orders of achievement and imposing arbitrary distinctions. Where is the logic in the equal ranking among Bradman's hundred hundreds accorded to a triple century in a Test against England and to a hundred for an Australian XI against pre-Sheffield Shield Tasmania? And what could be more arbitrary than the designation 'first-class' cricket? 'International cricket' might encompass the variation in standards between facing Glenn McGrath and Shane Warne one day and Stuart Matsikinyieri and Chris Mpofu the next, but it has the semblance of coherence constituted by a global structure and hierarchy.

Sure enough, day-in, day-out, Test runs are harder to come by than ODI runs. But it is difficult to believe that Tendulkar's astonishing double hundred in a fifty-over match against Dale Steyn, Jacques Kallis, Wayne Parnell and Charl Langeveldt at Gwalior was an innings inferior in quality to a hundred in a drawn Test off Mahsrafe Mortaza and Shahadat Hossain at Chittagong. So, far from being a corrective of discernment and discrimination, Kesevan's argument was simply snobbery and special pleading.

On the contrary: about this feat there is everything to honour. Tendulkar's quest for his century of centuries might have started as what the American historian Daniel Boorstin once called a 'pseudo-event', but it has achieved a kind of narrative arc by proving so elusive. Imagine what a squib it would have been had Tendulkar hit his hundredth hundred in Chennai a week after the ninety-ninth. By seeming so regularly within his reach then just eluding his grasp, Tendulkar's hundredth hundred has reminded us again and again that the game will not be hurried or defied, that it resists being packaged and commodified, that the players play, spectators attend and viewers watch in the knowledge that hopes are dashed at least as often as they are fulfilled.

Good sport is not one thrill or spectacle after another. It needs its disappointments, deferrals and delays. Nowadays, cricket administrators hold their publics in such subtle contempt that they worry about them reaching for an electronic game if forced to wait too long for their next six. On the contrary, it is the sense that the astonishing and the monumental are rare and that we are blessed when we witness them that lends sport its special quality. Tendulkar is bound to achieve his landmark at some stage, amid scenes of rejoicing and relief, but it will be the more cherishable for the waiting involved. At the eleventh hour, everything is sweeter.

The Australian, January 2012

THE ACHIEVEMENT

Great players have a habit of setting records. Only very, very special ones have records made for them – actually created in their honour. Nobody dreamed of one hundred first-class centuries becoming a landmark until W G Grace made it conceivable. Likewise the milestone of one hundred international centuries . . . that is, until Sachin Tendulkar glimpsed it in the distance, and set off in pursuit.

Then the game was afoot, and as Tendulkar surged towards the summit, so the summit seemed to shrink a little in proportion, by its growing attainability. That's another quality of the very, very special. They cut life down to size, recalibrate it by their capabilities. Tendulkar is called 'The Little Master', but he is also a master of littling, of scaling achievement down so it grows thinkable, accessible and permissible.

That said, there is something about *this* record, above all others, that is additionally monumental. Blazing his way to an unprecedented one-day double-hundred, Tendulkar crashed a barrier others will ford. Pushing past a hundred hundreds, he concludes an epic of endurance and excellence, like the *Mahabarata* and *Ramayana* rolled into one. You must factor in the distance travelled since the first, at Old Trafford in August 1990, and tensions absorbed in that time, from the scale of the hopes accumulated round him in that time, greater than those coped by than any cricketer.

The century is cricket's most incorruptible unit of currency. It has a universal historic and cultural utility: it is the glimmer in the batsman's eye every time he takes block. A century of centuries at the game's elite level has an undilutable and utter wholeness. It is like a round-the-world journey or a perfect smile: complete in itself, theoretically repeatable but essentially unimprovable.

Then you can appreciate the irony of the fact that the country in ecstasy over Tendulkar's accomplishment has done most to ensure that this is a record never to be repeated. Thanks to the ascendancy of the Indian Premier League, the next generation of cricketers will play more T20 and less international cricket. Tendulkar's career coincided with the gradual glutting of the global calendar by forms of the game of a duration conducive to the compilation of hundreds. It is all but impossible to imagine his heirs and successors emulating him in playing on for approaching a quarter of a century, let alone facing international opponents in more than 600 games of at least a day in length – not unless the act of making a hundred was made radically easier, which would in any case debase its value.

The shortening of our pleasures has entailed a contraction in cricket's scope. It was always a possibility that there would never be another Tendulkar, but perhaps now there cannot be. While Tendulkar has played, it has been possible to forget the forces compressing and commodifying cricket, turning it into just another form of television content and generator of TRPs. He has constructed a career along the lines of one of Europe's great gothic cathedrals, built to last, to serve future generations, full of splendour, grandeur, romance. And all cricket can now think of doing is surrounding that cathedral with lookalike apartments and selling these at a huge mark-up.

There's something mean and paltry about that, because, like those cathedral builders, Tendulkar has been built along lines generous, inspirational and ennobling, for fans, teammates and opponents too, filling them with a sense of being in the presence of the ineffable. Anil Kumble described Tendulkar as impressing on bowlers 'the sheer futility of having any fielders at all'. 'It was humbling to witness first-hand just how amazing he was,' says Graeme Swann of bowling to Tendulkar in his recent autobiography. 'Everyone knows he has been the best player going in the modern era, but when you actually bowl to him on a wicket in your favour, and he appears to know what you're thinking the minute before you think it, it's like playing poker against a full-time professional.'

Tendulkar has become an exceedingly wealthy man, but in a sense because he had to be, because that is the way our aspirational, materialist societies reward our heroes. He has continued to understand value in a world obsessed with price. He has taken nothing that was not insistently offered, and in the totality of his career will come out comfortably as a giver, the game perennially in his debt. What comes after him will not be of the same character. In so altering the financial stakes of his game, in fact, Tendulkar has inadvertently ensured it. In their book *The Business of Cricket* (2010), Shyam Balasubramanian and Vijay Santhanam cite a table prepared by TAM Sports pointing up 'the Sachin Factor': that Tests and one-day internationals with Tendulkar playing out-rate those in which he does not by a huge degree – in 2010, by three to one. They also present a graphic they call 'The Tendulkar Ecosystem', in the centre of which sits Sachin, sluicing value, financial and psychic, between Team India, fans, sponsors, media houses and state associations.

It looks very complex, but it's all quite simple, and scary too. Because without one small man who enters his fortieth year next April, it cannot work. Want *really* to grasp Tendulkar's importance to the modern game? Imagine it without him.

In writing of the immediate post-Bradman era, Ray Robinson described Australian cricket as like a man bumping around a darkened room. Something similar has taken place in Australia since 2006, when it was realised that cricket could not always be trusted to promote itself. To pump up its new Big Bash League, Cricket Australia had to wheel out Shane Warne, because nothing has come along to replace him in national affections. The same sense of loss and anti-climax can be expected in India – indeed, don't doubt that administrators and players live in silent dread of the announcement.

Sixty-five per cent of India's population is younger than thirty-five. They can recall no cricket without the Little Master. When he retires, it will be for them not just the loss of a sporting hero but an intimation of mortality. Amazing to say, Tendulkar might then grow even greater – it is the way of the memory of greatness that the recollection of success gradually effaces that of failure. It will then be the task of that generation to recapture for the next the sense of thanksgiving around Tendulkar's hundredth hundred, and his other accomplishments. Take it in. Think about it. Enjoy this moment and make it last.

India Today, March 2012

Rahul Dravid
THE WALL GAME

Rahul Dravid is a thinking cricketer. But one person I learned last season that he does not spend a lot of time thinking about is . . . Rahul Dravid.

It was shortly after the Boxing Day Test and we were having dinner with a mutual friend near my home, at a spaghetti joint in Lygon Street, Carlton. As happens when you're in distinguished sporting company, the subject of conversation turned to setting down some thoughts about that career when it ended – as Dravid announced yesterday, it was.

Test cricket's second tallest scorer, and the man who faced more deliveries than any other, would seem to have a tale to tell. Dravid did not agree. What, after all, had he done? He had had a comfortable upbringing, a good education, a loving marriage and . . . well, yes, he'd made more than 24 000 international runs with forty-eight hundreds, but what of it?

Dravid had read Andre Agassi's autobiography, *Open*, recently. Now, *that* was a story, he thought: drugs, girls, money, triumph, disaster. By comparison, Dravid said lightly, he had hardly lived at all.

It seems almost churlish to dissent such a commonsense view, but on this occasion let's quietly beg to differ. For most of his fifteen years at the top, Dravid was the most immaculate cricketer in the game, a batsman of preternatural serenity and a sportsman of model decorum.

That wonderful Indian cricket writer Sujit Mukherjee once said of Dravid's great antecedent Vijay Hazare that his innings had 'no beginning and no end', because 'whether his score was 2 or 20 or 200, he [Hazare] was assessing the bowling with the same exacting concern that characterized his every moment at the crease'. The same was true of Dravid. He batted as a river runs, at an immemorial pace. You could tune into an innings of his at any time and be unsure whether he had batted six hours or six minutes. He carried himself with the same easy dignity in success or failure, in India or abroad: unlike the other members of his country's prestigious batting elite of Tendulkar, Sehwag, Laxman and Ganguly, he boasted a higher average away than home.

Dravid's decision to retire will not come as a great surprise to those who watched him struggle through the Australian summer, as his stumps kept getting hit, as status was reduced from 'The Wall', to privet hedge, to herbaceous border. He is too perceptive not to have sensed it, despite his valiant struggles. He was, as ever, a model guest, his Bradman Oration being quite possibly the season's outstanding Indian performance. It is also characteristic that Dravid waited until the Australian summer was completely done with before making any announcement; the individual is at the game's service, not vice versa.

Not every cricketer's cricket faithfully reflects their personality, but Dravid's would seem to. In company, he thinks before speaking, gives his interlocutors undivided attention, is humble, unhurried and unflappable. That evening, dining al fresco, we were perfectly at the mercy of passing rubberneckers. Every two minutes, it seemed, someone would ask Dravid for an autograph, want him to pose for a photo or simply stop to gawk. Even the chef came out to shake his hand.

Dravid gave every petitioner perfect partial attention, not once growing flustered, not once losing the thread of a conversation – dealing with them rather like balls wide of off stump, giving them their due but no more.

There was, I realised after a while, a well-honed technique to it. Dravid acquiesced to each request politely but straightforwardly, volunteering nothing in addition. People got the message; it was impressive.

Various subjects were discussed that evening, which it seems impolite to divulge, and may even be unenlightening to, because Dravid is so reticent about his career and so respectful of opponents. About one opponent, though, he was forthcoming, and that was Ricky Ponting. He recalled being accosted by Ponting, whom he hardly knew and had barely conversed with, during Australia's tour of India in 2010. 'I want to talk to you,' Ponting had insisted.

Dravid wondered what he had done wrong; on the contrary, Ponting wanted to tell him what he was doing right. Dravid was having a poor series; Ponting urged him to hang in there. 'I know you're not making runs, and I know there's probably a bit of pressure on you at the moment,' Ponting told Dravid. 'But let me tell you: every time you come in, I tell the guys that you look like you're going to get runs today. You've been getting out, but I reckon there are some big scores around the corner for you.'

Dravid was moved by the grace of Ponting's gesture – as indeed were we, his companions that night, to hear of it. He went and proved Ponting right, too, enjoying in 2011 the second-most prolific calendar year of his Test career. Just over a week after our dinner, Ponting dived headlong for his crease at the SCG, just beating a throw and achieving his first Test century in nearly two years. It was noticeable that while most of the Indian fielders assumed excrutiated poses, hands on heads, looking martyred, Dravid moved in from mid-off clapping appreciatively, and perhaps also gratefully.

You would think that having a cricketer play at international level for more than fifteen years might conduce to a little succession planning; this being Indian cricket, you would think wrongly. Nobody stands out in this Indian line-up as an inheritor of his mantle. His retirement will leave the same breach in his team as it would have a decade ago.

All the same, there is perhaps no modern cricketer better equipped intellectually and temperamentally to make a contribution to the game's governance and direction. Dravid's greatest impact on cricket might lie ahead of him. And that would be a story worth telling.

The Australian, March 2012

Jacques Kallis
ONE-MAN TEAM

Perhaps the most surprising sentiment in Australia's much-discussed 'secret' dossier about their South African opponents is the observation that Jacques Kallis 'never gets the wraps he really deserves'.

Really? Hardly a day goes past when he's not compared to Sir Donald Bradman or Sir Garfield Sobers. That's some pretty fancy (w)raps he's being swathed in.

Not that they are undeserved. Kallis has spent half his career batting on South African pitches, the friendliest to pace in the world, and still has a batting record superior to Ricky Ponting's. Kallis has vied for the ball with some of cricket's slipperiest pace bowlers yet his bowling record is little inferior to Brett Lee's. Ponder that a moment: Kallis equals Ponting times Lee. Einstein could hardly have conceived of an equation so compelling.

The comparison with the greatest appeal, it would seem, is between Kallis and Sobers, first of all because it attracts the world's feral abacuses to their respective Test figures. Their averages – Kallis's 12 641 runs at 57 and 280 wickets at 33, Sober's 8032 runs at

58 and 235 wickets at 34 – are separated by a fag paper.

The comparison is made additionally enticing by involving two brilliant opposites: Sobers all prowling grace and feline elasticity, with his 360-degree bat-swing and three-in-one bowling; Kallis all looming bulk and latent power, constructed like a work of neo-brutalist architecture. Yet what they are just as much opposites of are their respective eras. Sobers was the most explosive cricketer of a more staid age, the more mercurial because of the orthodoxy and rigidity round him; Kallis is the most remorseless and unyielding cricketer of an era more ostentatious and histrionic. Sobers was a cavalier among roundheads; Kallis has steadily become a roundhead among cavaliers.

The immortal Amarillo Slim once counselled players of Texas Hold' Em to 'play fast in a slow game, slow in a fast game'. It's not the worst advice for cricket. By altering expectations, batsmen out of step with their peers force bowlers to aim for different lengths, and challenge captains to set different fields. In Kallis's era, strokeplay has taken on almost compulsive qualities. Batsmen are playing shots from the get-go; bowling 'dry' has become a standard counter-offensive. The pacific Kallis craves no such ego gratification. His strike rate of 46 has barely altered during his career. It is a steady, sober, almost God-fearing sort of strike rate: nothing fancy, flashy or greedy. Kallis has no need to swank. He knows he will get there in the end.

Kallis has profited from cricket in ways Sobers never did and never could have. But Kallis has by some measures had the more demanding popular task. Everyone loved Sobers. Such athleticism. Such élan. If wraps for Kallis have always been in ready enough supply, it is also true that he has been more readily appreciated than adored.

In a sense, he has never quite outgrown his origins – nor has he wished to. His formative years were in a South Africa deprived of international cricket competition. He never saw Viv Richards swagger. He never saw David Gower glide. He was coached by his father Henry, and his intensely functional methods have a touch of filial piety to them, as well as an intense respect for the game.

Today he achieves a remarkable record, by playing Test cricket at fifty different venues – only the third cricketer to do so, after Rahul Dravid and Sachin Tendulkar. Yet he remains very much a homebody, wedded to the south of Cape Town, and the familiar sights and sounds of low-key, suburban Mowbray, which he apparently knows down to the last street sign and post-box. His is the cricket of a similarly high boredom threshold; he has never tired of the playing, practising and travelling that has been his lot for so long.

At thirty-seven, Kallis is at last feeling the passage of time and has taken steps to cope. He has assimilated the disciplines of T20; he has guarded his body against excessive bowling loads; he has had his scalp fetchingly reupholstered.

But some things have changed despite him. This is the first tour Kallis has begun without his old mucker Mark Boucher, invalided home from England in July with a desperate eye injury. Their double act – spikey Boucher, bashful Kallis – had for years been a source of wry amusement to their fellows. 'What are you drinking, Jacques?' 'Oh, whatever Bouch is having.' 'What would you like to eat, Jacques?' 'Bouch?' If Australia are planning to 'really test him out' during this series, as their dossier recommends, it might be as simple as placing a menu in front of him.

Given that Kallis is in all probability on his last visit here, the cricketer whom Ponting rates as 'Australia's number-one opponent' could also feel some pressure to burnish his record against them. Down the years, Australian teams have done well to prevent Kallis being quite the same calibre matchwinner he has been elsewhere. His record against Australia is, to be sure, perfectly respectable: twenty-six Tests, 1722 runs at 39.14 and forty-nine wickets at 38. What it pales in comparison with is Kallis' record against all other comers: 10 919 runs at 61.34 and 231 wickets at 31.41. Three of Kallis's four Test centuries against Australia have been in losing causes. Nor has he ever taken more than three wickets in an innings against this country.

Today is a noteworthy event in the annals of South African cricket. It is the first time the team has entered a Test match as the format's undisputed number one. The Proteas fell upwards into the slot just over three years ago when Australia slipped downwards by losing to England at the Oval, but had been dislodged by India before they played their next Test. This Test commences with their regained mantle secure. If Kallis were to mark that event with a performance against Australia worthy of his stupendous accomplishments, some truly royal wraps would be his for the asking.

The Australian, November 2012

Kumar Sangakkara

READY FOR ANYTHING

The modern cricketer, detractors say, is a rather sorry specimen, good for cricket, but not much else, so that polishing a commentary stool with his backside is about the only option when his playing days are done. Those detractors are pulled up rather short by Sri Lanka's Kumar Sangakkara.

On his day, and these are not infrequent, Sangakkara is the world's best batsman, patient enough to have batted more than 360 minutes on a score of occasions in his Test career, supple enough to access almost all 360 degrees of the field, powerful enough to hit a long ball both straight and square, precise enough to beat extra cover fieldsmen by a metre or two left and right. He also belongs to a far smaller elite whose most consequential and productive years may actually be after his cricket career ends.

It's hard to imagine him reverting to the law studies he commenced at University of Colombo in 1998, then postponed when cricket became his calling. But he has the poise, and perhaps also the ambition, of one with a career in public life ahead. He thinks logically. He speaks fluently. In person, he is charm personified, but with a depth of seriousness. When he delivered the Spirit of Cricket Lecture at the Marylebone Cricket Club eighteen months ago, he filled in the turbulent civil and political backdrop to his country's cricket, then made trenchant criticisms of 'partisan cronies' in its administration. When he and teammates arrived in Melbourne last summer, his first stop was a charity event with the local expatriate community. With his friend and captain Mahela Jayawardene, he continued chatting, signing autographs and welcoming photographs long after most modern cricketers would have decamped in the direction of the hotel.

Sangakkara appears to have been predestined for distinction. Son of a distinguished jurist, he became head boy at Kandy's prestigious Trinity College, whose alumni include former Sri Lankan captains Ranjan Madugalle and Ravi Ratnayeke, and whose cricket ground, Asgirya Stadium, is of quality sufficient to host Test matches – indeed, Sangakkara can claim the surely rare distinction of having made hundreds for his school and his country on the same square.

Sangakkara first found his international niche as a lithe and elastic keeper; he and his precursor Romesh Kaluwitharana remain the only glovemen to have executed more than 100 international stumpings. Since hanging up his gloves, however, he has averaged nearly 70 in Test cricket, his keenly orthodox left-handed batting, eyes aligned with the right shoulder, bat face and elbow prominent, ever smoother and surer.

Batting has become a more brutal art in the last decade – at times, almost sadistic. With Sangakkara it remains a timeless, effortless, nearly noiseless affair. Historically, Sri Lanka has not abounded in left-handers, Sanath Jayasuriya and Arjuna Ranatunga, one explosive, the other abrasive, being the exceptions.

Sangakkara has provided his country a compact and conductive core, especially in collaboration with Jayawardene, with whom he has thirty times put on three-figures in international fixtures. The most celebrated of their alliances, at South Africa's expense six and a half years ago, spanning eleven hours, 624 runs and dinner at a Thai restaurant between times, is the most vast in the entire history of first-class cricket.

Yet it may be that the decisive event in Sangakkara's life occurred beyond a boundary. Boxing Day will mark eight years since he, Jayawardene and their colleagues, then in a dressing room at Auckland's Eden Park after a one-day international, first learned of the devastation visited on their country by a tsunami: eventually, the death toll would be 230 000; estimates are that as many as a million Sri Lankans were directly affected. In his MCC address, Sangakkara described landing in a stricken, stygian Colombo a few days afterwards, and joining Jayawardene in the relief work in Trincomalee, Batticaloa, Galle and Hambantota organised by the Foundation of Goodness, run by Muttiah Muralitharan and his manager Kushil Gunasekara.

> Vacant and empty eyes filled with a sorrow and longing for homes and loved ones and livelihoods lost to the terrible waves. Yet for us, their cricketers, they managed a smile . . . They did not exaggerate their own plight nor did they wallow in it. Their concern was equal for all those around them. This was true in all the camps we visited. Through their devastation shone the Sri Lankan spirit of indomitable resilience, of love, compassion, generosity and hospitality and gentleness. This is the same spirit in which we play our cricket . . . I experienced all this and vowed to myself that never would I be tempted to abuse the privilege that these very people had given me.

As patron of the Foundation since, his work has taken a variety of directions, most recently a programme he and his wife Yehali initiated, Bikes for Life, which is three-fifths of the way to distributing 1500 bicycles in provinces in the north of Sri Lanka, also ravaged by the country's protracted civil war. Sangakkara has also been a spokesman for the UNICEF programmes ThinkWise (HIV/AIDS prevention) and Healthy Hat-Trick (nutrition and sanitation). Unlike Ranatunga and Jayasuriya, he has held aloof from politics, while inevitably being exposed to them: Sri Lanka's sports minister, Mahindananda Aluthgamage, ordered an investigation of Sangakkara's critique of the country's cricket administration before backing off.

At thirty-five, Sangakkara still has some cricket worlds to conquer. Ranked the world's number-one Test batsman by the ICC's Reliance for the last year, he has nonetheless been only a moderate performer against Australia, averaging 42.7 from nine Tests, compared to 58.25 against all other comers; one epic innings aside, his 192 at Bellerive Oval in November 2007, this falls to 33.4. He will know he has not much time to set this to rights. His life? In some respects, it has hardly begun.

From *ABC Cricket Book* (2012–13)

Graeme Smith

HIS OWN MAN

A popular myth of science is that, on aerodynamic principles, the bumblebee should not be able to fly, but does anyway.

Although it's hokum – so please don't write in – something similar applies to Graeme Smith. Almost everything about his technique seems to militate against success: the shambling bulk, the crooked bat, the choking grip, the flat feet.

Yet here he was again yesterday, at Adelaide Oval, proving as he has for more than a decade, that it's not how, but how many. If his unbeaten 111 has not rivalled the innings of his opposite number Michael Clarke's in scale, it has been its match in intent.

If you glimpsed South Africa's captain in a club match, you would hardly give him a second look. He looks ungainly, even a bit lazy. He drapes himself across his stumps like he's sprawled on a living room couch; as the ball is released he works his way still further over, as though stretching for the remote.

Working not just straight balls but balls wide of off stump to leg, he looks a prime lbw candidate. Driving with half a bat, he appears a huge chance of nicking off. Sauntering heavily between wickets, he excites the ambitions of enterprising fielders.

Then you look up – as yesterday – and he's 20, 30, 40, 50. You're not quite sure how long you've been watching. You can't remember any stroke in particular. You just have a general sense of a very large man obscuring the stumps so as almost to render them invisible. That, and a growing sensation of the inevitable.

This was a characteristic Smith entrenchment. During Australia's first innings, he had pocketed four catches at first slip with unspectacular aplomb; he started on a similar note, squirting Pattinson to the mid-wicket boundary. Then he played and missed. Then he nicked one to the rope at third man. Then he nudged another for four to leg. Smith 12. Pattinson remonstrating with the fates. Easy as you like.

Smith look slyly pleased. He is a cussed opponent, seldom lost for a word, barely fazed by a retort. He also has that attribute of resilient batsmen of living in a rolling present, sealing off the previous ball behind him, even if he does not quite forget it. Certainly, he never neglects his strengths. These were all on show yesterday. Off the pads. Off the hip. The occasional cut, sometimes subtle, sometimes severe.

Smith is a better off-side player than when he first made the Test grade, against Australia in 2002. Back then he drove like a Trabant; now it's more like a second-hand Datsun 120Y. Yesterday he slapped once with a diagonal bat and an overpowering bottom hand through cover – ugly but effective. A couple of times he pushed down the field, and on an outfield seemingly of glass rather than grass the ball raced away – circumspect but positive.

Otherwise it was whilst driving that he placed himself in gravest peril, being reprieved first by Matthew Wade, then by the unequal burden of proof of the decision review system, which because it found insufficient evidence to uphold Richard Kettleborough's caught behind decision overturned it.

As the game descended into forensic farce, Smith remained nonchalantly unmoving, his face fit for five-card stud. He re-marked his guard a few times. He adjusted his protective gear. He surveyed the scene. The alarm passed. He resumed, caution reinforced. Steadily, in fact, the time seemed to move into synch with Smith rather than vice versa. After he reached his century with a signature square slash, the afternoon's last half hour of the day took place in a state of suspended animation, like a delayed playing out of the accumulated pauses the first day had lacked.

Otherwise, this was a day when the luckiest Australian bowler may have been the onlooking Mitchell Starc, and the greatest danger to batsmen was posed by their own fluctuations of concentration. During the four overs the Proteas faced before lunch, Alviro Petersen fetched his fifth delivery from Pattinson rather casually in front of square leg. It would have been a tasty wicket for the Australians to chew on at the adjournment, but the chance just eluded Cowan's grasp. Smith's partner looked best thereafter when playing in the V, with a full face and minimal backlift, and glancing fine, which he does with cool delicacy, until he was again too casual, taking the high road when he should have taken the low road while hazarding a single to mid-on.

There has been a good deal of scholarly debate around the respective rights of way of bowlers and batsmen whilst runs are being taken; less consideration of who goes where when batsmen approach along the same line. But a jink would have sufficed where Petersen took a detour. He would, furthermore, still have made his ground with ease had he slid his bat rather than tapping it in like a blind man's cane. Having twice donated his wicket to the Australians in Brisbane, Petersen is averaging 41 for the series when he should by now have scored at least one century.

This opportunistic breaking of South Africa's opening partnership also represented a continuation of an encouraging Australian knack of conjuring up wickets against the trend of their games. On this occasion, the instigator was Mike Hussey, with a side-arm direct hit that, like almost everything he does, belied his thirty-seven years. Next David Warner gained the prize scalp of a nonplussed Hashim Amla, the seventeenth wicket to fall to a part-time bowler in Clarke's seventeen-Test captaincy career. For all Smith's success with the bat yesterday, this kind of jeu d'esprit continues to elude him as captain.

It is Clarke's capacity for invention, almost as much as his capacity for run-making, that has Australia still *just* ahead as the mid-point of this series approaches. He is like the bee too: always busy.

The Australian, November 2012

Chris Gayle

GAYLE'S WORLD

'Me vex bad!!!!!! Kiss Teeth!!!!!!!!!!!!! :(:(!!!'
'One luv peeps...Sweet Azz!!'
'Any chew chew?'
'Lol u a lone clapping loL. Bro.'
Were a prize going round for the zeitgeistiest player in modern cricket, second would be daylight behind Chris Gayle, whose charismatic unintelligibility on Twitter is the perfect complement to his sellable on-field swagger.

If you wanted a map of cricket's fast-changing terrain, too, there could hardly be a better guide than Gayle's engagements for the last six months. Where money is on offer and sixes in demand, Gayle is lololoing all the way to the bank.

The T20 trade winds first blew Gayle to India for three weeks from late September, where he represented his Indian Premier League franchise, the Royal Challengers Bangalore, in the Champions League. He hit twenty-four sixes in six games. Yay.

From late November through early December, he then played

for the Matabeleland Tuskers in Zimbabwe's Stanbic Bank T20 tournament. He hit nineteen sixes in six games. Wow.

In seven games over five weeks here representing the Sydney Thunder in the Big Bash League, Gayle hit twenty-two sixes. Sensed a theme emerging?

This month he has been doing his stuff for the Barisal Burners in the Bangladesh Premier League, hitting twenty-six sixes in five games. Yes, happy days.

Gayle should currently be turning out for the Dolphins in South Africa's MiWay T20 Challenge, but instead is nursing a groin strain – which must be a result of carrying the several million dollars he has accumulated from his exertions, because it sure as hell can't be from running between wickets.

Between times, Gayle actually flitted home to Kingston on a couple of occasions to represent Jamaica, first in the West Indies' Regional Super50, then in the Regional Four-Day Competition, albeit that these visits seemed more like the kind of infrequent personal mercies a successful son affords an ailing parent. The game Gayle played for Jamaica against the Windwards in the first week of February, in which he made 2 and 165, was actually his first first-class fixture outside a Test match in almost four years – which is part of the reason that the WICB can no longer find sponsorship support for its domestic competitions.

For his countrymen, of course, the issue is not where Gayle is, but where he isn't. That is, when West Indies host Australia for the First Test in Barbados in five weeks' time, Gayle will be in Bangalore, for home IPL fixtures against the Delhi Daredevils then the Kolkata Knight Riders.

In commercial terms, of course, Gayle is simply cashing in on a gift he has for hitting white balls out of small grounds with a supercharged bat that were it an Olympic athlete would be dope-tested every other day. Yet if you follow cricket more broadly, Gayle is turning into a slightly eerie figure – like one of those collectable novelty Pez dispensers, intensely sought after by a besotted community of interest, spitting out sixes rather than sugar hits.

On this last tour down under with the West Indies, Gayle looked like a Test batsman coming into his prime. These days it seems like every time you turn on your pay television or boot up your computer, he is clubbing a six at Godknowswhere Stadium in the local Bash for Cash, materialising on Twitter soon after to talk about what he's eaten at Nandos.

Does he know where he is? Does he know where he's going? It must be at least a little disorienting because he always appears to be in roughly the same company. His countrymen Keiron Pollard and Dwayne Bravo will be thereabouts. Rana Naved-ul-Hasan and Shahid Afridi won't be far away either.

Fresh from the Big Bash League, Brad Hogg, Owais Shah, Alfonso Thomas, Paul Collingwood and Luke Wright are all playing in South Africa's new forty-four game, six-week MiWay Challenge at the moment. Collingwood, the epitome of duty and defiance with England for a decade, who led his country to the World T20 crown two years ago, now leads a muck-up bunch called New Age Impi who have lost every game they have played.

And as great a change as this represents for cricket, it is perhaps just as much a change for cricketers. Not so long ago, swapping states, counties or provinces was not done lightly. But in a world of proliferating supranational T20 tournaments full of instant teams with soundalike names and lookalike uniforms, emotional attachment may well be an impediment.

Some international players have already played for three IPL franchises. It is not uncommon to see *Cricinfo* player profiles with as many as ten different team associations. That may not mean much to Gayle, who always looked like he cared a bit more about what cricket could do for him rather than what he could do for cricket. But it begets a kind of cynicism that with the best will in the world will leave its imprint on the game.

Passengers on the new T20 merry-go-round have various objects, a big one being the securing of an invitation to the IPL. Team success in a domestic tournament can also provide an entree into the lucrative Champions League.

In the case of the Bangladesh Premier League, however, among the chief beneficiaries appear to have been gamblers, one of whom is now under arrest, and unknown numbers of whom aren't. Despite teams having salary caps twice the size of the Big Bash League, players have yet to be paid. The tournament took a bizarre turn towards its conclusion when one semi-finalist was substituted for another, the organisers having apparently misread their own playing conditions.

If you are playing for fast money, what's to distinguish it from other classes of fast money, particular at a level of cricket where anti-corruption checks and balances are so few, and administration is so haphazard? From a surfeit of meaningless cricket, some fortunate individuals will get rich, but the tendency of short-term financial profits is to lead to longer-term moral losses. Or, to put it in Gaylic, :-(.

The Australian, March 2012

END PIECES

END PIECES

Australian Cricket
CLUBBED TO LIFE

I need hardly say what an honour it is to deliver the tenth Bradman Oration. I won't say it's daunting. That would be unfaithful to the spirit of perhaps the most dauntless cricketer who ever lived. But it is a privilege and an onerous one.

Last year, Rahul Dravid delivered perhaps the best and certainly the most watched of all Bradman Orations, a superbly crafted double-century of a speech on which, I remember thinking at the time, it would be hard to improve.

Now I find myself coming in *after* Rahul, a job so huge that India has traditionally left it to Sachin Tendulkar. By that marker, I can really only disappoint. All I have in common with the Little Master is that we are both grimly staving off retirement – although, of course, the potential end of Tendulkar's career is a matter of moment to 1.2 billion Indians, while the potential end of mine concerns only my wife who would then need to find something for me to do around the house at weekends.

I'm a cricketer. The game is the longest continuous extrafamilial thread in my life and I'm attached to it as tightly as ever. I started pre-season training in April. I own a cat called Trumper. And while it's hardly uncommon to have a cricket bat in the house, not everyone can claim to have one in the kitchen, one in the living room, one in the bedroom and one in the outside dunny.

I represented my first club, the St James Presbyterian under-12Bs in Geelong, when I was nine; I played my first game at the mighty Yarras in 1993 and I'll play my next one this weekend. The rest of my life has been contoured accordingly. I married my wife during a Christmas break; we became parents during the next Christmas break; on neither occasion did I miss a training, let alone a game. We delayed our honeymoon until it was a bit more conveni-ent. Until an Ashes series in England, anyway. *I* certainly thought it was convenient.

They *do* say that the first step to dealing with addiction is admitting you have a problem. OK, here's my problem. I'm no bloody good. Oh, I'm not terrible. But, I mean, you can be terrible in a hilarious and companionable kind of way. Me, I'm just medio-cre in a hanging-on-for-dear-life-oh-God-let-it-end-soon kind of way, one of those park cricketers who answers to the designation 'all-rounder' because I basically do nothing very well, everything equally badly.

The ineptitude, moreover, is now exacerbated by physical decrepitude. I don't even need to be playing now to be reminded of my age. This was brought home to me a few years ago when the Yar-ras were joined by a gangling youth, name of James Harris. Following my time-honoured philosophy that the lamest and most obvious nickname usually has the best chance of sticking, I naturally dubbed him Rolf – which I quickly regretted, as a look of incompre-hension crossed his face.

Anyway, I'm hanging in there. Sir Donald's contemporary

Ernie McCormick once said that the moment to retire came when you took off one boot, then the other fifteen minutes later. I'm stable at around about ten minutes. And, y'know, lack of ability can add something to one's cricket experience. When Michael Clarke hits one through the covers, he's simply doing what he and everyone else expects; me, I'm getting a pleasant surprise. The top-level player inhabits a world of pitiless absolutes; for me, and the likes of me, for we are legion . . . we're in the realm of the relative, where 'not-so-bad' is good enough.

That's particularly so because of what I might call the compensatory pleasures. A few seasons ago, I broke the Yarras' games record – a triumph of availability over ability if ever there was. On doing so, I was forwarded a spreadsheet of all the guys I'd played with in that time: about 400 of them. A few brought back no memories at all – that's another function of getting older. But so, *so* many brought back happy memories, of shared struggles, shared gags, moments of joy, of disappointment, of relief, of redemption. There were a couple of dickheads in there too – no club is without them, I dare say. But the proportion I've encountered at the Yarras has been vanishingly small. And, well, as we also know, that club dickhead might be a dickhead, but he's *your* dickhead. I've always liked a remark by Freddie Jakeman, who played for Nottinghamshire in the 1950s. He said: 'Out of every hundred cricketers there's probably two shits. And if the 98 of us can't look after those two, we're a poor bunch.'

I'm sure you understand what I mean. The club. We *all* have one. We might not see it much any more. But it's like a first love – never forgotten. As a junior cricketer, I always took for granted that there would be a game for me. As a senior, the most rewarding parts of cricket have been keeping the show going at a club that's mainly had moths in its trophy cabinet and IOUs in its till.

For grassroots cricket in the twenteens, I can tell you, is as precarious as it ever was. It's not so long since we had a $3500 utilities bill turn up when we had $50 in the bank. Could we, wondered the president, become the first club to operate without electricity? Really, added the treasurer, the most profitable option would be to play no games at all and simply to hold barbecues. The secretary rather liked the sound of this, having himself been unanimously elected at the annual meeting while on his honeymoon in Bali, and still to evolve an exit strategy. Alas for him anyway, we dug deep and found a way, which you tend to over time.

Clubs are dependent on the goodwill of sponsors, who ask for little, offer much, and deserve whatever exposure you can give them. And I think everyone gains from knowing that the friendly staff at the Windsor Community Bank can assist with all your financial needs, that the calamari at the Union Hotel is delicious, that Lachlan Fisher at Fisher Cricket Bat and Willow is a prince among men . . . and that FlosFlorum is not only tops for flowers but lent us their van so we could retrieve our new bowling mats. Of course, I may be wrong about that, but when you're personally in charge of your club's sponsorships you have to be a bit shameless, don't you think?

Clubs are likewise dependent on the good offices of their local council. Sometimes these remind me of an old gag. How many council recreation officers does it take to change a light bulb? Answer: none because it's no longer their job to change light bulbs; there's an independent contractor for that, but his tender was so low that you'll get a candle only if you ask nicely. Actually that's not an old gag – I made it up. But it sounds like it resonates with a few people.

Mainly, of course, they're dependent on people, and it's often where you find those people at their best, because they are putting others' interests first, and giving the gift of time, in which we generally these days feel so poor.

I find the generosity of people towards their fellow man and woman through the medium of cricket deeply moving and motivating. Behind the apparently ordinary individuals who volunteer their aid to the cause of sport, furthermore, unsuspected gifts can also lie.

I like that story that Tony Greig tells about arriving in Adelaide for the Rest of the World tour in 1971, and being met at the airport by this dowdy, bespectacled old chap whom he took as some local association gofer there to carry his bag. When they had a bit of a chat, the old codger seemed to know a thing or two about the game. [South African accent:] 'Play some cricket, did you, old man?' Greigy asked. [Reedy voice:] 'Oh, y'know, a bit,' said the old bloke. Just then Garry Sobers arrived and headed straight towards Greigy's companion. 'Hello, Sir Donald,' he said.

Sir Donald's epic career, in fact, was bookended by administrative roles. Some of you will know that his first job at Bowral Cricket Club was as the first-team scorer; I dare say that his books added up too. He was picked for his first game as a twelve-year-old, in the time-honoured tradition, when the XI was a man short. When Sir Donald's playing day was done, the master of the game became its foremost servant. While everyone revels in 6996 and 99.94 – and we were never going to get through the evening without an invocation of those totemic numbers – a stat *I* love is that he *also* attended, for nothing, 1713 meetings of the South Australian Cricket Association. I *also* love the fact that someone bothered to make that into a stat.

We inhabit a modern world in which vast and minute attention falls on a very thin layer of highly paid, wildly promoted and hugely glamorised elite athletes who regard the attribute of 'professionalism' as the highest praise. I mean, *everyone* wants to be a professional nowadays: to do a *professional* job, to obtain *professional* standards, to produce work of *professional* quality, to exhibit *professional* pride. The porn star Randy Spears has explained that he manages to work up some lust for thirty per cent of the women he has sex with in X-rated movies; the rest of the time, he is 'just being a professional'. Yet even now, amateurism endures, and mightily. About a quarter of Australians participate in a sport organised by a club, association or other organisation each year. What proportion is paid for it, do you think? Probably closer to 0.1 per cent than one per cent.

Club cricket remains our game's biggest participation sector, with 3820 clubs in 570 associations enumerated at the most recent cricket census. And I suspect there's something about battling through and totally arseing everything, just scraping teams together and barely making books balance, that becomes part of the pageant. You're aiming to keep petrol in the roller, beer in the fridge and change in the till. But you're maintaining a preparedness to laugh when, due to a breakdown in communication, it ends up that there's change in the fridge, the till's full of petrol and the roller's full of beer.

We like our clubs to be successful, of course, but maybe not *so* successful that they become big, rich, complex, impersonal. That might become a little *too* much like everyday life – from which, when we take the cricket field on the weekend, we are usually seeking some distance. There's an interesting contrast, I fancy, between those groups we form ourselves, for our own enjoyment and beneficiation, and those formed for us, for maximum economic efficiency. The modern corporate world has developed to a fine art the act of building empires of strangers. For our own parts, we seem to prefer environments where it remains possible to know everyone's name, where we're connected by the intangibles of friendship and mutual reciprocity rather than by the formality of titles, ranks, reporting lines and organisational matrices.

I'd go further. This is something Australians have historically been good at. The theory and practice of forming cricket clubs is in our blood and in our history. Within two years of this city's settlement, citizens had founded the Melbourne Cricket Club, dedicated by one of its founders to 'men of all classes, the plebeian mingling with the peer, in respectful feeling and good fellowship' – a character which it's arguable it *has* maintained . . . assuming you can wait twenty years to find out.

Melbourne's first significant rival was Brighton Cricket Club, still prospering, 170 years young. Tasmania's oldest surviving clubs date from round the same time, South Australia's oldest surviving clubs from about a century and a half ago. They are older, therefore, than a majority of Australia's legislatures, an overwhelming number of our municipalities, and all but a tiny handful of our commercial enterprises.

The overwhelming proportion of clubs, of course, do not endure anywhere near so long. They rise and fall because of geography, demography, availability of participants, accessibility of organisers, facilities and funds. But the habits they instil are those that build communities: of giving and sharing, of volunteering and responding, of balancing interests, nurturing culture, respecting history and generally joining in common purpose. Grassroots cricket can even, I fancy, claim an influence on the foundation of the Australian commonwealth.

Cricket has always taken a certain pride in having provided an inspiriting example to the inchoate nation, the idea of a unified Australian team pre-empting that of a unified Australia. But there's more to this. When you focus on the political actors in the period around federation, it is striking how varied and how deep were their cricket connections. Four key figures in federation, George Reid,

END PIECES

Edmund Barton, Charles Kingston and Thomas Playford, also served as at least vice-presidents of the cricket associations in their respective states. Whilst a 22-year-old assistant accountant in the colonial treasury, for example, Reid was elected delegate to the New South Wales Cricket Association by the Warwick Cricket Club – the same club, incidentally, as Dave Gregory, Australia's first captain. After nine years, Reid became association treasurer, and he continued serving as association president whilst he was the premier of New South Wales, resigning only in the year before he became prime minister. Reid was not himself a noted player although he might have made a handy sightscreen, being roughly as wide as he was tall, and he certainly sledged like an Australian cricketer. Once while addressing an audience from a hotel balcony in Newcastle, he nonchalantly propped his belly on the balustrade. 'What'll you name it, George?' called a heckler. Reid replied: 'If it's all piss and wind as I expect, I'll name it after you, young feller.'

Consult the NSW Cricket Association annual reports in Reid's time, furthermore, and you'll find three future premiers, James McGowen, Joseph Carruthers and John Storey, acting as delegates for their clubs, Redfern, University and Balmain respectively. Carruthers and Storey, interestingly, were born rivals: Carruthers a hotshot lawyer and dyed-in-the-wool conservative, Storey a state-school-educated boilermaker and a self-described 'evolutionary socialist'. What made them unlikely lifelong friends was representing the same parliamentary XI. As Carruthers wrote in his memoirs: 'There were other men of different shades of political belief in the cricket team, and I can say of them as I say of Storey and myself, that the bitterness of party strife disappeared during contact with one another in the cricket field.'

In *this* city, around the turn of the century, the presidents of the St Kilda, East Melbourne, Richmond and Prahran Cricket Clubs were respectively also Australia's first treasurer (Sir George Turner), Melbourne's first federal member (Sir Malcolm McEachern), and the local members for their suburbs (George Bennett and Donald Mackinnon). Again, cricket exerted a surprisingly broad appeal: Turner was a stolid bookkeeper, McEachern a bold entrepreneur, Bennett a radical Catholic from Banffshire who championed the eight-hour day, Mackinnon a silver-haired Presbyterian educated in classics at Oxford, later to become both president of the Victorian Cricket Association and Australia's wartime director-general of recruiting.

Admittedly, the era's foremost political figure, Alfred Deakin, professed no great love for cricket. But when he wanted to describe Australian politics in the era of its split between the ALP, free traders and protectionists, Deakin deployed a famous cricket metaphor: it was, he said, like a cricket match featuring three XIs – an idea so outlandish that it has not even occurred to Mike McKenna yet. In Deakin's ministry, meanwhile, was a Queenslander rejoicing in the name Colonel Justin Fox Greenlaw Foxton, who in cricket rose highest of all: he was simultaneously chairman of the Australian Board of Control and Grand Registrar of the United Grand Lodge of Queensland after nearly thirty years in local and federal politics.

While researching this oration, I dug out press reports of the Athenian Cricket Club which Foxton helped to found in Ipswich in the 1860s when he was a teenaged articled clerk. There obviously wasn't much happening in Queensland a hundred and fifty years ago, because Brisbane's *Courier* gave extensive coverage to the Athenians' inaugural annual meeting, held in Ipswich's Church of England schoolroom in March 1867, where Foxton, then just seventeen, presented the treasurer's report, which was deemed 'most satisfactory'.

The report continued: 'There has been a decided improvement

in the play in the last twelve months both on account of the accession of new members and the natural result of practice. It is to be regretted that practice is not more numerously attended; the ground has not been in good order and this has rendered play unsteady.' Colonel Justin Fox Greenlaw Foxton would not have recognised what cricket has become today, but he would have been right at home at the Yarras committee meeting I attended last week. Ground's a bit rough – tick. Attendance at training a bit spotty – tick. Unsteady play – big tick. Otherwise, ticking over nicely.

Cricket and politics have never interpenetrated in this country as deeply as in others – thankfully so. But there *is* something significant, I think, about club cricket having loomed so large in the lives of so many involved in the early fashioning of this nation. As I observed previously, in order that *everyone* bats, bowls and fields in club cricket, *some* must get organised, elect officials, hold meetings, weigh interests, manage finances and delegate responsibilities – skills readily transferable to wider fields.

We can couch this more generally too. For numberless millions of Australians since, a sports club has been their original and most tangible experience of day-to-day democracy, and their greatest means of investment in civic amenity. The historian John Hirst has called this country a 'democracy of manners'. Australia, he observes, is short on inspirational rhetoric where democracy is concerned: our constitution is silent on citizenship; our curricula have no great tradition of civic education. What we have instead, says Hirst, is a way that 'Australians blot out differences when people meet face to face' and 'talk to each other as if they are equals'. In no environment has this tended to happen more spontaneously than when individuals band together in pursuit of a sporting goal. Club sport remains, I would argue, the most inclusive, evolved and constructive means by which Australians express their instinct to associate.

Better yet, our clubs are distinguished to this day by actually *working*. In our daily lives we are regularly beset by institutions that leave us feeling powerless, voiceless, helpless. Government institutions. Commercial institutions. Financial institutions. Religious institutions. Media institutions. It's easy to think: What does it matter what I do? What influence can I *possibly* have? At the little sporting institutions we make for ourselves, we aren't powerless; we can *and do* make a difference; we can put a shoulder to the wheel and feel the thing move.

It's a sorry reflection on the times that so few, outside an immediate circle, seem to grasp that. As if the thrall of the television remote and the atomisation of the working week were not enough, community sport has suffered gravely from the climate of financial stringency and sterile user-pays philosophies. 'But we subsidise sporting clubs in our community,' complain local governments, oblivious to the way sporting clubs subsidise local governments by mobilising free labour and local expertise, contributing to social cohesion and civic texture. In fact, the minuscule funding support local sport receives has colossal multiplier effects. And if this can't readily be ascertained by economic models, then the answer is new models, because the old ones aren't working any more.

But I can't hold local governments wholly responsible. I also fear that from time to time a sort of mechanistic view of grassroots cricket prevails within cricket itself. It is regarded simply as kind of a squeaky and unpainted front gate to one of those glorious 'pathways' one hears so much of – ah, the pathway, paved with gold, strewn with primrose petals. 'New markets' is the clarion call; but what of the old? All we've got to recommend us is that we love the game – and we wonder, from time to time, whether the game still loves us.

Some of you would have seen the figures of the recent

Australian cricket census, which were touted as showing cricket to be the country's biggest participation sport at the same time as it disclosed a 3.5 per cent decline in the club cricket population. We don't have the advantage of exit interviews, of course, but I wonder how many of those individuals passed out of the game because they don't like the way it is run, and promoted, and headed. I don't wish to spread alarm, but this would not wish to be remembered as the cricket generation that grew so obsessed with flogging KFC and accumulating Facebook likes that it let its core constituencies fade away.

Tomorrow, an annual meeting of Cricket Australia will finally phase out the system by which it has been governed since 1905, under which its board has been composed of the nominees of state associations drawn from the delegates of their premier, district and grade clubs. It's a system that has had a lot of critics, me among them, and I'm not about to mourn its passing. But it has always exhibited one *particular* virtue – that of recognising the integral role of the club in the cricket of this country, and the value of the volunteer in a sporting economy that could not otherwise function. And it would be remiss of cricket if it simply marched into its corporatist future without a backward glance, or a sideways acknowledgement of cricket's hardiest faithful.

In that spirit, I'd like to close this speech the old-fashioned way, by proposing a toast. To the club. It's the beginning of us all. To *your* club. For all that it has done for you; to all that you have done, and might yet do, for it.

Bradman Oration, October 2012

FIGHT THE POWER

Say what? You start about 11 a.m. and go till around 6 p.m, right? Why? Oh, never mind . . .

You break for lunch? *And* for afternoon tea? You play in the open air, so that rain and darkness can ruin everything? And you play for *five days* and *still* might not get a result?

Look, no offence, fella, but it will never catch on. You have to understand: we're too time-poor; we're too attention-challenged; there aren't enough sixes; there isn't enough colour; you can't squeeze it into a Tweet. I think you have to face it: sports marketing isn't for you. Have you considered a career weaving baskets?

The Test match, eh? Not even Lalit Modi could sell it. Fortunately he doesn't have to. Here we stand on the brink of the 2000th and, frankly, the prospect could hardly be more mouth-watering. Tendulkar at Lord's? No dancing girls required here; no cricketainment necessary.

Cricket spaced 803 Tests over its first century, meaning that 1197 have been shoehorned into the thirty-four years since, despite more than 3100 one-day internationals having been wedged in over the same period. But there don't seem too many Tests; arguably there are too few, even if this is probably better than a surfeit.

Not everything is rosy in the garden, of course. During their recent series in the Caribbean, West Indies and Pakistan looked like schoolboys trying to solve differential equations by counting on their fingers, so technically and temperamentally ill-suited were they to the rigours of five-day cricket. But the essence of a Test is that some must fail. Identifying inadequacy helps us recognise excellence.

In an age in which it has been deemed obsolete countless times, the Test match somehow sails on, not so much a mighty ship of state any more as a reconditioned windjammer – not the fastest thing around, but somehow the lovelier for that. Administrators busily infatuated with cricketainment have rather neglected it of late – no bad thing, really, given the damage administrators do without trying.

Players, praise be, still value it. You could feel the joy in England's cricket this last Australian summer. You could see this week how much runs at Lord's mattered to Tillakaratne Dilshan. And some days just sweep you away, like the last at Cardiff, where four days of slumber preluded a fifth of nightmares. Test matches do loudquietloud better than the Pixies.

Test matches survived a nasty brush with malpractice last year better than seemed possible at the time; India's number-one status has been a boon for interest and relevance; Australia's decline probably has, too, in addition to representing a stern cautionary tale, a punishment for hubris. For what a falling off is here. England might have invented cricket, but it was Australia that more or less invented the Test match, as a literal 'test' of its prowess, as an expression of rivalry and fealty.

The origins of Test cricket lie in the primordial ooze that was early Anglo-Australian competition. There was then no structure, no schedule, no overarching organising body – just an interest in settling who was better and, let it be said, making a few quid. The Marylebone Cricket Club would not come along with its ideas of fostering the bonds of empire until early in the twentieth century; likewise there was no notion of providing for the rest of the game out of the profits on Test matches until the advent of the Australian Board of Control for International Cricket in 1905. The first thirty years of Test cricket are in the main the work of private entrepreneurs, jobbing professionals and local officials, all busily making up the rules as they went along.

The edge in competition mattered to the English, but to Australians always mattered that little bit more. So it is that cricket owes an unacknowledged debt to the Adelaide sports journalist Clarence Moody, who wrote under the pseudonym 'Point' in the *South Australian Register*. As a kind of five-finger exercise, Moody set out in a section of his book *South Australian Cricket* (1898) a list of what he regarded as the 'Test matches' played to that time. Moody was hard to impress. He must have been tempted, out of national pride, to instate Australia's 1878 defeat of MCC at Lord's, honouring Spofforth's ten wickets for 20, but on Australia's inaugural tour of England he decided that no Tests had been played; nor would he recognise the games played against 'Combined XIs' by the rival English touring teams of 1887–88. Perhaps because he was so discriminate, and also in the absence of anything better, the list became canonical.

The other aid in the propagation of the Test match was, strange to say in an era that regards it as staid and unchanging, its pliability. Draw what inferences you will about the national characteristics they reflect, but the English preferred their Test matches to last three

days, in order to minimise interference with the County Championship, while Australians insisted on a result and cared not how
long it took to obtain. All cricket down under was timeless, in fact:
the First Test of the 1886–87 series, for example, actually began at
1.45 p.m. after the completion earlier that day of the Victoria–New
South Wales intercolonial match. When Sydney's gift to Somerset,
Sammy Woods, originated his oft-quoted *mot* about draw(er)s being
useful only for bathing, he was expressing a national not just a personal partiality.

The Test match resisted standardisation, furthermore, well into
its evolution. Only after more than a century was the five-day format made entirely uniform; only in the last quarter-century have
ninety overs in a day been the enforced minimum. And while International Council Cricket playing conditions make certain
stipulations about arena dimensions, cricket in general has uncon-
sciously preserved a pre-modern variety in the specifications of its
grounds – a reminder of cricket's bucolic origins that Test cricket in
its unregulated early development helped preserve.

Well established after half a century – no, nothing about this
game happens in a hurry – Test cricket then took its other seminal
step. Two Imperial Cricket Conferences at Lord's in 1926 agreed to
England's exchange of visits with West Indies, New Zealand and
India – a remarkable, seemingly unconscious expansion of the game
on the stroke of a pen and a handshake or two. Had the step been
contemplated twice, it may not have happened; as it was, cricket
began an imperceptibly slow tilt from its Anglo-Australian axis.

What is sometimes ignored in the modern relativist custom of
embracing cricket's 'three forms', in fact, is that cricket owes the Test
match everything. The one-day international was born into the
global estate Test cricket created, like an heir with all the advantages;
T20 has come along in the last five years like the proverbial

third-generation thickhead with a silver-spoon sense of entitlement. Its future, moreover, will depend on the degree to which cricket can be preserved as something other than a scam for sharkskin-suited spivs and third-rate politicians. One of the several ways in which cricket has been turned topsy-turvy in recent times is that after a hundred and more years as a bastion of conservatism, the sanctum sanctorum of the establishment, the Test match is the rebel game: uncompromising, unpredictable, ineffably appealing, immutably long, difficult to understand, resistant to commodification, and apparently unfriendly to the young, or at least to the condescending conception of the young as too dumb for anything but the bleeding obvious.

Here it stands, plumb in the way of the marketers and money-men, who see their role as sucking up to people who don't like cricket and quite probably never will. Here it stands, relentless in its demands on players for excellence in an era that encourages, and even worships, mass mediocrity. Here it stands, kept alive by a love of the game that can't be bought, or feigned, or mimicked, or manu-factured. Want to be the man? Want to fight the power? Celebrate Test cricket.

ON WARNE
Gideon Haigh

Now that the Australian cricketer who dominated airwaves and headlines for twenty years has turned full-time celebrity and media event, Shane Warne's sporting conquests and controversies are receding steadily into the past.

But what was it like to watch Warne at his long peak, the man of a thousand international wickets, the incarnation of Australian audacity and cheek? Gideon Haigh lived and loved the Warne era, when the impossible was everyday, and the sensational every other day.

In *On Warne*, he relives the era's highs, its lows, its fun and its follies. Drawing on interviews conducted with Warne over the course of a decade, and two decades of watching him play, Haigh assesses this greatest of sportsmen as cricketer, character, comrade, newsmaker and national figure – a natural in an increasingly regimented time, a simplifier in a growingly complicated world. The result is one of the finest cricket books ever written, a whole new way of looking at its subject, at sport, and at Australia.

One day, you might be asked what cricket in the time of Warne was like. *On Warne* is the definitive account.

'Bloody brilliant . . . As good as anything I have read on the game.'
Andy Bull, *The Guardian*

'A masterful book . . . ceaselessly insightful . . . Perhaps it is a cliche to refer to a biography as definitive; in this case it would be remiss not to do so.'
Rob Smyth, *The Cricketer*

Winner of the Cricket Society and MCC Book of the Year Award

The Cricket Book of the Year, British Sports Book Awards